Investing in
Developing Countries

The authors wish to thank the following for contributing material for use in this book:

Asim Erdilek

Nancy Gordon

Robert Grosse

Gary Hawes

John P. Starke, Sr.

William Stoever

Research for this book was supported by a grant from the Overseas Private Investment Corporation.

Investing in Developing Countries

A Guide for Executives

Thomas L. Brewer
Georgetown University

Kenneth David
Michigan State University

Linda Y.C. Lim
University of Michigan

with the assistance of
Robert S. Corredera

Lexington Books

D.C. Heath and Company/Lexington, Massachusetts/Toronto

Library of Congress Cataloging-in-Publication Data

Brewer, Thomas L., 1941–
   Investing in developing countries.

  Bibliography: p.
  Includes index.
  1. Investments, Foreign—Developing countries.
I. David, Kenneth II. Lim, Linda. III. Title.
HG5993.B74 1986   658.1'52   85-46008
ISBN 0-669-12770-1 (alk. paper)

Published simultaneously in Canada
Printed in the United States of America
Casebound International Standard Book Number: 0-669-12770-1
Library of Congress Catalog Card Number: 85-46008

The paper used in this publication meets the minimum requirements of American National Standard for Information Sciences—Permanence of Paper for Printed Library Materials, ANSI Z39.48-1984.
∞™

The last numbers on the right below indicate the number and date of printing.

10 9 8 7 6 5 4 3 2 1

95 94 93 92 91 90 89 88 87 86

Contents

Figure and Tables

Figure

Tables

Exhibits

Foreword

For many small and medium-sized U.S. businesses, investing overseas, particularly in developing countries, appears to be the kind of opportunity that is available only to large multinational companies backed by substantial financial, technical, and personnel resources. "How can I afford to invest in Barbados or Bangladesh when I can't afford to invest in Boston?" is an often heard refrain. One answer is that it may be less costly to invest in a developing country than in the United States. Another answer may be that unless you find new markets your competition may make it difficult for your business even to survive. Increasingly, the world's growth markets are to be found in the approximately one hundred countries of the so-called Third World. Indeed, some small and medium-sized U.S. businesses are finding that they can no longer afford to pass up these emerging opportunities.

Another factor inhibiting many otherwise strong and confident companies from venturing into the developing world is the fear of encountering risks that such firms do not normally deal with in the United States. In addition to normal business risks, there are additional ones posed by unstable political conditions in many developing countries. Fortunately, there are considerable resources available to U.S. companies, such as political risk insurance, which can be obtained from the Overseas Private Investment Corporation (OPIC); some private insurers can also help offset these risks. Other U.S. government agencies, such as the Commerce Department, the Private Enterprise Bureau of AID, and the Trade and Development Program, to name just a few, offer information, communications, and financial services that are designed to help small and medium-sized companies identify, assess, and act on overseas business opportunities.

OPIC is interested in encouraging smaller U.S. companies to consider the advantages of investing in developing countries. OPIC's business includes direct loans, loan guarantees, and other forms of investment encouragement as well as political risk insurance, and an increasing proportion of this business involves small firms. We encounter hundreds of small companies each year that have good ideas for overseas investment projects, but very little idea of how to implement them. While the government programs mentioned earlier can help, the would-be manager of an overseas investment needs to do a considerable amount of homework in order to take successful advantage of these programs. The developing world markets are for the most part new, dynamic, and in some ways unconventional by the standards of American business. Not even the best business school education can prepare you to participate in these markets without some hands-on experience, or the next best thing: the wisdom of those successful businesses that have had such experiences.

This realization led us to develop, in consultation with Dr. Thomas Brewer, the idea for this book. As a well-known author, he has written a considerable number of books and articles on international business issues. Based on his understanding of the foreign investment process, Dr. Brewer then worked with a number of managers of small and medium-sized businesses who have operated successfully in developing countries and interviewed them. Of course not all of their stories were about success, and the failures described herein provide some of the most useful lessons in the book. As a result, the reader has the benefit of a great deal of firsthand information about the opportunities and risks of investing in developing countries.

This large amount of information is not, to my knowledge, available in such comprehensive form in any other publication. But in addition, the book is full of good, commonsense advice, do's and don'ts for each stage of the investment planning and operations process. I dare say that we at OPIC would be delighted if each prospective investor we deal with had the benefit of reading this book before coming to us with an investment proposal. We consider this book a significant resource for identifying, evaluating, planning, and implementing successful business ventures in developing countries.

Gerald T. West
Vice President for Development
Overseas Private Investment Corporation

Preface

Y ou should find this book useful if you are a businessperson in any of
the following situations: (1) the domestic market for your product is
saturated, and you are wondering about opportunities in markets
outside the United States; (2) you are exporting to a foreign market, but
foreign firms or trade restrictions have made it difficult for you to compete;
(3) domestic production costs have made it difficult for you to compete in
the U.S. market or to compete in foreign markets through exports; (4) you
know about an opportunity to invest in a developing country, but you are
not sure how to take advantage of it.

This book will introduce you to the process of making and managing
investments in developing countries. It is intended especially for executives
and managers with little or no previous experience with such projects, though
more experienced businesspeople may also find portions of it useful. The
book presents a concise yet comprehensive survey of the managerial problems
you will confront in planning, implementing, and operating an investment
project—it also presents solutions to those problems.

A central theme is that the often difficult problems involved in investing
in developing countries *are manageable*. If you are an experienced businessperson, your knowledge can be applied to an investment project in a developing country. This book explains how you can do it and how you can manage the additional and sometimes novel problems as well, if you are willing
to make the necessary commitment.

The individual chapters of the book contain descriptions and illustrations
that are focused on the specific managerial problems that you will need to
address. Statistical information is also provided, as are checklists and actual
case experiences. There are also lists of reading materials and organizations
that you can consult for further information. (Since some U.S. government
programs were undergoing major changes as this book went to press, you
may want to check on their current status.)

The first chapter introduces the reader to opportunities for establishing
production facilities in developing countries. The subsequent chapters are ar-

ranged according to the sequence of stages involved in a project—from strategic planning to decisions about whether to abandon or stay with an existing project.

The chapters can be read selectively and independently of one another. For instance, if you are generally familiar with opportunities and other conditions in developing countries, you may want to skip portions of the first chapter. Or if you already have a proposal from a prospective joint venture partner in a developing country, you might want to begin by reading the chapter on joint ventures and then read chapters as appropriate. The book is short and nontechnical, however, so it can be read in its entirety in a few hours.

The book is applicable to all types of investment projects in developing countries; no particular sectors, industries, or products have been singled out for special discussion. You may therefore find that no mention is made of your particular type of firm, but you should be able to apply the guidelines and solutions to your specific situation without difficulty.

Also, no particular countries have been singled out for detailed analysis. However, numerous examples drawn from specific individual countries have been included to illustrate general points.

In view of the large number of authors and contributors, it is appropriate to provide additional information about their specific roles. Thomas L. Brewer was the coordinator and editor for the project and the principal author of chapters 1, 4, 6, and 10; he also contributed materials for other chapters. Kenneth David was the principal author of chapters 2, 3, and 9. Linda Y.C. Lim was the principal author of chapters 5, 7, and 8.

Robert S. Corredera contributed several cases as well as extensive notes based on his experience in international operations. His materials were integrated into nearly all of the chapters in one form or another; he also provided detailed comments on chapter drafts.

Asim Erdilek contributed material on Turkey for chapter 10. Nancy Gordon contributed materials on promotional techniques for chapter 9. Robert Grosse contributed cases and other materials for chapters 1, 4, and 10. Gary Hawes' materials were used for sections on land and housing problems and the political consequences of investment projects in chapters 1, 5, and 7. John P. Starke, Sr., read chapter drafts, contributed materials, and made numerous helpful suggestions for all chapters. William Stoever prepared the case on Ghana for chapter 1.

As coordinator of the project, I am indebted to my colleagues and contributors for their cooperation. I am also grateful to the numerous people whose assistance is acknowledged below.

Acknowledgments

The book was made possible by financial support from the U.S. Overseas Private Investment Corporation (OPIC). Also, several OPIC staff members offered critical advice; in particular, Gerald West, Harvey Himberg, and Margaret Walsh read chapter drafts with great care and made numerous constructive suggestions. Thomas Brewer's discussions with Gerald West and Harvey Himberg were especially helpful in shaping the book and bringing it to publication.

Jürgen Voss at the World Bank and Dale Weigel at the International Finance Corporation made helpful suggestions on several points in the initial stages of the project. John Baker of Gelman Sciences read a draft of the chapter on joint ventures and made numerous suggestions that were incorporated in the final version. Others provided assistance for the chapter on obtaining funds: Carl Bazarian and Thomas Evans of East–West Financial Services, Gordon Hunt of Caribbean Central American Action, Peter Nelson of the International Development Institute, Ben Hardy of Equator Bank, Judith Katz of the Bank of New England, Wilfred Lewis and Phiroze Medhora of the International Finance Corporation, Hugh Henry-May of the Caribbean Project Development Facility, David Ramsaur of the Bank of Hawaii, Samuel Hale of International Resources Group, Phillips Perera of Interfin, Timothy Hopkins of Comerica, and Lawrence Taepke of the National Bank of Detroit. Others who checked material for accuracy and made suggestions on particular points were Russell Anderson of the Bureau for Private Enterprise in the U.S. Department of State, and John Hardy, Jr., of the U.S. Trade and Development Program.

Chwo-Ming Yu provided excellent research assistance and proofreading for the project, and also lightened the burden of other projects underway at the same time.

The capable and conscientious people who helped produce the numerous manuscript drafts were Christi Bemister, Karen Custer, Debra Deneau, Brenda Guzal, Kim Hoyt, Amy McDonald, and Mary Jo Robinson.

Everyone at Lexington Books was also consistently helpful. Bruce Katz supported the project with enthusiasm from the outset. Karen Maloney was always attentive to editorial punctilios in the production process. Margo Shearman substantially improved the manuscript in the copy editing stage.

Fariborz Ghadar and Charles Feigenoff read chapter drafts and suggested numerous improvements.

Investing in
Developing Countries

1
An Introduction to the Opportunities

This chapter provides an introduction to the opportunities for establishing operations in developing countries. It includes illustrative management problems as well as preliminary planning considerations.

Opportunities for Projects

There are many developing countries and there is enormous diversity among them; as a result, numerous and varied opportunities are available to potential investors. Specific sources of additional information about the opportunities are listed at the end of the chapter. Here we merely highlight a few important facts and trends.[1]

Over one half of the world population lives in developing countries. The total GNP of the more than one hundred developing countries is well over $2 trillion per year, and the real growth rates in many developing countries have been higher in recent years than growth rates in industrial economies.

More important for you if you are considering investing abroad are the forecasts for the future. The World Bank forecasts real growth rates of 5 to 6 percent in the GNPs of the developing countries as a group, compared with 3 to 5 percent in the industrial countries, over the next decade. Such growth will occur in spite of the developing countries' debt crisis.

The populations in developing countries are also going to increase substantially. By the year 2000, five billion people will live in developing countries—two billion in China (PRC) and India, and another three billion in other developing countries.

Gross National Product (GNP). The following countries already have GNPs of hundreds of billions of dollars per year: Brazil, Mexico, China, and India.

Thomas L. Brewer, principal author.

Many other countries have GNPs approaching $100 billion a year in the late 1980s. These countries include Nigeria, Turkey, South Korea, Yugoslavia, and Argentina. As a group, the countries in the Association of Southeast Asian Nations (ASEAN) are also this large in economic terms.

Real Growth Rates. Some of the most promising opportunities for foreign direct investors, however, lie in countries that are not especially large in terms of population or GNP, but have very rapidly growing economies. Consider, for example, Lesotho, which enjoyed a real growth rate of more than 8 percent per year during the 1970s, as did Egypt, Ecuador, and most of the countries in Southeast Asia.

Sectoral Growth. Some countries have particular sectors or market niches that are fast emerging. The manufacturing sector, for example, grew at an average annual rate of 14 percent in Indonesia during the 1970–81 period and by more than 10 percent in many other developing countries—compared with only 3 percent in the United States for the same period. The agricultural sector and the services sector have also experienced unusually high growth rates in some developing countries. The agricultural and services sectors were growing at an average annual rate of more than 5 percent in Tanzania, Syria, and Paraguay.

Urbanization. One of the most important facts about many developing countries is the extent to which they are already urbanized—and they are becoming even more urbanized. For example, there are more than 125 cities in developing countries with populations greater than a million. By the end of the century, there will be nearly three hundred cities that size. Their urban populations create market opportunities, while their infrastructural facilities and services can support production plants.

Literacy. In some developing countries, literacy rates are quite high. Argentina, for example, has a literacy rate of over 90 percent, as do Uruguay and Costa Rica. Although literacy rates barely reach 10 percent in some countries, most have literacy rates well over 50 percent.

Summary Projection. Recent forecasts by a major accounting-consulting firm provide a good summary statement of the increasing opportunities for projects in developing countries:

> Probably the most fundamental change in the world economy that will set the tone for the world business climate for the next two decades is the rising importance of [developing countries]. Traditionally sources of raw materials,

commodities and cheap labor for certain industries, many [developing countries] have recently become strong manufacturers in their own right. They now produce goods that compete with those of the [industrialized] countries in world markets and, very important, are building strong middle-class consumer economies in their own developing domestic markets. Developing countries, especially those in Asia and Latin America, have risen rapidly as producers of the world's wealth and income, moving from 17 percent of world Gross Product (GDP) in 1960 to approximately 22 percent in 1981. Third World GDP could reach one-third of world GDP as early as 1990 and exceed 40 percent of world GDP by the year 2000.[2] [See table 1–1 for details.]

Illustrative Opportunities. In recent years, several countries in East and Southeast Asia have been especially attractive locations for investment projects. For instance, the six countries of Indonesia, Malaysia, the Philippines, Brunei, Singapore, and Thailand have formed the Association of Southeast Asian Nations (ASEAN), which offers a rapidly growing market of more than 200 million people. Since trade barriers among the countries are being lowered, a single production facility may be able to serve the entire market more competitively than in the past.

In the Middle East, to give another example, Morocco recently changed its industrial investment code. The new code allows full foreign ownership of firms in Morocco; it also grants tax and other incentives for foreign investors. Another code for the tourist sector in particular also grants tax incentives and other inducements for foreign firms to establish facilities in Morocco.

The existence of many different types of specific opportunities for projects in Latin American countries is evident in table 1–2 and in exhibit 1–1. A recent "shopping list" of investment opportunities in Peru in table 1–2 is based on that government's development plans, and it suggests the variety of opportunities available there. Descriptions of free trade zones for manufacturing facilities suggesting yet other possibilities in Central America and the Caribbean are found in exhibit 1–1. (See also appendix 1A at the end of the chapter.)

As table 1–3 indicates, U.S. firms in many industries have already taken advantage of opportunities in the Middle East, Southeast Asia, and other parts of the world as well.

Finding Specific Opportunities

You must of course be able to identify and assess quite specific opportunities for your firm—whether you are looking for new markets or for a low-cost production location.

Table 1–1
Regional Economic Projections

Regions	Percentage of World Total						Average GDP Growth	
	Population		Gross Product		GDP per Capita			
	1980	2000	1980	2000	1980	2000	1970–85	1985–2000
Indian Sub-Continent	23.81%	25.95%	1.93%	3.95%	$201	$549	4.00%	7.65%
(India)	17.69	18.66	1.47	3.15	$206	$609	3.89%	7.98%
Central America	2.40	2.79	1.95	2.68	$2,010	$3,467	4.49%	6.39%
South America	6.14	6.56	5.32	6.37	$2,145	$3,506	3.75%	5.92%
Asia/Pacific	11.97	11.58	15.68	21.45	$3,249	$6,688	4.76%	5.41%
(NICs)	8.44	8.78	3.33	7.05	$980	$2,900	7.04%	7.78%
North Africa	2.38	2.83	1.27	1.49	$1,324	$1,897	5.40%	5.18%
China	25.67	22.45	2.67	3.61	$258	$581	5.37%	4.96%
Sub-Saharan Africa	9.47	12.68	2.47	2.60	$648	$742	2.78%	4.63%
Mid-East	2.09	2.48	3.03	3.22	$3,590	$4,687	5.99%	4.42%
Caribbean	0.36	0.37	0.20	0.19	$1,345	$1,827	3.06%	3.97%
North America	6.59	5.45	34.80	30.62	$13,087	$20,307	3.08%	2.85%
Western Europe	9.11	6.87	30.68	23.82	$8,350	$12,521	2.38%	2.57%
(FRG, UK, Fr.)	4.49	3.30	17.61	12.88	$9,728	$14,096	2.25%	2.19%
Total/Averages	100.00%	100.00%	100.00%	100.00%	$2,480	$3,611	3.34%	3.86%

Source: Coopers & Lybrand, 1985 *Annual Report on the World Wide Economic and Business Climate* (Washington, D.C.: Coopers & Lybrand, 1985), 9. Used with permission.

Table 1–2
Sample of Projects in Peru Needing Foreign Investors

Projects	Projected Investment ($ millions)	Needs
Sawnwood production	0.4	Equity participation; loans; market access; training
Wood pillars and technology	2.0	Equity participation; loans; technology
Railway rolling stock plant	8.9	Equity participation; loans; market access
Dairy products plant	6.1	Foreign market access; loans; technology, machinery
Olive oil processing plant	0.5	Loans; market access; technology; machinery
Fresh fruit processing (pineapple, orange juice/oils, fruit concentrate)	1.8	Equity participation; loans; market access
Hotel construction	7.0	Equity participation; loans; market access
Pectin production (apples, citrus residues)	0.8	Equity participation; loans; services; training
Salt production plant	0.7	Equity participation; loans; technology; management; market access
Yuca flour plant	4.0	Equity participation; loans

Source: Adapted from *Business Latin America,* September 21, 1983, p. 303. Used with the permission of the publisher, Business International Corporation, New York.

Exhibit 1–1
Free Trade Zones for Manufacturing in the Caribbean and in Central America

Companies investigating production-sharing possibilities in the Caribbean or in Central America should take a close look at the Free Trade Zones that the region has to offer. For one thing, firms will find competitive wage rates and generous tax incentives across the board. But . . . other specific benefits can vary greatly from country to country, and even from zone to zone; the suitability of an FTZ for particular business operations must be weighed carefully as well.

Several general points regarding Caribbean Basin FTZs are worth noting:

1. *Tariff and tax incentives.* Duty-free import of parts, materials and machinery for export is standard fare. In some cases (for example, in the Nether-

lands Antilles), a portion of a firm's production can enter the local market duty-free. Tax holidays are granted liberally throughout the region; firms can often win additional breaks by making large capital outlays or by initiating training programs.

2. *Export-market incentives.* The U.S. Caribbean Basin Initiative (CBI), of which all of the countries listed are beneficiaries, allows duty-free import into the United States for a wide range of products. However, textiles, apparel and leather goods are not included. In the case of the English-speaking Caribbean and the Netherlands Antilles, access to the European market is facilitated by their association with the European Economic Community (EEC).

3. *The Eastern Caribbean countries* do not have FTZs per se, but they normally grant duty-free import privileges to enclave industries located anywhere on the island. The Bahamas and a number of other countries have industrial parks that in many ways function as FTZs.

4. *Labor is abundant, but job training is frequently needed,* particularly as offshore production grows more sophisticated. Local labor regulations vary, but firms can generally expect a 40–48 hour workweek; employer-paid benefits normally include a Christmas bonus ("thirteenth month"), social security, and health benefits.

5. *The availability of production space and factory shells* should not be taken for granted. The Honduran FTZ in Puerto Cortes is reportedly booked up, as is at least one of the Dominican Republic's four zones.

6. *Look beyond labor cost savings* when deciding where to set up a free zone operation. The U.S. Department of Commerce's Caribbean Basin Unit warns prospective FTZ operators not to overlook communication costs, shipping, availability and reliability of electric power, water and transportation, and living conditions for expatriate managers.

Adapted from *Business Latin America,* June 6, 1984, pp. 183–84. Used with the permission of the publisher, Business International Corporation, New York.

Table 1–3
Illustrative Statistics on U.S. Firms' Facilities in Developing Countries

	Value in US$ (millions)		
	Singapore	*Egypt*	*Nigeria*
All industries	1803	1272	492
Food and related products	9	1	*
Chemicals and related products	22	*	*
Primary and fabricated metals	*	0	*
Machinery, except electrical	54	0	1
Electric and electronic equipment	277	1	1
Transportation equipment	*	0	0

Source: U.S. Department of Commerce, *Survey of Current Business,* August 1983, p. 24.
*Amount deleted to avoid disclosure of information about individual corporations.

Using the U.S. Government. The U.S. Commerce Department has services that can be quite helpful in assessing foreign market opportunities. Each of its *Country Market Surveys* (CMSs) provides a summary report on a single industry in a single country. Each *International Market Research Survey* (IMR) provides in-depth analyses of up to four hundred pages of the markets for a given product category in a given country. Each IMR contains statistical information and also analyzes the market for select products, end-users and their purchasing plans, marketing practices, and trade restrictions. IMRs also list key potential buyers, government purchasing agencies, and similar relevant organizations. The Commerce Department also has other market information services for specific countries or products; it even has customized services for your particular needs.

The U.S. Overseas Private Investment Corporation (OPIC) has an Opportunity Bank, though the program's activity has been curtailed as part of the broad effort to reduce government expenditures.

The Trade and Development Program (TDP) in the U.S. International Development Cooperation Agency also has programs that can help prospective U.S. investors find opportunities for projects in developing countries. Regional Directors of TDP are available for consultations with representatives from U.S. firms. TDP activities are concentrated in developing countries that have already achieved substantial levels of economic development and no longer receive much U.S. economic aid. There are more than forty countries in which the TDP is active, but special emphasis is being placed on Caribbean and Central American countries at present. A project must involve not only the establishment of facilities in these countries, but also the creation of U.S. exports to those facilities in order to qualify for TDP assistance. You can easily determine whether your project meets these and other requirements by contacting TDP officials.

The Agriculture Department may be able to help you if you have an agribusiness firm. Although the Agriculture Department strongly emphasizes the promotion of commodity exports from the United States, it does have information and services that might be pertinent to an agribusiness investment project in a developing country. The Office of International Cooperation and Development is a good place to start. The Information Services Staff of the Foreign Agricultural Service may also be helpful.

More information about how to contact these and other U.S. government programs is provided at the end of the chapter. See also the highly informative book on U.S. government programs by William A. Delphos, *Washington's Best Kept Secrets: A U.S. Government Guide to International Business*, for further details.[3]

Using International Organizations. The World Bank, regional development banks, and several United Nations agencies operate programs that create numerous and diverse business opportunities in developing countries. Many of the projects sponsored by these agencies are large infrastructure or industrial projects, but these agencies' projects also generate demand for a tremendous variety of goods and services. If you have facilities in a country where such projects are underway, you will be in a strong competitive position to bid on procurement contracts. A convenient and comprehensive source of information about the business opportunities generated by these projects is *International Business Opportunities Service,* which contains advance project announcements and procurement notices from the World Bank and other international agencies. More than $2 billion per month in sales opportunities are presented here. Other related services are also available. The United Nations Industrial Development Organization has an investment promotion office in New York. (Again, see the Sources of Additional Information at the end of this chapter for address and phone number.)

Using Your Own Experience. You should know from your own experience in selling your products domestically or exporting to foreign markets what the most pertinent factors affecting demand are. Indeed, your export experience may give you clear impressions about market prospects in individual foreign countries. On the other hand, your export experience may be limited to a single country or to a short period of time, and it may have resulted more from coincidence or accidental factors rather than from a careful market analysis. You should therefore undertake a thorough market analysis of all relevant countries, if the purpose of the project is to expand into new markets. (See chapters 2 and 9 for further advice.) Of course, cost factors must also be considered: you want to locate in countries that have in relative abundance the inputs into the production process that you need. Your needs and the countries' resources need to be matched. Your own experience and analysis of your previous and potential production processes will be the best guide to your needs. (See especially chapters 7 and 8.)

Rewards

If you can find the opportunities and manage the problems of operating facilities in developing countries, the rewards can be substantial. The rate of return on operations in developing countries is often much higher than in industrial countries. In 1981, for example, U.S. firms earned about 20 percent on their investments in developing countries, and their returns averaged 15 percent in the following year, even though these were recession years around the world. A study of returns on U.S. investments in fourteen developing countries covering over more than a decade found that the rate of returns on investments in ten of the developing countries was greater than in the U.S.— more than 10 percent greater in several cases.[4] Another study found that U.S.

firms' joint ventures in India enjoyed an average increase of 20 percent per year in their after-tax profits.[5]

Furthermore, diversifying operations into countries outside the United States or other industrial countries can reduce the aggregate risks of your firm. Since business cycles in individual developing countries are not perfectly correlated with U.S. cycles, you can partially alleviate the impact of cyclical downturns in the U.S. economy.

Problems

In order to reap such rewards, you will of course have to deal with numerous problems. Some of the problems that you will encounter in developing countries may be different from those that you are accustomed to, but they are not necessarily greater. In any case, they are usually manageable. Some especially important ones—such as war, expropriation, and controls on profit remittances—will be discussed in detail in chapter 10. Here we will simply point out some illustrative problems.

Finding a suitable plot of land, for instance, could be a problem, especially if you are looking for expansive tracts of land in order to enter the direct production of agricultural products. In most of Southeast Asia, for instance, the land frontier has closed. The desire to protect forests and preserve watersheds, plus the expansion of urban areas, means that the land available for cultivation may actually be declining. This situation, coupled with a still rapid rate of population growth, creates intense competition for land.

If the real estate market were fully operational, the competition for land would not necessarily pose serious problems for you. In many developing countries, however, the occupant of a piece of land may not be the owner. Yet the occupant may feel that he has other, equally legitimate claims to this same piece of land. He or his ancestors may have cleared the land and made it productive, but unfortunately, they did not have the necessary knowledge or political connections to gain legal title to the land. Or, the occupant of a piece of land may have lost clear title to the land because of harassment or connivance between local elites and administrative officials. The occupant may not have a legal claim to the land, but in his mind there is a moral claim even stronger than the legal title—and he may be determined not to relinquish his claim. The settlers' rights are clear and strong in many countries.

Several other types of potential problems are illustrated by the experience of the firm in exhibit 1–2. In particular, the case demonstrates the importance of thoroughly analyzing costs, market potential, and government policies *before* making a commitment to a foreign investment project.

Exhibit 1–2
Problems with a Manufacturing Project in Country X

The ABC firm was involved in a joint venture to manufacture and sell a proprietary product as a supplier to manufacturers in country X. The firm was enticed by the government of X with incentives that seemed too good to pass up. The incentives included: management control based on 55 percent ownership; royalties of 6 percent; an up-front technical fee of US$600,000; a multiyear tax exemption; the government's promise to protect domestic manufacturers from imports; promised relief from government price controls; and the opportunity to borrow from a special government agency at favorable rates of interest.

In light of these highly attractive incentives, the firm went ahead with the project and built a factory without careful analysis of the government policies, the projected costs, or market potential of the project.

Within six months of starting up its operations, the firm discovered that the government agency responsible for the special lending was obligated to its capacity and that its funds were coming in at a trickle. Furthermore, the protection of "domestic manufacturers" was not specifically incorporated in any law, and the government was having trouble granting the protection because of strong lobbying pressure from local business organizations. In addition, the cost of manufacturing in the early stages of the project turned out to be more expensive than it had been in the United States. Outside competition was flooding the market with similar products at lower prices. The net result was that the company was operating at a loss. The firm was forced to eliminate products, reduce production, and ultimately shut down its operations.

In retrospect, company officials recognized that they had not done enough research about conducting business in country X when they decided to go ahead with the project in the first place. Because they had been successful in the U.S. market, they assumed that their success in the foreign country's market was assured. Of course, they were wrong. The costs of production, the distribution system, government practices, and the market for the product were all quite different. The firm still believes that country X is a good location for an investment, but it now recognizes that careful, detailed homework is mandatory for a successful venture. It also recognizes that market potential and costs—not government incentives—should be the principal considerations in undertaking investments.

Based on material contributed by Robert S. Corredera.

Formulating a Preliminary Plan

It may be useful to write up a brief, tentative plan, for it will help you to clarify your own ideas about the project. Such a document can be the basis for obtaining the initial commitment and go-ahead from all responsible people within your own organization; it will also provide a common reference for people in the firm who will be responsible for pursuing the more detailed planning of the project. Exhibit 1–3 lists the kinds of questions that you will need to address. They receive detailed analysis in later chapters.

Exhibit 1–3
Project Plan Checklist

I. Market
   1. What is the basic market orientation—export, local national, or local regional?
   2. What is the projected production volume and market share?
   3. Who are the potential users of the product?
   4. What distribution system will be used?
   5. What is the present competition, and what is it likely to be in the future?
   6. What role do government policies have in affecting your competitive position?

II. Facilities and resources
   1. Are land, buildings, water, electricity, fuel, waste disposal, telephone, telegraph, radio, and communications available? At what cost?
   2. Are necessary transportation facilities and services available—ports (including container-handling facilities), railroads, airports, roads, and public transportation for workers? At what cost?
   3. Are new materials, equipment and other supplies available? From suppliers in the country or from imports? What are the costs?
   4. Are workers with appropriate skills available? How can local workers be trained if necessary? What are labor costs likely to be? What labor relations laws and practices are pertinent?

III. Finance
   1. What is the total cost of the project—broken down into land, building, equipment, and working capital?
   2. What is the financial structure, including sources and terms of debt and equity financing?
   3. What are the expected operating costs and revenues?
   4. What are the sources and costs of funds from U.S. sources—private and governmental?
   5. What are the sources and costs of funds from foreign sources—banks, partners, and government?
   6. What kinds of insurance are available from private or governmental sources to cover remittances of profits, capital repatriation, and other risks?

II. Government policies
   1. Does the project fit into the host government's development plans?
   2. How will the project be affected by government investment incentives, restrictions, and guarantees?
   3. How will the project be affected by other government policies—such as tariffs, export or import regulations, taxes, budget expenditures, or health, environmental, and labor regulations?

4. What relations does the country have with the United States, other foreign governments, and international organizations such as the World Bank and the International Monetary Fund?

Adapted from International Finance Corporation, *Preliminary Project Information Required*, pamphlet, June 1982. Used with permission.

You can formulate a very preliminary plan on the basis of only a limited analysis. Whatever the outcome of the preliminary analysis, however, you should be careful not to jump to final conclusions, either positive or negative, about the project. Any conclusions based on this preliminary analysis should be regarded as highly tentative. As you proceed to a more careful and detailed analysis, you may find that many of your preliminary conclusions need to be substantially revised.

For instance, you may already have a specific country in mind as a possible location for your investment project. You should be careful, however, not to exclude other countries from consideration without at least some analysis. You might find that a country you have not considered at all will turn out to be the best location for your project. You may also find that other neighboring countries will provide good market opportunities in addition to the country where you locate your facilities.

Consulting with People in the United States. Many kinds of information will have to be collected through consultations with people outside your firm. These consultations should take place first within the United States, particularly with your banker, certain U.S. government agencies, the offices of foreign government agencies in the United States, and perhaps private consultants as well.

Your consultations with such people will focus on the major areas of your plan. A consultant, for example, may want to focus on your basic strategy, market analysis, and country selection. Your banker will be interested in these matters too, in addition to the financial plan. U.S. government agencies may be especially interested in whether your project will generate U.S. exports. The foreign government investment promotion offices or embassy personnel will want to know how your project will contribute to their development goals, including employment, exports, and technology transfer.

As your consultations and information collection continue, you may find that the plans for the project change a great deal. Your plans may need to be reformulated on the basis of the consultations in the United States and also on the basis of a visit to a prospective host foreign country.

Visiting the Foreign Country. Several OPIC programs exist to facilitate on-site discussions and evaluations, although funding for these programs has been curtailed. They include Investment Missions, Reconnaissance Surveys, and Feasibility Studies. Further advice concerning visits to foreign countries is contained in subsequent chapters.

Conclusion

There are many diverse opportunities for producing and selling your goods or services in developing countries. Like any serious business venture, though, investing in developing countries requires commitment and careful planning. Chapter 2 provides a detailed guide to the planning process.

The appendixes to this chapter provide case studies of investment projects and also suggestions for sources of additional information.

Appendix 1A
Using Costa Rica for Offshore Sourcing

B oasting the advantages of political stability, favorable climate, competitive labor rates and fair treatment of foreign companies, Costa Rica intends to offer itself as the most attractive site for Caribbean Basin Initiative sourcing when U.S. import duties on many products from the Caribbean region are reduced to zero. . . . In anticipation of the expected benefits, some companies (including a few successful Asian firms with U.S. import quota problems) are already seeking Costa Rican plant sites or contract-manufacturing arrangements in this Central American country.

Two outside studies recently completed for Costa Rica's export minister underline the country's cost advantages as a CBI-sourcing site. The first study shows, for example, that under existing conditions a hypothetical electronics manufacturer in its third year of operation would have lower sales costs in Costa Rica than in any of its CBI rival nations, including Panama, Jamaica, the Dominican Republic and Haiti. Only Haiti would have a marginal total advantage because of its proximity and, hence, cheaper costs for transporting goods to the U.S. market.

The second study identifies 143 product lines, including electronics, transport equipment, instruments, luggage and toys, in which Costa Rica presently has an overall labor and freight advantage compared with 21 Asian, Caribbean and Latin American countries that are now supplying the U.S. market. The report notes, however, that Costa Rica's advantage is wage-sensitive and could evaporate if labor costs rise relative to those in rival sourcing sites.

The following case is included for instructional purposes. It does not necessarily illustrate good management practices in all respects. You might want to identify the issues and alternatives needing analysis before making a decision to proceed with the project.

Adapted from *Business Latin America,* November 30, 1983, p. 382. Used with the permission of the publisher, Business International Corporation, New York.

Case: Offshore Assembly in Costa Rica for Florida Electronics Corporation?

Florida Electronics Corporation (FEC) is a small Miami-based manufacturer of circuit boards for microcomputers and other light electronics applications. The firm has developed a market niche for supplying a number of small and medium-sized U.S. makers of electronic equipment and several wholesale dealers of computer-related supplies. In business since 1974, FEC has achieved annual sales of about $3.9 million with a growth rate of about 11 percent per year. Recent income statement and balance sheet data appear in tables 1A–1 and 1A–2.

During the past two years, the firm has faced increasing competition from manufacturers with plants in Korea and Hong Kong. It appears that FEC will encounter a severe loss in market share unless it can cut production costs. For this reason the general manager, George Barnes, has decided to consider building an assembly plant in Central America.

FEC's financial manager is a Costa Rican who chose to move to the politically stable United States. The financial manager believes that Costa Rica would make the best choice among Central American countries because of its long democratic tradition, high educational level, and reasonable infrastructure. He also believes that despite its proximity to Nicaragua and the pressing foreign debt problem, Costa Rica probably offers the most stable environment and most developed economic infrastructure of countries in the region (not including Mexico).

Given the company's lack of experience in foreign business, Barnes was quite lost in trying to decide how to proceed. He thought, however, that he needed to secure a feasibility study for a plant in Costa Rica.

Table 1A–1
Florida Electronics Corp. Income Statement, 1983

Item	Amount
Sales	
Circuit boards	$2,600,000
RS-232 cables	850,000
Other products	430,000
Production costs	
Labor	1,100,000
Computer chips	640,000
Other materials	810,000
Administrative costs	240,000
Licensing fee	100,000
Depreciation	160,000
Interest expense	190,000
Net income before tax	640,000
Corporate income tax	230,000
Net income after tax	410,000

Table 1A–2
Florida Electronics Corp. Balance Sheet, December 31, 1983

Assets		Liabilities	
Cash	$ 50,000	Accounts payable	$ 250,000
Marketable securities	570,000	Notes payable, short-term	450,000
Accounts receivable	890,000	Current taxes due	130,000
Inventory	610,000	Notes payable, long-term	1,220,000
Plant & equipment	970,000	Net worth (shareholders' equity)	1,040,000
Total	$3,090,000	Total	$3,090,000

Table 1A–3
Pro Forma Income Statement, FEC Costa Rica, 1984
(thousands of colones)

Item	Amount
Investment (in 1983)	90,000
Sales to Miami office	130,000
Cost of production in San José	
Labor	9,500
Imported components	49,000
Local materials	5,000
Cost of insurance and freight	4,500
Administrative costs in San José	2,600
Financing costs	To be determined
Net income before tax	To be determined
Costa Rican income tax (40%)	To be determined
Net income after tax	To be determined

The main difficulty of conducting a feasibility study was to locate a capable, knowledgeable analyst to carry it out. Fortunately for FEC, the financial manager's brother worked as a principal in an economic consulting firm in San José, and he would be happy to do a careful study. Also, Barnes discovered that a Costa Rican agency called CINDE, which is funded primarily from the U.S. Agency for International Development (AID), offers to help finance feasibility studies for projects that lead to exports from Costa Rica. As a result, he could borrow 90 percent of the money to finance the cost of the study from CINDE, and if he actually built the plant, he would not have to repay the loan. These very favorable terms induced Barnes to have the study done immediately; the resulting pro forma income statement for the proposed plant is shown in table 1A–3.

Contributed by Robert E. Grosse

Appendix 1B
Case: A Fertilizer Plant in Ghana for Nitrofix?

T he following case is included for instructional purposes. It does not necessarily illustrate good management practices in all respects. You might want to identify the issues and alternatives needing analysis before making a decision to proceed with the project.

Nitrofix, Inc., is a medium-sized U.S. manufacturer of nitrogenous fertilizers that has made a specialization of setting up plants to serve the local markets in smaller countries. In the 1960s their first international ventures went into the smaller countries of Western Europe, but in the 1970s they expanded into friendly Third World countries, such as the Philippines, Indonesia, Thailand, and Venezuela. The company thoroughly analyzed its overseas investments, and they had generally panned out well, contributing most of Nitrofix's growth in sales and profits for two decades. In the 1960s, Nitrofix executives usually insisted on 100 percent ownership of each overseas subsidiary, but in the 1970s they came to recognize both the necessity and the desirability of entering into joint ventures with local partners when terms and conditions were suitable.

Proposal from the Government

A Ghanaian government representative first approached Nitrofix about establishing a fertilizer plant in 1981, two years after Dr. Hilla Limann became the country's first democratically elected president in over a decade. The Limann government was actively seeking foreign investment, reversing previous governments' socialist practices and antipathy to private investment. However, Nitrofix was hesitant to enter an agreement because of Ghana's past political and economic instability, and negotiations proceeded fitfully. The Limann government was overthrown in a military coup on December 31, 1981. Nitrofix executives assumed that that was the end of the matter until the Ghana Trade and Investment Office contacted them again in mid-1982 and mentioned that some very favorable terms might now be possible for the investment.

Craig Michael Lee, the project advisor to the vice president of Nitrofix's international division, had a long meeting in mid-1982 with Bawol Cabiri, the commercial consul at the Ghana Trade and Investment Office in New York City. Lee hoped that the talk would enable him to decide whether it might be worthwhile to pursue an investment opportunity in Ghana. His meeting with Cabiri focused on the possibility that Nitrofix might invest in a plant in Ghana to be operated as a joint venture with either private Ghanaian entrepreneurs or with the government. A tentative name was agreed upon: Nitrofix (Ghana) Ltd.

The Investment Climate

Lee had been impressed by Cabiri's knowledge and understanding and by the potential profitability of the project. However, he knew that he had to evaluate a number of issues of vital importance: the condition of the Ghanaian economy, the political climate in Ghana and West Africa, the existence of a Ghanaian and/or West African market for fertilizer, Ghana's policies toward foreign investment, and the financial arrangements. He also knew that if his company decided to follow up on the possibility, it would have to prepare for negotiations on a wide range of matters.

From a variety of sources, Lee pieced together some information about Ghana's political and economic situation. The country had gained independence from Great Britain in 1957, the first black colony in Africa to become independent. Its first prime minister (later president) was Dr. Kwame Nkrumah, an eloquent spokesman and leader for the emerging aspirations of Africa. Thanks largely to its position as the world's largest cocoa exporter, Ghana was the richest country in Africa at the time of independence. Continuing a British colonial tradition, the new government invested a substantial part of its revenues in education at all levels from primary school through university. As a result Ghana had an unusually high level of literacy for a developing country, though the literacy rate among farmers remained low.

In subsequent years, the government's policies toward private enterprise (both Ghanaian and foreign) reflected a basic ambivalence that has persisted for two decades. On one hand, the Ghanaians recognized their need for the capital, entrepreneurial initiative, managerial know-how, and technology that domestic and foreign companies could supply; but on the other hand, they were impressed with the socialist, state-directed model of development and were concerned that private capitalists, if left unchecked, would accumulate and keep most of the country's wealth and benefits of development for themselves.

At the time when Nitrofix was considering the project, the existing investment code assured foreign investors protection and a fair return on their investment. It specifically eliminated any restrictions on transfers out of Ghana of fees, charges, capital, and profits to the investor's country of origin. It established a Ghana Investing Center, chaired by the vice president of Ghana, to dismantle regulatory and administrative barriers to investment and to review investment projects; the Centre would decide which projects qualified for special incentives. All approved enterprises were to receive five-year exemptions from customs duties for machinery and equipment imported for use in the enterprises, three years' customs exemption for spare parts, guaranteed manufacturing or establishment licenses, guaranteed immigration of necessary expatriate personnel, and certain tax exemptions and remittance guarantees for such personnel. In the manufacturing sector the government sought industries in which the country had a raw material advantage, underutilized existing plant capacity, or the capacity to conserve and/or earn foreign exchange. Projects qualifying for investment included agro-based industries, those processing raw materials originating in Ghana, such as animal feed and fertilizer, among others. Companies in the export sector could be exempted from company income tax during an initial period provided they declared no dividends during that period.

The Market for Fertilizer

Agriculture is a way of life for the people of Ghana, employing 60 percent of the labor force and producing 42 percent of the gross domestic product of 1980. However, out of the 23 million hectares suitable for farming, only 3 million hectares, or 13 percent, were under cultivation. Methods of cultivation were divided into two general categories: traditional (or subsistence) and new improved practices. Traditional methods were characterized by the use of simple tools; they relied almost entirely on human labor, resulting in inefficient processing and storage methods and in low crop yields. The new methods stressed the use of chemicals (fertilizers and pesticides) as well as farm machinery and implements.

Over 90 percent of the farming was undertaken by subsistence-level private farmers cultivating small plots of land, generally between three and four hectares. Soil fertility on these farms was generally maintained by crop rotation and burning of vegetation cover; the latter practice returned potash and some minerals to the soil, but it caused the loss of important organic matter and other minerals. Burning was especially damaging if done too frequently or at the wrong season, practices likely to increase as land use intensifies.

While the cultivation of tree crops (cocoa, coffee, rubber, and palm oil) is labor intensive, mechanization was introduced in the cultivation of field crops such as maize and rice. Mechanical cultivation leads to rapid deterioration of the organic matter in the soil and to depletion of soil nutrients. Therefore fertilizers must be used to replenish lost minerals, or else crop yields will decline.

The Limann government declared that agriculture would be the number one priority for development and investment. The government encouraged the development of large-scale commercial farming, which requires the use of modern techniques. In order to boost overall productivity and expand agricultural output, the government supplied many inputs, including hoes, seed rice, and groundnuts (peanuts). It also distributed more than 1 million bags of fertilizer to small producers, commercial farms, and parastatal organizations.

These steps alone, however, would not be sufficient to improve productivity or increase the usage of fertilizers; raising the educational level of the farm population is a fundamental necessity for increasing the understanding and acceptance of fertilizers. Such an educational program would require a massive effort by the government. But the more energetic and literate members of the younger generation who might be more amenable to adopting new practices have been leaving the countryside for the cities. Furthermore, the archaic land tenure system is based on traditions and customs that discourage innovation and thus constitute a formidable obstacle to the acceptance of fertilizer by small farmers.

Cocoa is raised both by small farmers who convert a portion of their subsistence holdings to production of the cash crop and by larger plantations and state farms. The cocoa industry is the main source of Ghana's foreign exchange earnings, accounting for approximately 65 percent in an average year. It employs 11 percent of the nation's labor force and is believed to account for a large part of its fertilizer usage. However, cocoa production has declined steadily since the early 1960s, and by 1980 Ghana had fallen from first to third place among the world's major exporters of cocoa. The factors responsible for the decline in output include low producer prices, poor maintenance of cocoa firms, aging of cocoa trees and cocoa farmers, scarcity of farm labor in the major producing areas, and ineffective control of pests and diseases. Poor transportation and a lack of infrastructure are problems, as is smuggling to neighboring countries where better prices are obtainable. Storage facilities have also deteriorated.

Questions to Be Considered

After reviewing all this information, Lee concluded that there would be many imponderables in any effort to estimate the growth potential of the Ghanaian fertilizer market. So much would depend on noneconomic factors, such as the effort and expense the government might decide to put into promoting the use of fertilizer and the pace at which Ghanaian farmers would accept it. Lee did find some tables apparently indicating that the use of fertilizers was growing in Ghana and enabling comparisons to other countries. However, he also found another source that said that Ghanaian consumption of nitrogenous fertilizers had peaked at eleven thousand metric tons in 1975–76 and had declined somewhat for several years thereafter. Consumption of potash and phosphate fertilizers had also decreased since 1975–76.

Lee also wondered whether some Ghanaian fertilizer production might be exportable to other West African countries. Ghana had joined the Economic Community of West African States (ECOWAS) at its inception in 1975. This community had a total of sixteen member states: Benin, Cape Verde, Gambia, Ghana, Guinea, Guinea-Bissau, Ivory Coast, Liberia, Mali, Mauritania, Niger, Nigeria, Senegal, Sierra Leone, Togo, and Upper Volta (now Burkina Faso). Many of these states, however, were even smaller and poorer than Ghana. It was supposed to become a common market with the elimination of trade barriers among its members and a common external tariff, and its members were supposed to work cooperatively for agricultural development, the construction of infrastructure to improve regional transportation, communications, and industrial growth. However, most of the members could not afford to lower their own tariff barriers or to take any real steps to implement the regional integration plans. Furthermore, Nigeria, with its oil wealth and naptha feedstocks, would be likely to grab the lead as the dominant nitrogenous fertilizer exporter in the region.

Contributed by William A. Stoever.

Appendix 1C
A Comparison of Successful and Unsuccessful Projects in India

Two separate investments in India, both by the same company, developed along dissimilar paths—one is eminently successful, the other a complete failure. A look at the likely reasons should prove instructive.

Company A . . . pioneered the industry in India during the 1950s when it started companies F and S as two investments in related but different lines. Firm S is now on top of the ladder in India. Firm F, which is now being wound up, is a case example of a firm that has committed three cardinal sins in India's complex environment: (1) It picked the wrong partner, (2) picked the wrong location, and (3) failed in public affairs, particularly in host government relations.

The Right Partner

Any partner in India is usually in a relatively strong position because of his knowledge of the complexities of the Indian environment. The right partner with that know-how is immensely helpful. But the single mistake of picking the wrong one can endanger a venture from the start. To make matters worse, foreign companies frequently find it difficult to recognize when their Indian partner is a problem, and dislodging an established one is even more difficult.

Company A held majority equity in firm F, but gave the Indian minority shareholder a managing agency role. The partner, it turned out, never really understood the capital-intensive and technologically oriented nature of the business, which was unlike most industries in India at the time. Company A was able to change the management of firm F only after years. The new partner was far more efficient than the first one, but the problems had gone too far, and company F continued to lose market share to more recent entrants in the industry it had pioneered.

Adapted from *Business Asia*, May 20, 1983, p. 159. Used with permission of the publisher, Business International Corporation, New York.

Locations

Choosing a location can be even more difficult than selecting a partner because the site may come with a host of troubles—labor, power supply, the incentive package, or state government relations—that must be considered ten or even thirty years out; yet the place of investment is of key importance. Company S, which is located in Bombay, may not have been viable if sited (like company F) outside Calcutta. In fact, Calcutta once was a prime industrial site. On the other hand, companies now locating in the Thane-Belapur belt near Bombay may in a few years' time run into some of the same problems firm F encountered in Calcutta.

Company F's plant was located some distance from Calcutta, near its source of raw material. To help the managing agent, company A sent a stream of technical managers from the parent firm. But since none of them wished to stay longer than two years in the inhospitable environment of a company compound, the lack of continuity of management expertise exacerbated the other problems.

Labor trouble (related to the strength of the Communists of West Bengal) started early and continued throughout. It caused not only production problems, but made living in the company compound even more uncomfortable for the expatriate staff, especially when the unions resorted to so-called *gherao* tactics—that is, locking managers into their offices, sometimes for days. Attempts to buy off labor resulted in gross overmanning. With production slowdowns, company F never really became profitable.

The Government

India's amount of red tape gives the government many opportunities to make doing business miserable for companies considered unfavorably. The Communist government of West Bengal was not favorably disposed toward company F because it was majority-owned by a multinational corporation. Moreover, coordination between the federal and the state government was bad because opposing parties were in power.

Since firm F did not succeed in developing good government relations, or did not try, getting anything done became a problem. Management did try to make the project work, and further investment in the early 1960s added new processes. Exports, mainly to southeast Asia, were pushed to nearly 25 percent of total sales, which should have pleased the government.

However, it was to no avail, and by the mid-1960s company A decided to sell out. With F not profitable, the stock market was no option, and government financial institutions showed no interest when approached. A workers' cooperative was mooted, but before a solution could be found, the unions in the early 1980s launched their largest and last strike, locked out management, and took over the plant.

The workers knew that non-use of the equipment would destroy it over a period of time; hence they tried to keep the machinery going. But without a throughput of material, the equipment was eventually ruined.

It was the end of the factory. Company A is now trying to sell what is left of the fixed assets—land, buildings, and peripheral machinery—and the technology to rebuild the project to one of its erstwhile competitors.

With company S, all the mistakes of company F were avoided. To comply with India's Foreign Exchange Regulation Act (FERA), company A had to dilute its original majority ownership, yet it plans to retain and expand this investment because it is pleased with progress. Here's why:

Company A avoided the difficult choosing of a partner by itself assuming management control from the start.

Politically and regarding labor, the location near Bombay was favorable. Expatriate managers found the climate hospitable and the life-style pleasant, and they stayed in India for long terms—one as long as eight years.

The government of Maharashtra, the state in which Bombay is located, generally has a better attitude toward business than does the strongly Communist rule in West Bengal.

Sources of Additional Information

Astriab, Christopher P., comp. and ed. *Annotated Investor's Information Guide.* Washington, D.C.: U.S. Overseas Private Investment Corporation, 1983. 1615 M St. NW, Washington, D.C. 20527. Phone: (800) 424-6742 or (202) 457-7010.

Bartz, Carl. *Washington Embassies: A Guide for the Private Sector.* Washington Association Research Foundation, 1133 15th St. NW, Washington, D.C. 20005.

Business America. Periodical published by the U.S. Department of Commerce. Available through district offices of the Commerce Department's International Trade Administration or from the Superintendent of Documents, U.S. Government Printing Office, Washington, D.C. 20402. Phone: (202) 783-3238.

Business International. *Indicators of Market Size.* New York: Business International, Annual. One Dag Hammarskjold Plaza, New York, NY 10017. Phone: (212) 750-6300.

Delphos, William A., ed. *Washington's Best Kept Secrets: A U.S. Government Guide to International Business.* New York: Wiley, 1983.

International Business Opportunities Service. The Johns Hopkins University Press, Journals Publishing Division, 701 W. 40th Street, Baltimore, MD 21211. Notices concerning procurement associated with projects funded by the World Bank and other international agencies.

The International Entrepreneur. Periodical published by the International Trade Council of Mid-America, Inc., in cooperation with the International Trade Institute of Kansas State University. Available free from the International Trade Council of Mid-America, 1627 Anderson Ave. Manhattan, Kansas 66502. Phone: (913) 532-6799.

Lambert's World of Trade, Finance and Economic Development: An International Directory of Government Contacts. Business Press International, 205 E. 42d St. New York, NY 10016. Phone (212) 867-2080.

Maffry, Ann Dwyer. *Foreign Commerce Handbook.* 17th ed. Washington, D.C.: Chamber of Commerce of the United States, 1981. 1615 H St. NW, Washington, D.C. 20062. Phone (202) 659-6111.

Robinson, Richard D. *Internationalization of Business: An Introduction.* New York: Dryden Press, 1984.

Root, Franklin R. *Foreign Market Entry Strategies.* New York: AMACOM, 1982.

Third World Development. 1985. 3 vols. Business Press International (USA), 205 E. 42d St. New York, NY 10017. Phone: (212) 867-2080.

United Nations Industrial Development Organization (UNIDO), Investment Promotion Service, 821 United Nations Plaza, New York, NY 10017. Phone: (212) 754-5966.

U.S. Department of Agriculture. Office of Private Sector Relations in the Office for International Cooperation and Development, Washington, D.C. 20250. Phone: (202) 475-4191. Media and Public Affairs Office of the Foreign Agricultural Service. Phone: (202) 447-7937.

U.S. Department of Commerce. Statistical profiles from market identification program: *Country Market Surveys* and *International Market Research Surveys.* Available through district offices of the Commerce Department's International Trade Administration or from the Office of Trade Information Services, U.S. Department of Commerce, P.O. Box 14207, Washington, D.C. 20044. Phone: (202) 377-2432 or 2665. Also consult Publications Officer, Office of Export Administration, U.S. Department of Commerce, Washington, D.C. 20230. Phone: (202) 337-2574.

U.S. Department of State, Office of Investment Affairs, Washington, D.C. 20520. Phone: (202) 632-1128. Also the Office of Business and Export Affairs. Phone (202) 632-0354.

U.S. Small Business Administration, Office of International Trade, 1441 L St. NW, Washington, D.C. 20416. Phone: (202) 653-7794. See also its field offices in nearly one hundred cities.

U.S. Trade and Development Program, International Development Cooperation Agency, Washington, D.C. 20523. Phone: (703) 235-3663.

World Bank. *World Development Report.* New York: Oxford University Press, Annual. World Bank Publications, P.O. Box 37525, Washington, D.C. 20013. Phone: (202) 477-1234.

2
Planning the Project

I t is important to put a great deal of thought into the strategic planning process since strategic planning is one of the single most important determinants of the ultimate success of a foreign investment project. Your plan should reflect carefully formulated objectives, but should also be flexible and subject to revision. This chapter provides step-by-step procedures for developing a plan, and it discusses key elements of the plan in detail.

As you consider going outside the United States, you need to be explicit about your business strategy, your technical competence, your intended marketing plan, and your own strengths and weaknesses. Such self-awareness is necessary for several reasons. When a small to medium-sized firm considers doing business abroad, it is well advised not to change its product or technology drastically. Such a firm should not go beyond its proven competence and experience in product or technology because it faces problems of operating in a new environment. On the other hand, a firm may have to modify its business strategy in order to operate successfully in the new environment.

You must also be certain that your financial structure and cash flow permit the investment. The investment should not be so big that you bet the future of your company. Because cash flows from abroad can be delayed, sufficient slack in the cash flow should be budgeted.

In addition, you should be sure that your firm is culturally flexible enough to undertake a foreign investment. American executives are often strongly wedded to the American values of individual achievement and mastery of personal destiny, and these values can make it difficult for American executives to understand people from other cultures. Cultural parochialism impedes foreign business. Methods of self-assessment and environmental assessment that can reduce problems of cultural miscommunication will be discussed in chapter 3.

Kenneth David, principal author.

Choosing Foreign Investment over the Alternatives

In order to take advantage of market opportunities and/or cost-reducing possibilities in developing countries, a firm needs a carefully considered strategy. There are many strategic alternatives available to a firm wanting to serve these markets, but the three principal ones are exporting, licensing, and direct investment. Individual direct investment projects frequently evolve from existing export strategies, but exporting does not necessarily have to precede direct investment in a particular country.

A careful comparison of the strategic alternatives is important. All strategic alternatives involve trade-offs, and each alternative has its own distinctive combination of advantages and disadvantages. Although direct investment does involve some distinct problems, it also solves the problems associated with other ways of doing business.

Key Questions. One of the first questions you should ask yourself as a potential investor in a developing country is: What is my principal objective? Are you hoping to increase your revenues by entering or expanding in foreign markets? Or are you interested in finding a low-cost location for producing your goods? A combination of these two objectives is also possible. For the sake of simplifying the analysis, however, it is helpful to keep those two objectives separate. But the objectives must be clear in the minds of all the potential investors. The objectives must be widely shared and agreed upon—by the chairman and chief executive officer and other senior executives.

Potential investors thus need to consider in their preliminary analysis four closely related questions about a direct investment project: (1) *Why* this project would be undertaken. Is it for market-seeking and/or cost-reducing purposes? (2) *Whether* the foreign market prospects are better than the market prospects at home—and/or whether foreign costs of production would be lower than those at home. (3) *Where* the market prospects—and/or the costs—would be most attractive, that is, in which particular countries. (4) *How* the expansion in that foreign country should occur. Which strategic alternative—direct investment, exporting, or licensing—should be adopted on the basis of its effects on revenues and/or costs?

Exporting versus Investing. If you are currently exporting your goods, deciding whether to continue to serve the foreign market by export or to serve the foreign market by foreign production is a key question.

Exporting is frequently a highly attractive way for a firm to enter and serve a foreign market for several reasons. In the first place, exporting may not require any substantial initial investment in plant and equipment. A firm may have excess capacity, or perhaps it can simply increase production runs in order to produce additional goods for a foreign market beyond the production levels for the domestic market relatively easily. Fixed costs, furthermore, may be relatively low. The perceived risks associated with an export strategy may be relatively low also.

On the other hand, exporting does have disadvantages. Particularly if transportation costs are a substantial part of the total cost structure, the variable costs associated with exporting may be relatively high. What's more, the revenues associated with exporting may be constrained by the firm's lack of direct involvement in the foreign market. That is to say, serving a market from a distance may put the firm at a disadvantage compared with its competitors in that market if those competitors have a direct market presence in the form of facilities and marketing personnel. Also, import barriers may make it difficult to serve the market.

There are therefore transfer costs and political considerations associated with both the export and the investment options. Table 2–1 summarizes these considerations. Let us compare the elements of the transfer cost calculations and political considerations.

First, the home country government offers various incentives to increase export trade, such as low-cost loans and business insurance for qualifying businesses. Host country governments also offer incentives, such as tax holidays and low-cost rental sites, particularly if the business uses national suppliers of materials and plans to export some or all of the product. The relative value of these incentive packages can be calculated.

Table 2–1
Serving Foreign Markets by Export or by Foreign Production

Export	*Foreign Production*
Transfer Cost Calculations	
Projected revenues by export	Projected revenues by foreign production
Plus export incentives offered by home country government	Plus investment incentives offered by host country government
Less costs of production at home	Less costs of production abroad
Less international transport and tariff costs	Less local transport costs
Less costs of doing business at a distance	Less costs of doing business at a distance
Equals export profit	Equals foreign production profit
Political Considerations	
Home government support for increase of export trade	Union disapproval of exporting jobs
Problems of trade protection by host country government	Problems of intervention with operations or ownership by host country government

Second, the lower cost of production abroad and the absence of international transport and tariff costs are prime motivations for serving foreign markets via foreign production. The price of lowering these variable costs can be calculated next to the additional fixed costs of financing foreign operating facilities.

Third, there are costs of doing business at a distance in both cases. Both exporters and foreign investors must bear the costs of adapting to foreign tastes and regulations with both options, though marketing research and midcourse corrections are easier if production is located abroad.

With export, the foreign firm must carefully select and monitor foreign distributors. The exporter does not control distribution and marketing directly and usually does not attain the level of sales revenue possible by foreign investment.

With the foreign investment option, there are costs of additional communication requirements—planning, directing, reporting on foreign operations. There are also additional staffing requirements, whether expatriate or local managers. Increasingly, large firms have chosen to train indigenous managers rather than bear the high expense of training and supporting home country managers who are assigned abroad. The family of the expatriate manager must also be considered. Studies have found that the most frequent cause of failure of foreign assignments is discontent on the part of the manager's family.[1] At least the spouses of candidates should be screened and given a cultural briefing prior to the assignment. A small firm commencing foreign investment may start by staffing key executive and managerial positions with home country personnel, but it should plan for future staffing by indigenous personnel.

Finally, a prime motivation for shifting from export to foreign production is often trade protectionism by the government of the foreign country. Firms with a profitable export trade learn that they must either set up facilities or face a restricted market. The host government frequently offers, as an additional incentive for investment, the imposition of a trade barrier to protect the market for the foreign investor.

Licensing. A third alternative, licensing, has the advantage of avoiding some of the risks associated with direct investment. In a typical licensing arrangement, the firm does not have physical facilities in the foreign country that would be at risk. Its costs of course, both fixed and variable, are extremely low, and it does not necessarily have to make any kind of substantial initial investment. By the same token, licensing tends to yield relatively low returns, especially if the licensee does not market the product or service as enthusiastically as the licensor would. On the other hand, if your licensee does well, you may find that you have a competitor in foreign markets where you wish to expand. Furthermore, licensees do not always remain within the markets set out in the licensing contract.

Changes over Time. There are also trade-offs over time among these three basic strategic alternatives. Although the initial investment is relatively high for direct investing, over the longer term the returns tend to be greater than with exporting or licensing. So, direct investment is a longer-term strategy, involving a permanent presence and therefore a greater commitment and greater returns. Exporting and licensing entail less substantial commitments in the short term, but as a consequence they also tend to yield less return over the long term. These comparisons are summarized in table 2–2.

Seeking Specific International Business Opportunities

If your firm selects the foreign production option, the next step is to seek a specific international business opportunity. Two approaches are available: (1) a systematic search for foreign projects or foreign partners, and (2) a global scan for opportunities.

Systematic Search. As chapter 1 made clear, many sources of information are available through U.S. government agencies that firms can use to learn of foreign business opportunities. Your firm can also systematically search for business opportunities by subscribing to a variety of publications (some of which are available on computer data bases) and by participating in seminars, trade fairs, or investment missions.

Global Scan. Alternatively—or, even better, in addition to the first method— your firm can conduct a truly global scan for foreign business opportunities

Table 2–2
Summary Comparisons of Direct Investment, Exporting, and Licensing as Strategic Alternatives

	Direct Investment	*Exporting*	*Licensing*
Initial investment	High	Medium	Low
Revenues	High	Medium	Low
Costs:			
Fixed	High	Medium	Low
Variable	Medium	High	Low

in order to cover all geographic areas. This method is advantageous if the first method produces results that could cause your firm to violate the rule stated earlier: your firm should not go beyond its proven competence and experience in product or technology because it is facing the problems of operating in a new environment.

Why should you do extensive global scanning? You may have heard that most large U.S. firms do not scan on a global basis, but either (1) accept or reject each project by some financial criterion such as a return on investment percentage, or (2) rank all currently analyzed projects by some financial criterion. However, small firms are advised to invest in global scanning for two reasons.

First, because large firms have a portfolio of foreign investments, inadequate returns on a particular investment do not materially affect their overall position. Small firms, especially when going international for the first time, require a higher degree of confidence in the investment.

Second, common practice is not always best practice. A fine example of the benefits of global scanning can be found in Kenichi Ohmae's book, *The Mind of the Strategist,* about a Japanese firm that performed a global scan on markets served, competitive activity, and services offered in the worldwide shipping industry.[2] The firm located an underserved market that was extremely profitable.

The first phase, global scanning, narrows the choice of production site to several candidate countries. The actual choice of a country for foreign production requires additional homework. Inexperienced firms (even those that have done some international trading) sometimes do not do their homework and choose their location simply because they have been exporting to that country or because they are responding to invitations or tips. Other firms choose to locate in an area with some cultural similarity, with political stability, and with geographical proximity. Faced with a choice between cultural distance and geographical distance, many inexperienced firms feel more comfortable operating in a culturally similar country even if it is farther away.

International business consultants can, of course, be hired to do the homework, but because their fees are high, it is prudent to limit the range of choices. Even small firms can do this using the following scanning techniques that employ public sources of information.

1. Develop criteria for initial country scanning in view of your investment objectives. The production site choice is independent of the target market choice. If your objective is market based, then the production location should be in or near the market. If your objective is to cut costs and if the foreign investment project is an export platform, then evaluate countries for operating costs plus shipping costs minus country incentives for export operations.

2. Develop criteria for initial country scanning in view of the type of

foreign business you are planning. Compared with a foreign manufacturing plant, where components are manufactured on-site, a foreign assembly plant, where all components are imported and simply assembled abroad, requires a lower level of infrastructural facilities and a lower level of worker skills. For manufacturing operations, advanced developing nations such as Hong Kong, Greece, Mexico, Nigeria, Portugal, Singapore, South Korea, or Taiwan may be more suitable. For assembly operations, less developed nations may be adequate.

3. Scan candidate countries for the level of economic development by market potential by considering the structure of production and employment by economic sector. For example, see table 2–3.

4. Scan candidate countries for the level of development of industrial energy and transportation facilities required by your business. Good measures of these facilities are the number of motor vehicles in use, the size of the merchant shipping fleet, and the volume of rail traffic. These are rough indicators of consumer mobility and the availability of transport for both sourcing of materials and the distribution of the physical product.

Because data on energy consumption and transportation facilities correlate closely with countries' levels of development and gross domestic product per capita, these measures are further indicators of market potential. For examples, see table 2–4.

5. Scan countries for the level of communications facilities required by your business. Multinational corporations gain a competitive edge over local firms by the control of strategic information in every business function: marketing intelligence, product management, financial management, and so forth. The extent to which a firm can obtain and use strategic information depends in part on the development of the communications and promotional infrastructure in the countries in which it is operating. Intracompany communications between headquarters and subsidiaries are dependent on local

Table 2–3
Levels of Economic Development

	Sectoral Composition			
	Percentage of GNP from		Percentage of workers employed in	
	Agriculture	Industry	Agriculture	Industry
Low-income countries (n = 34)	37	32	72	13
Middle-income countries (n = 38)	15	38	46	21

Source: World Bank, *World Development Report, 1984* (Washington, D.C.: World Bank, 1984), 222, 223.

Table 2–4
Industrial Infrastructure—Transportation and Energy Consumption

Country	Motor Vehicles in Use (1000)	Merchant Shipping Fleets (1000 gross tons)	Rail Traffic (freight-ton-kms)	Energy Consumption per Capita (kgs of coal equivalent)
United States	151,869	19,111	1,341,171	7,540
West Germany	24,762	7,707	57,264	4,342
Argentina	2,907	2,256	11,472	1,445
India	1,734	6,214	164,253	158
Nigeria	181	463	972	143
Other low-income countries (average of 34 countries)				80
Middle-income countries (average of 38 countries)				721
Upper-middle-income countries (average of 22 countries)				1,209

Sources: U.S. Bureau of the Census, *Statistical Abstract of the United States, 1984* (Washington, D.C.: U.S. Government Printing Office, 1984), 879, 880; World Bank, *World Development Report, 1984* (Washington, D.C.: World Bank, 1984), 232, 233. Data are for 1978–80.

facilities. See table 2–5 for examples of differences by country in communications facilities.

6. Scan candidate countries for the availability of natural resources. If the objective of foreign investment is cutting costs, the firm must determine whether natural resources are locally available. Many developing countries, being short of foreign exchange, frown on large-scale imports of raw materials.

7. Scan countries for the availability of human resources. When transferring technology to a developing country, it is necessary to know whether the work force is sufficiently skilled to employ the technology. A rough measure of work force skill is literacy rates. These figures are available in the World Bank's *World Development Report* and in reports of the International Labor Organization. The International Labor Organization also reports on country wage levels in different industries.

Depending on the industry, you may have to hire local scientists and technicians for local research and development. Table 2–6 illustrates the differing research and development potential of different countries.

The next step is to determine whether your firm has a competitive advantage.

Table 2–5
Distribution of Communications Media

Country	Telephones per 100 Population	Pieces of Mail Sent (millions)	Newspaper Copies per 1,000 Population	Radios per 1,000 Population	Television Sets per 1,000 Population
United States	78.5	88,970	282	2,099	624
West Germany	46.4	12,368	423	370	337
Argentina	9.3	620	NA	379	190
India	0.4	7,421	20	45	2
Nigeria	0.2	959	NA	73	6

Source: U.S. Bureau of the Census, *Statistical Abstract of the United States, 1984* (Washington, D.C.: U.S. Government Printing Office, 1984), 881, 882. Data are for 1979–80.

Table 2–6
Expenditures and Human Resources for Research and Development

Country	Expenditures for R&D As a Percentage of GNP	Personnel engaged in R&D (full-time equivalents)	
		Scientists and Engineers per Million Population	Technicians per Million Population
United States	2.5	2,875	NA
West Germany	2.4	1,989	1,883
Argentina	0.6	351[a]	491[a]
India	0.5	— (89[b])	—
Nigeria	0.3	31	19

Source: UNESCO, *Statistical Yearbook, 1983* (Paris: UNESCO Press, 1983), V114–19.
[a]Estimated figures.
[b]Scientists, engineers, and technicians per million population.

Competitive Advantage Audit

Whether it is going into a foreign country because market prospects are better there than at home or because costs are lower than at home, your firm must be certain that it has a competitive advantage over host country competitors. The question can be posed as follows: *Is your firm's projected revenue less its operating costs and less the cost of doing business at a distance, greater than local competitors' revenue less their operating costs?*

Evaluating the Revenues and Costs. The various sources of revenue and cost advantages for a firm located outside the U.S. include such factors as:

1. Sophisticated management skills and information management
2. Perceived higher quality of the firm's products or services
3. Proprietary rights via brand names, patents, and trademarks
4. Economies of scale in purchasing, production, promotion, research and development, and international marketing intelligence
5. Capability to renew technology via R&D
6. Capability to transfer technology internally without loss of control of proprietary knowledge
7. Capability to acquire the lowest-cost funds, materials, and labor within the system of headquarters and subsidiaries

Overall, your firm has a competitive advantage over local firms when it has superior skills and resources, and when it has the capability to take advantage of market imperfections and reduce risks by means of linkages between headquarters and subsidiaries.

For a profitable venture, these competitive advantages must offset the costs of doing business at a distance, such as:

1. Costs of avoiding losses from changes in the value of foreign currency
2. Information problems: costs of acquiring knowledge of local economic, political, social, legal, regulatory, and cultural conditions
3. Additional communication requirements: costs of insuring good communications in planning, directing, reporting, and controlling foreign operations
4. Adaptation costs: costs of adapting product or service to local needs, costs of adapting to local supply, labor, and distribution conditions
5. Need for complex managerial skills: high costs of training and supporting managers assigned to foreign locations or of training local managers

In short, a U.S. firm has a competitive advantage over local firms when it has revenue advantages or cost advantages over local firms that more than offset the costs of doing business at a distance. It is essential that a firm assess its competitive strengths and weaknesses before entering into a foreign venture.

Additional Competitive Factors. Another complication of foreign investment is that multinational corporations from other nations may already be operating in or preparing to operate in the same national market. Competitive scanning is necessary in order to avoid surprises. For example, American machine tool manufacturers considering an investment in India will find that, in addition to a technologically advanced Indian competitor—Hindustan Machine Tools—there are competitors with fairly high quality products at moderate prices from several Eastern European nations.

To know whether, how, and how much to modify your business strategy for the foreign business, your firm must therefore determine the competitive strategies both of local firms and of foreign firms operating in the country of interest. Chambers of Commerce, trade missions, and industry reports by the Department of Commerce may help you obtain a list of competitors in the candidate countries. You can also do research on the offerings of competitors in order to perform a competitive product–market analysis of product benefits to buyers in the countries of interest.

Competitive analysis may be easier than it sounds, for some of the competitors in your target market may also be competing in the U.S. marketplace. If so, it may not be too difficult to find out how these competitors change their product offering for the foreign target market.

It is essential to remember that even if your business strategy is successful in domestic operations, you are facing an environment in which the rules of the game differ. For example, a U.S. company can be rated highly in its industry if it is known to be a supplier to major firms. If it chooses to compete in another country, however, it may be evaluated by different criteria, such as the precision of its technical specifications and the ability of sales personnel to communicate those specifications expertly.

Analyzing Foreign Markets

The basic marketing philosophy applies for foreign investment: Satisfy the *customers'* needs and wants at a profit. Homework is necessary to find out what the foreign customers' needs are and to adapt your business strategy accordingly.

Depending on the countries chosen as target markets, the market research and analysis procedures may or may not differ greatly from procedures you already use. Market information available in advanced developing nations is fairly adequate, though not quite as extensive as is found in the United States; on the other hand, detailed market information about other less developed countries is not as readily available in published sources. (The chapter "Social Organization" in *The Cultural Environment of International Business* gives some hints for approaching these markets.)[3] For more details on how to adapt product offerings, see chapters 3 and 9. Modify your product offering if necessary.

If time is not crucial to your decision, one way to obtain information is to use export trade as a research tactic. If you have not already done so, consider exporting to several countries that are candidates for a foreign production site before investing in that location. This tactic is helpful, however, if and only if you choose a foreign sales agent who can teach you about that country. When you use export trade as a research tactic, you should select as a sales agent someone who, in addition to helping get the goods out the door, has knowledge of the local market and has business and government contacts—someone you might consider as a joint venture partner. Informing the person chosen of the possibility of a future jointly owned and operated investment should increase that person's motivation in the sales role.

If you wish to begin foreign operations sooner, because of competitive pressures, you will have to do the research in other ways. General trading companies or export management companies can provide this information for a percentage of the revenue. Large consulting companies primarily work for large firms, and their fees are in line with the large budgets of their clients; a decent job done by one of these companies may cost $100,000 or more. If this cost is beyond your means, other options are to make use of Management Assistance Programs sponsored by the Small Business Administration, such as the Service Corps of Retired Executives, the Active Corps of Executives, and the Small Business Institute. The Small Business Institute employs senior or graduate level international business students to do foreign marketing analysis. Some firms directly contact local business schools and hire international business professors to supervise a research project that will be carried out by students.

A U.S. government agency, the Overseas Private Investment Corporation (OPIC), has the Investor Information Service, which provides packets of informational materials on approximately a hundred countries and a dozen major market groups. The packets contain information concerning a given country's economy, business climate, trade situation, labor market, infrastructure, geography, culture, government, and other characteristics. In addition, country studies from Business International, Arthur Anderson, Ernst & Whinney, and Price Waterhouse can be helpful.

Other Elements of the Planning Process

You will need to determine which factors are crucial to the performance of your project and its products. These factors can be the criteria for the final selection of a country for the production site, that is, for evaluating the coun-

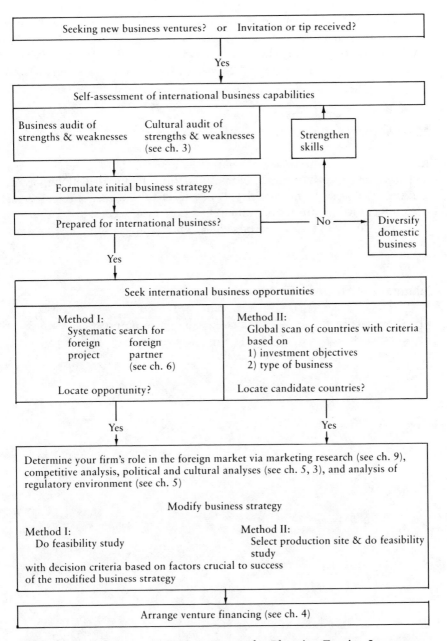

Figure 2–1. Decision and Task Sequence for Planning Foreign Investment

tries on your short list. In other words, these are the criteria for a detailed analysis of the investment climate in prospective countries.

You will also need to consider the technical feasibility of your project as well as financial arrangements and government policies. These topics are considered in later chapters.

Making the Commitment

After completing these several steps, then you are ready for a review, reformulation, and formal approval within your firm. It is extremely important that this final stage be taken seriously because having a very strong, serious commitment to the project by top-level executives is necessary if a decision is made to go ahead with it. Responsibility for the project should be assigned to a senior officer.

Summary of Strategic Planning Process

The flowchart in figure 2–1 summarizes the planning process presented in this chapter. It also provides a guide to subsequent chapters, where several topics are considered in further detail.

Sources of Additional Information

Ohmae, Kenichi. *The Mind of the Strategist*. New York: McGraw-Hill, 1982.

Price Waterhouse. *Doing Business in [Country X]*. Series.

Robinson, Richard D. *Internationalization of Business*. Chicago: Dryden, 1984.

Robock, Stephan H., and Kenneth Simmonds. *International Business and Multinational Enterprises*. Homewood, Ill.: Irwin, 1983.

Root, Franklin R. *Foreign Market Entry Strategies*. New York: AMACOM, 1982.

U.S. Department of Commerce. *The Investment Climate in Foreign Countries*. Series.

3
Managing Cultural Problems

ven firms with extensive international business experience sometimes blunder in intercultural communications. For example, Evitol shampoo unexpectedly sold poorly in Latin countries; the reason was that the sound of "evitol" was similar to words meaning "dandruff contraceptive." Similarly, the makers of Fresca soda found they were selling "lesbian soda."[1] Language barriers are sometimes the most difficult problems to deal with when firms conduct business outside their home countries. Planning for your first extensive international business operations therefore means learning to expect the unexpected.

When you engage in international business operations, you must modify many of the business tasks you are familiar with from domestic business operations. Firms tend to become proficient at the more quantifiable and culturally less sensitive business functions such as international finance, accounting, and logistics; they often have trouble, however, with the culturally sensitive business functions, such as international marketing and personnel management. It is thus important to pay careful attention to intercultural communications and other cultural problems before you start up your project.

The possibility of miscommunication that can unexpectedly impair your business operations is present whenever business people differ in cultural understandings and expectations. Managing cultural problems is therefore an essential task in your international business operations; mismanagement can cause you to make unwitting and possibly very costly mistakes. According to Jagdish Sheth, an expert on this problem, "The post mortems performed on past marketing mistakes strongly suggest that most mistakes occur in the process of carrying out marketing plans rather than in basic thinking. In other words, it is the execution of marketing plans in terms of interpersonal communication, negotiations and mass communication where most mistakes oc-

---

Kenneth David, principal author.

cur. Therefore, the message is clear: the cross-cultural setting creates situations in which the marketer must decide whether he should extend or adjust his way of doing business in a foreign market."[2]

The task of managing cultural problems is difficult even in domestic business relationships in such situations as mergers and acquisitions, where the parties differ in their individual corporate cultures, but are otherwise part of the same wider business and national cultures. Of course there are also often important regional differences that affect domestic business relations. However, the task of intercultural communications is generally more difficult in international business relationships, where the cultural differences involved in business relationships may be even greater.

This chapter will suggest ways to avoid intercultural communications blunders by addressing the following questions: (1) What are the causes of intercultural communications problems? How can you find out whether your firm's corporate culture will make problems? (2) How much should your firm be concerned about cultural problems in the foreign operations you are planning? How crucial are intercultural communications for the success of your venture? (3) What should you do about potential communications problems? Should you expect to impose your cultural understandings and practices or should you adapt to the foreign setting? (4) How much time, money, and energy should you spend to improve intercultural communication skills?

The Importance of Culture

Cultural differences can cause serious misunderstandings—as the following experience illustrates.

> An American businessperson was bemoaning the frequent giving of gifts to government officials as a way to reduce bureaucratic red tape in India. It seemed corrupt to him. His Indian joint venture partner patiently explained to him the continuity of this form of gift giving with the traditional exchanges of gifts by Brahmin priests. When the American remained unimpressed, the Indian added, "Here, we give gifts *after* a law has been passed and you call it corruption. In your country, you give gifts *before* a law has been passed and you call it lobbying!"[3]

To give another example, Japanese and U.S. management cultures differ. Japanese managers are classified into working groups. Codes of conduct emphasize harmony and cooperation within the working group. High priority is placed on the accomplishment of tasks by groups. By contrast, in the

United States managers are classified as individuals. According to a common code of conduct individuals are competing for power and position and may not necessarily cooperate in working on related tasks. Finally, priority is placed on the accomplishment of each individual's job. (Of course, the cultures of different Japanese corporations differ just as much among themselves as corporate cultures do in the United States.)

Distinctive corporate cultures do exist. Indeed, your own firm has a corporate culture. Ask yourself whether newcomers have to learn "how things get done around here." Watch newcomers make mistakes until they map the territory and discover the implicit assumptions and priorities that have become part of the landscape. Ask your experienced sales personnel whether they know about the way things get done in the companies where they have their major accounts. The answers to these questions will clearly reveal that corporate cultures make a difference in your business.

Various elements of your corporate culture can be identified. Corporate culture classifies events by the use of special language or jargon;[4] one company, for example, refers to all of its crises as "challenges." Moreover, besides formal policies that govern behavior, there are also informal codes of conduct. Newcomers to your firm learn about these codes in the recruitment and training processes; they hear corporate stories of your heroes, successes, and failures that define the proper and improper behavior for employees.[5] Organizationally smart managers often imitate the behavior of successful managers that they encounter.[6] They also learn the real channels of communication that may or may not coincide with formal reporting relationships. These informal codes of conduct are just as important as the formal systems of evaluation, reward, and promotion in directing the behavior of your personnel. Finally, your firm's value priorities and deeply held assumptions are sometimes consciously imparted in corporate rituals such as board meetings and occasions where superior performance is recognized, and in qualitatively stated corporate objectives (for example, "IBM means service!"), as opposed to quantitatively stated objectives (for example, "Increase market share by 4 percent this year!").[7] On the other hand, important priorities and assumptions about how things work in your firm are frequently part of the landscape, something of which the members of the organization are not conscious, except during times of crises.[8]

What are the implications of these issues for your firm if it is going to be involved in extensive intercultural business relationships as part of an investment project in a developing country? In the early planning stages, your firm should perform an audit of its cultural strengths and weaknesses, for you will need to develop a cultural policy that fits in with your foreign business strategy.

Conducting a Cultural Audit

The first objective of a cultural audit, to put it bluntly, is to find out whether your personnel are so parochial that you might face serious problems in the investment project you are planning. The cultural audit can be conducted by your own personnel and/or by outsiders. Professional consultants are available to help you select and train personnel for foreign assignments. Even after training, those individuals will still have to adjust the way things are done in your company. It helps to take time to examine your corporate culture.

The second objective is to determine whether your organization is open to foreign ways of doing things, whether it can learn from foreign experiences. The terms *strong* and *weak* corporate cultures can be helpful in understanding the role of your corporate culture in intercultural communications.[9] If your firm has a strong corporate culture, your assumptions, values, and codes for behavior are widely shared and the personnel are committed to carrying them out. If your firm has a weak corporate culture, then your personnel neither widely share the assumptions, values, and codes nor are committed to them. You may assume that for firms operating only in a single national market strong cultures improve profitability, but studies of firms providing services internationally suggest that corporate cultures can be too strong. Although members of a firm with a strong corporate culture can understand one another well, they may have problems learning from the environment. An openness to learning from foreign cultures, however, is especially important to your success in developing countries. A cultural audit of your firm may make you more aware of potential obstacles to such learning.

If you have a small firm, you may not feel that you have the time or resources to hire an outside consultant to perform a cultural audit. If you want to do it yourself, there are several ways to reveal the underlying assumptions of your corporate culture. Assign *several* people to do the following: (1) Review the backgrounds of the founders of the company. What are their strongly held values? How forcefully do they communicate these values to the rest of the organization? (2) Review any periods when the company was undergoing difficulties. Is there any pattern to the choices made during such a period? Have these choices become part of the landscape and now influence "how things are done around here"? (3) Follow the process of making a major decision that requires a significant amount of the company's resources. What is the path of communication that such a decision takes? Where are pockets of unseen influence?

One word of caution: outside consultants and newcomers to a firm may not know the inside story of how things work in your firm. On the other hand, long-time members of your firm may be partially blind to deeply held assumptions because those assumptions are part of the landscape; in this case, an outsider may be helpful in mapping the territory.

Developing Your Firm's Cultural Policy

Your firm faces the need to develop an appropriate cultural policy, just as it faces the need to develop an appropriate technology policy and an appropriate product policy. Your corporate culture, which may be appropriate within the U.S. cultural framework, will be alien in a developing country. Your expatriate managers and your partners in international joint ventures will be managing organizations where different cultures meet, and what's more, your managers' social relationships with suppliers, customers, and government officials are crucial to the operations of your enterprise. Intercultural communication is therefore an important business task that needs to be managed well. Consider, for example, the case in exhibit 3–1.

Exhibit 3–1
The Importance of Having a Culturally Competent Managing Director

A United States manager with an M.B.A. from a well-known university and twenty years of experience in business in the United States was appointed to be the managing director of a foreign subsidiary. He was in charge of running a new plant and a recently refurbished old plant (which had been taken over from a local firm). The total work force of the two plants was 890, all local people who had been trained by the firm to work in the two facilities. After six months of operations, the managing director was the only expatriate manager from the United States remaining at the facilities.

The managing director was a stranger to the country. The language was new, the culture was new, the way of doing business and the people were new. Putting in practice all of his experience in the United States and his M.B.A. training, the managing director started to issue instructions on the assumption that the orders would be carried out, as they were in the United States, since they were the same orders that had been issued in the United States. He did not stop to think, however, that his memos would be read and interpreted by people with different concepts of work, faith, loyalty, dedication, and goals, and he soon concluded that his "proven instructions" were not being executed as they should be. No other way was possible, he thought, for his twenty years of experience in the United States showed that this way worked. Therefore, he decided to "enforce the rules."

Friction between the managing director and his staff and plant operating group became severe. It was exacerbated by the fact that profits were well below plan. By the beginning of the third year, the subsidiary was in the red, and product rejections because of quality problems were reaching the level of 30 percent. The firm was therefore forced to import components by air, which substantially increased costs. Losses increased dramatically.

As losses mounted, the managing director issued more and more instructions to the work force. After he and two of his staff members were physically threatened by workers, the managing director hired bodyguards who accompanied him to his office. The local press, the government, and the political opposition were all becoming critical of the firm and its operations. The losses continued to increase, and the public image of the firm continued to deteriorate. In view of the circumstances, no local buyers could be found to take over the firm. Nor was the local majority partner interested in increasing its share.

The managing director was finally replaced by a new manager, who knew the language, the culture, and the business practices of the country. He knew how to communicate with people, and he knew how to motivate them. Within twelve months, the firm was nearly profitable. The company was in good standing with its work force, the union, the press, and the government. The firm was later sold for a good price to the local partner.

The U.S. parent firm had originally made a simple but expensive mistake. It had given major responsibility for operating a plant in a foreign country to a manager who had no previous business experience or training outside the United States and who had the naive, ethnocentric idea that management practices that had been successful in the United States would also be successful in a foreign culture.

Contributed by Robert S. Corredera.

Key Questions. In most situations, your firm cannot and should not simply try to impose its corporate culture on foreign business collaborators. Should you totally adapt? Hold your own? Seek to work out a compromise corporate culture with foreign business collaborators? Build a portfolio of adaptive techniques from experience in the various societies in which you operate? There is no single answer. Cultural policy cannot be stated categorically in such a way that it will apply to all business situations. Different situations call for different cultural policies.

Assessing the Cultural Environment. In order to answer these key questions, you will need to assess the cultural environment and adjust your cultural policy accordingly. You should assess three kinds of relationships: your relationship with the host country government; your relationship with foreign business collaborators, such as partners, managers, workers, suppliers, sales agents, and distributors; and your relationship with consumers or clients. Each kind of relationship should be analyzed so that you can determine how much your firm should adapt to local practices in the developing country.

You should first assess the strength of your bargaining power with the people you will be dealing with in the foreign country; next, you should determine the importance of the intercultural communication tasks that will be necessary to implement your firm's strategy. The less your bargaining power and the more critical the communication tasks, the more you should adapt to the foreign culture; in other words, your cultural policy should be more responsive. To implement such a responsive cultural policy, you will need more time and money for the selection and training of personnel for foreign assignments.

The Company–Host Country Relationship. Chapter 5 and portions of several other chapters deal more fully with aspects of your relationship with the host country government. You should note, however, that your firm cannot operate in a country without the approval of its government, so you should consider that relationship as early as possible. You should be sensitive to the importance of cultural differences in your relations with the host government.

For instance, developing nations often value consumer choice less than the effect of consumers' purchases on national economic plans and may prohibit products that do not fit with their plans and priorities. Coca-Cola was thus considered a luxurious product in India and undesirable within the context of government economic plans.

Type of Business Relationship. Your decision to adapt your business practices will also depend in part on the type of business relationship involved. There are two questions here. How closely must you and your business collaborators understand one another? Can one party impose its culture and practices on the other?

Communications are less critical between a firm and its foreign sales agent than they are with a joint venture partner or a foreign subsidiary. Furthermore, while corporate headquarters has the authority to impose its culture (via intensive training) on a wholly owned foreign subsidiary, it cannot impose its corporate culture on a joint venture partner. Communications intensity will be low in the relation between you and a foreign sales agent. In this relationship, precise communications are important but the bargaining power is generally on the side of the export firm. You need not spend much to facilitate the communications. Similarly, in the relationship between an American firm and foreign suppliers, the American firm generally can expect the suppliers to adapt.

In an international business venture that is jointly owned by firms from two countries, however, the need for coordinated activity will be high. As exhibit 3–2 illustrates, neither firm can impose its culture on the other. A case study of a successful Indo-American joint venture found that the firms not only engaged in a long process of negotiating the contractual terms of the venture, but they also in effect negotiated understandings and expectations. They thereby negotiated the corporate culture for the venture.

Your Relationship with Customers and Clients. The decison to adapt business practices also depends on the nature of the product or service you render and your relationship with your customers or clients. If your products or services are standardized and tangible, then you should invest more in marketing re-

Exhibit 3–2
The Importance of Culture in Business Relationships

The following incident makes clear (1) that culture makes a difference in international business relationships, and (2) that joint venture partners cannot impose their culture on one another, but must negotiate how to understand one another in addition to negotiating the business partnership.

The president of a North American construction firm was arriving in Delhi, where the firm was engaged in a joint venture with a large Indian firm to build a pipeline. Another North American, who was second in command in the construction firm, was stationed in India for the duration of the two-year project. He had worked out operating details with his Indian counterpart for the second phase of the project. The North American chief executive's plan was to confirm the arrangements in a meeting with the chief executive of the Indian firm and to depart the next evening for Singapore.

When the North Americans called the Indian firm, they learned that the Indian chief executive was requesting three days "to review the operating details." The North American second in command was furious and accused the Indian joint venture partners of a lack of common decency and more.

By questioning the participants a consultant revealed that there was nothing shared in the two firms' priorities and interpretations of the situation.

The North American side prioritized time and underplayed hierarchy.

The North American chief executive was quite willing to delegate negotiations to his second in command and basically did not care if the Indian chief executive was fully informed of the minute details.

The Indian chief executive, on the other hand, wanted to be fully briefed on the details.

Partially because he did not have confidence in his subordinate and partially because he wanted to display full knowledge of the situation to both the visiting North American chief executive and to his own subordinate during the formal meeting, the Indian chief executive downplayed a time delay. For him, imposing a delay on a visiting chief executive was a small ritual intended to impress his Indian subordinate.

Among joint venture partners, therefore, neither side can impose its corporate culture on the partner, although a joint corporate culture can be developed through discussions.

Adapted from Vern Terpstra and Kenneth David, *The Cultural Environment of International Business*, 2d ed. (Cincinnati: South-Western Publishing Company, 1985), 1. Used with permission.

search and in mass advertising in order to communicate with your customers or clients. If your products or services are unique and intangible, then you should invest more in corporate organizational design features to facilitate interpersonal communications.

Industries differ in the degree to which firms can standardize their products or must respond to consumer needs. Oil producers are free to produce highly standardized products for customers around the world. Producers of such consumer goods as soap or perfume, in contrast, face culturally varying wants and needs. Firms cannot adapt to the precise needs of every country in which they operate without losing a competitive edge (via cost economies of large-scale operations) over local firms. An alternative is product standardization at the level of world regions, with packaging, distribution, and promotional campaigns tailored to each country market.

In foreign operations, as in domestic ones, it is necessary to match the expected buying decision behavior with appropriate promotional activity. Consumer goods that are bought frequently and with little consideration are promoted by mass advertising techniques and only rarely by the more expensive personal selling technique (for example, door-to-door vacuum cleaner salesmen). Industrial goods sold to producers, on the other hand, require personal selling because the buying decision is extended and subject to multiple scrutiny. Interpersonal, intercultural communication skills are crucial to performing these functions effectively, especially if the industrial good is customized for the client. (See Appendix 3A.)

In service industries, the necessary degree of adaptation to client needs also varies by the type of the service rendered. In machine-intensive service industries, such as the mechanized car wash industry, the service rendered is not unique, and so the need for adaptations for customer response is minimal.

In human-intensive service industries, personal communications are more important. In overseas construction projects, for example, the project team must first engage in long-range economic planning and feasibility studies with government planners before submitting actual engineering plans and a bid for the project. The service to be provided is ambiguous and must be carefully negotiated with the client.

Communications are most intense when a service such as a large-scale, customized computer software program is provided. Here, the service is unique and intangible. The firm cannot impose business practices, but must be very responsive and appear credible to the client.

Conclusion

There are two stages in the management of intercultural problems: performing a cultural audit and developing an appropriate cultural policy. You will need to be sensitive to host governments' desires that you employ technology that is appropriate to the employment needs of the country and that you modify products to meet local consumers' needs and wants. A nationally responsive business strategy, furthermore, requires better communication not only with the ultimate consumers but also with government agencies.

Your need to manage intercultural problems will also vary by the type of business relationship. Your need will be greater when many of your activities must be coordinated with firms from different cultures. Your best method of communicating with foreign customers and clients will also vary, depending on the nature of your product or service offered. Regardless of your particular situation, however, you will need to give some careful attention to intercultural communications problems.

Appendix 3A
Communications Tasks in Different Foreign Business Relationships

To amplify the discussion of types of business relationships, this appendix contrasts two major forms of international business relationships: (1) intrafirm relationships between corporate headquarters and their foreign (wholly owned) subsidiaries in manufacturing industries, and (2) interfirm relationships in service industries.

First, the communications tasks vary with the complexity of the reporting relationships. In multinational manufacturing firms, reporting relationships between headquarters and subsidiaries are fully within the control of headquarters. Reporting relationships are most frequently formalized in some kind of division structure (divisions by business functions, by geographical areas, or by international product divisions). In these administrative structures, communications paths and reporting relationships are unambiguous because a manager reports to one person. When a manufacturing firm employs a matrix structure, there is greater ambiguity in communications because many managers have two reporting relationships; for example, a country manager may report to an international product manager and to a geographical region manager. In these firms, project teams are assembled for occasional tasks.

In international service firms, the project team is the stable unit of organization. The project team in a service-providing firm is usually in direct contact with a user team, a set of persons from the client firm (or government agency) who will be directly affected by the service provided. The project team is also expected to present periodic progress reports to the upper management of the client firm. The project team has a more formal reporting relationship with the upper management of its own firm.

Second, communications tasks differ in the amount of time that can be allotted for accomplishing them. Because of the long-term relationship between headquarters and its subsidiaries, headquarters can fine-tune the communications over a long period. With providers of services, the relationship may last two weeks or two years. Service providers must know how to learn the client firm's culture quickly.

Third, communications tasks differ in the degree to which complexities and uncertainties can be anticipated. Foreign manufacturing operations are located in fixed sites. Complexities and uncertainties in the host country environments can be managed over an extended period. International service contracts occur in various sites, in various cultures. Scattered site provision of service requires flexibility on the part of the project team to deal with complexities and uncertainties that cannot be anticipated far in advance.

Fourth, communications tasks are affected by relative bargaining power. A manufacturing firm's headquarters can impose its corporate culture on its foreign subsidiaries; a service provider cannot. The provider must make some attempt to understand and respond to the recipient's culture if the know-how is to be transferred and the service is to be successfully provided.

In short, communications tasks are more or less critical in international business relationships, depending on the degree of coordination of activities required and on the relative power of the parties to the transaction. In different situations, a firm may have the power to impose its culture, may have to negotiate a joint corporate culture, or may have to respond and adapt to another corporate culture.

Sources of Additional Information

Adler, Nancy J. "Cultural Synergy: The Management of Cross-Cultural Organizations." In *Trends and Issues in OD: Current Theory and Practice*, edited by W. Warner Burke and Leonard D. Goldstein, 163–84. San Diego, Calif.: University Associates, 1980.

Doz, Y.L., C.A. Bartlett, and C.K. Prahalad. "Global Competitive Pressure vs. Host Country Demands: Managing Tensions in MNCs." *California Management Review* (1981): 63–74.

Hofstede, Geert. *Culture's Consequences: International Differences in Work-Related Values*. London: Sage, 1980.

Landis, Dan, and Richard W. Brislin, eds. *Handbook of Intercultural Training*, 3 vols. New York: Pergamon Press, 1983.

Reynolds, John I. *Indo-American Joint Ventures: Business Policy Relationships*. Washington, D.C.: University Press of America, 1979.

Sheth, Jagdish N. "Cross-cultural Influences on the Buyer-Seller Interaction/Negotiation Process." *Asian Pacific Journal of Management* 1 (1983): 46–55.

Terpstra, Vern, and Kenneth David. *The Cultural Environment of International Business*. 2d edition. Cincinnati: South-Western Publishing Company, 1985.

Thomas, Dan R.E. "Strategy Is Different in Service Industries." *Harvard Business Review* 56 (July–August 1978): 158–65.

Triandis, H.C. "Interpersonal Relations in International Organizations." *Organizational Behavior and Human Performance* 2 (1967): 26–55.

Tung, Rosalie. "Selection and Training of Personnel for Overseas Assignments." *Columbia Journal of World Business* 6 (Spring 1981): 68–78.

4
Obtaining Financing

O f all the issues that you will encounter in connection with a direct
investment project in a developing country, financial issues are
probably the most technically complex. Because of this complexity
you may need assistance in managing financial problems—assistance that is
readily available from bankers and other specialists in international finance.

This chapter presents materials that will give you a basic understanding
of funding sources so that you can converse with such specialists. (Chapter
10 focuses on foreign exchange and tax issues.) One of the themes of this
chapter is that although distinctive problems are associated with raising funds
for foreign production facilities, there are also unusual opportunities. Indeed,
the diversity and the terms of alternative funding sources may surprise you.

There are numerous possible sources for funding a project in a developing
country. One possible source would be the firm itself; this source could be
the parent firm in the United States, or it could be a partner in the project
being established in the foreign country, or it could even be an existing foreign
affiliate. A variety of possible sources of funds external to the firm may be
found as well. See the outline of sources in table 4–1.

Furthermore, organizations exist that can help you find a partner able to
provide financing, and they can help you locate yet other organizations that
would be potential sources of funds.

Private Sources in the United States

Your Local Bank. Within the United States, you should go to your own private banker first. Since your local bank may not have had any experience in
financing projects in developing countries, it may be skeptical about your
plans. Even so, it is an appropriate place to begin your search for financing

---

Thomas L. Brewer, principal author.

Table 4–1
Outline of Possible Sources of Financing

Internal corporate sources

Parent firm in United States
   Equity in form of cash, equipment, or goods
   Loans to foreign affiliate
   Leads (lags) in paying affiliate (parent) accounts

Related affiliates in other countries
   Loans
   Leads (lags) in paying related affiliates' accounts

Foreign affiliate borrowing with guarantees by U.S. parent firm

External sources

Loans from U.S. sources
   Private
   Governmental

Loans from host country and other foreign sources
   Private
   Governmental

Joint venture partner

Loans

Equity

Source: Adapted from David K. Eiteman and Arthur I. Stonehill, *Multinational Business Finance,* 2d ed. (Reading, Mass.: Addison-Wesley, 1979), 372.

sources because it can help you to clarify your financing needs and perhaps put you in touch with other potential sources of funds.

If your local bank is interested in the possibility of helping to finance the project, it will want to see multiyear financial statements. More generally, bank officers will want to be assured that you have established a successful track record in your domestic operations and of course in any previous international business activities. They will also be especially interested in any prospective joint venture partner that may participate in the project and in any involvement by U.S. or foreign government agencies. The market prospects, the financial plan, and the technical feasibility of the project will of course also be of interest. It is therefore important for you to do some homework on the foreign country and the market for your product before you begin your search for financing.

If your local bank itself has foreign branches and if it is interested in your project, then it will arrange an introduction for you with its branch in the foreign country where the project would be located. The branch would in turn introduce you to an indigenous bank in that country, for you will need to deal with a local foreign bank as well as a U.S.–based bank.

Larger Banks. If your bank is not interested in helping to finance your project, it should be able to introduce you to a larger commercial bank or investment bank in New York or in another major financial center in the United States. However, such banks tend to be interested mostly in large projects, such as those of their own large multinational corporate clients.

Merchant Banks and Other Specialists. A more promising alternative than either your local bank or a larger money-center bank may be one of the merchant banks or other organizations that specialize in smaller projects in developing countries and that are especially responsive to the needs of small and medium-sized firms with no previous experience in such projects.[1] These specialists are generally quite knowledgeable about the diverse sources of funds that may be available to finance your project. They are also often particularly knowledgeable about specific foreign countries and industries.

They are therefore able to provide a variety of services—from the initial planning stage through the first few years of operations and in subsequent years if additional financing needs arise. Even before you undertake detailed marketing or feasibility studies, you may find that they can help you assess the prospects for the basic concept of a proposed project. If the project seems sufficiently promising, they can then help with marketing and technical feasibility studies, and they can also help in the search for a foreign joint venture partner. (See chapter 6 for further information on selecting joint venture partners.)

The key function of these specialists, however, is obviously to assist you in developing a financial plan and arranging a financing package. They can thus provide assistance in structuring the debt and equity for the project. For instance, you may be able to obtain a loan from the U.S. Overseas Private Investment Corporation for a portion of the debt (as will be discussed in a later section of this chapter). But this still leaves a need for additional U.S. dollar loans and perhaps for foreign currency loans as well. In addition, the forms of equity contributions need to be addressed—for instance, the proportions of cash, equipment, and services contributed by you and any prospective partners. Managing these and other problems involved in putting together a financial package is a particular area of competence of the specialty merchant banks. Some guidelines for financial structuring are suggested in table 4–2.

Of course, to use the services of the merchant banks effectively you will need to do some homework before visiting them. These bankers will ask you many of the same questions your local bank would ask. They will be especially interested in how much you know about the market for your product in the foreign country and in your willingness to adapt it to suit foreign mar-

Table 4–2
Guidelines for Structuring the Financing for Projects in the Middle East

Avoid excessive leveraging (70/30 debt-equity ratio should be the maximum).

Debt financing should include the following: concessionary interest rates, grace period during construction and six months into production, foreign exchange and local currency borrowing based on uses of funds.

Equity capital contributions should be made concurrently with the conclusion of the joint venture agreement. Cash contributions are preferable to contributions in kind.

Cost overrun expenses should be shared by partners on the basis of their shares in the joint venture.

Contributions should be insured/guaranteed through governmental and/or private organizations.

Source: Adapted from Carl J. Bazarian, "Financial Aspects of Joint-Venture Formation in the Arab World," unpublished paper, East-West Financial Services, Washington, D.C. Used with permission.

ket needs. They will probably also emphasize the importance of exporting a portion of the project's output *from* the foreign country, since foreign governments strongly favor export-oriented projects. Like other bankers, then, these merchant bank specialists will want to discuss not only the financial aspects of your project, but many other aspects as well.

After the preliminary discussions, they will of course charge fees, including perhaps retainer or consulting fees for their contributions to planning, market analysis, or feasibility studies, and then fees for obtaining sources of equity and debt. In addition to cash, the fees might be in the form of a share of equity in the project or a portion of its profits. See the Sources of Additional Information at the end of the chapter for names and addresses.

Foreign Sources

Most developing countries' governments have some form of lending program for foreign investors—often at highly attractive rates. Sometimes these government agencies are able to lend in hard currencies, though they normally lend in the local currency. See the sources in Pakistan, for instance, in table 4–3.

There are of course many private sources of funds as well—not only in the United States and in the country in which the project will be located, but also in third countries. Note, for example, the facility described in exhibit 4–1.

Table 4–3
Summary of Sources of Financing in Pakistan

Name	Ownership	Total Available Resources[a] (million rupees)	Types of Financing	Usual Interest Rates	
				Local Currency	Foreign Currency
Pakistan Industrial Credit and Investment Corp. (PICIC)	35% private foreign investors, balance in Pakistan government	7,348.9	Long- and short-term loans; equity participation; debenture underwriting	12.5%	2% above bank rate
Industrial Development Bank of Pakistan (IDBP)	Pakistan government	2,540.31	Long- and short-term loans	10–12%	3.5% above bank rate
Investment Corp of Pakistan (ICP)	Pakistan government	1,420.6	Underwriting debentures; equity participation	Interest-free	—
National Investment Trust (NIT)	Pakistan government	1,519.6	Mutual funds; equity participation	Interest-free	—
National Development Finance Corp. (NDFC)	Pakistan government	5,554.0	Equity, guarantees, local and foreign currency loans	—	2% above rate associated with line of credit
Bankers Equity Ltd. (BEL)	Pakistan government	359.6	Equity underwriting	—	—
Pakistan-Libya Holding Co. Ltd. (PLHC)	Pakistan/Libya governments	1,080.0	Bridge finance; equity underwriting; local and foreign currency loans	—	—
Pakistan-Kuwait Investment Co. Ltd. (PKIC)	Pakistan/Kuwait governments	284.5	Direct equity participation; debentures	—	—
Saudi-Pak Industrial & Agricultural Investment Co. Ltd. (SAPICO)	Pakistan/Saudi governments	200.0	Equity financing	—	—

Source: Adapted from *Business Asia*, December 2, 1983, p. 382. Used with the permission of the publisher, Business International Corporation, New York.

[a]Paid-up capital plus reserves, local and foreign bank borrowings, and lines of credit from international financial institutions.

Exhibit 4–1
Private Investment Company for Asia (PICA)

U.S. companies operating in Asia should take note of a new source of loans offering attractive long maturities and grace periods. The Private Investment Company for Asia (PICA) has been granted a US$15 million credit facility from the Overseas Private Investment Corporation, a U.S. government agency that provides financial services and political risk insurance to encourage U.S. private investment in developing countries.

PICA will use the funds primarily for on-lending to subsidiaries or joint ventures of U.S. firms in Hong Kong, Indonesia, Korea, Malaysia, Papua New Guinea, the Philippines, Singapore, Sri Lanka, Taiwan, and Thailand. Typical credits will be in the US$2–3 million range. Loan maturities may extend up to fourteen years.

The PICA lending program will focus on establishing projects that will contribute to the host countries' developmental objectives—by creating jobs, generating capital, and imparting new skills—as well as grant U.S. investors access to new markets. Targeted sectors include energy and natural resources, construction materials, food processing and agriculture, medical and health care products, and distributorships and leasing operations for companies handling U.S.–made equipment.

PICA, incorporated in 1968, is an international development finance and investment banking institution with nine offices in Asia and headquarters in Singapore. As of August 1983, PICA had equity and/or long-term loans in more than sixty companies involved in thirty industries.

Adapted from *Business Asia*, December 2, 1983. Used with the permission of the publisher, Business International Corporation, New York.

Eurocurrency Loans

It may be possible to obtain through your local banker or through another institution a so-called Eurocurrency loan. Such a loan is one that is denominated in a currency other than that of the country in which the loan contract is executed. For instance, it may be possible to borrow U.S. dollars through a bank in Britain, such as the London branch of a U.S. bank. Although loans in the Euromarkets tend to be limited to rather large amounts borrowed by large corporations, it is sometimes possible for smaller firms to obtain them. The advantage is that the interest rates are somewhat lower than those on comparable loans executed within the United States or other home country of the given currency. These lower rates are possible because the "offshore" banks that lend the funds are not subject to the usual bank regulatory laws and thus enjoy lower operating costs. (See appendix 4A for an illustrative case.)

U.S. Government Sources

Agency for International Development (AID). Through its Office of Development Finance, the Agency for International Development (AID) can lend to private investors in developing countries. A relatively new program within AID is the Bureau for Private Enterprise (PRE), which works directly with foreign governments and businesspeople. One of its activities is to help develop foreign credit institutions that would be available for funding projects involving local and U.S. firms. In Jamaica and in Thailand, for instance, PRE has helped to create investment funds in insurance companies and banks for agribusiness loans at market rates. Other funding possibilities are being developed in Central America. PRE is especially interested in encouraging small and medium-sized U.S. firms to invest in developing countries.

Although most PRE loans go to private intermediate financial institutions in developing countries, some PRE loans go directly to nonfinancial business enterprises. Agribusiness enterprises are of special interest. U.S. firms can be involved in those enterprises as long as the project includes substantial local private ownership. The enterprise must also have a strong developmental impact in the foreign country, such as creating jobs, earning foreign exchange through exports, transferring technology, or improving managerial skills. The loans are typically less than $3 million and cannot exceed one-fourth of the total invested in a project. Interest rates are generally near the rates for U.S. Treasury notes, with terms for up to ten years.

Overseas Private Investment Corporation (OPIC). You should also contact the U.S. Overseas Private Investment Corporation to determine your eligibility for its finance program.[2] OPIC offers a variety of loan and loan guarantee techniques that provide medium- to long-term funding to ventures involving substantial equity and management participation by U.S.–based firms.

OPIC participation is often in the form of project financing that is based primarily on the economic, technical, marketing, and financial soundness of the project itself. OPIC must therefore determine that there is an adequate cash flow expected to pay all operating costs and service all debt.

OPIC can offer you loans through its direct investment fund and/or issue a loan guarantee to a U.S. financial institution that is making you an eligible loan. In addition, although OPIC does not purchase equity in a project, it may purchase convertible notes, or certain other debt instruments with equity participation features. OPIC's participation in a specific financing package is often through a combination of such instruments, all of which provide suitable grace periods on principal and repayment schedules consistent with sound credit practices and principles.

An example of OPIC financing is described in exhibit 4–2.

Exhibit 4–2
Illustrative OPIC Financial Package

The Liberia Company obtained a loan and loan guarantee for the rehabilitation and expansion of an existing rubber plantation and of plant processing capacity. The company is owned by several U.S. companies and individuals. In addition to direct loans of $900,000, OPIC guaranteed a loan of $1 million. Total cost of the project was $3.3 million. The grace period of five years before loan repayment will allow completion of renovation and substantial expansion of the plantation before payments begin. As a result, the company was able to proceed with its expansion plans.

Selection Criteria. OPIC applies several criteria in determining the eligibility of a given project for its financing program. The project must be commercially and financially sound, and it must be within the demonstrated competence of the management, which in turn must have a proven record of success in the same business as well as a significant continuing financial stake in the project. Furthermore, the project and OPIC's financial commitment to help fund it must be approved by the host country.

OPIC is especially interested in projects in the poorest of the developing countries and also in projects involving cooperatives or small and medium-sized U.S. firms. OPIC is prepared to help fund a wide variety of projects, such as manufacturing, agriculture, fishing, forestry, mining, energy development, processing, storage, and certain service industries that involve significant capital investments, such as hotels, tourist facilities, and equipment maintenance and distributorship facilities.

However, there are some kinds of projects that are excluded from OPIC eligibility—for example, projects involving munitions, alcoholic beverages, or sugar for export to the United States. OPIC is prohibited from funding a project that represents the substitution of a foreign plant to produce for the United States or export markets in place of an existing U.S. facility. Nor does OPIC fund housing or infrastructure projects. OPIC is willing to help finance projects involving foreign governments as local joint venture partners; the management and ownership of such a project, however, should be substantially private.

Size of the Commitment and Other Considerations. The size of OPIC's financial commitment varies, taking into consideration the contribution to the host country's development, the financial requirements, and the extent to which the financial risks and benefits are shared among the investors and lenders. However, OPIC will assist in designing the financial plan. OPIC's financing commitment in a new venture is typically 50 percent of total project costs. A greater OPIC participation may be considered in the case of expansion of a successful existing project to a maximum of 75 percent. In any case, project sponsors are encouraged to arrange for additional financial participation from other U.S. and foreign sources.

Recognizing that cost overruns may occur despite careful planning and allowance for contingencies in the financial plan, OPIC requires that the principal sponsors enter into an agreement under which they are jointly and severally obligated to provide any additional financing necessary to complete a project, and they are required to have adequate working capital when certain operating tests are met.

When it evaluates a proposed project, OPIC will consider the contribution of the project to the economic and social development of the foreign country. It will thus consider such factors as the creation of employment opportunities and the development of skills through training, the transfer of technological and managerial skills, foreign exchange earnings or savings, increases in host country tax revenues, and the stimulation of other local enterprises in the foreign country. OPIC must also consider environmental effects, technical feasibility, market demand, and other aspects of the project that will ultimately determine its success. In some cases, OPIC will retain independent consultants to assist in its analysis and review of the project.

Furthermore, OPIC will consider the balance of payments and employment effects of the project on the U.S. economy as well as on the host government. Thus, such factors as the extent of procurement of U.S. goods and services, the net financial flows, and the net project exports to the United States are also taken into consideration.

OPIC loans generally range from $100,000 to $4 million, and OPIC can guarantee loans up to $50 million. OPIC loans and guaranteed loans usually provide for approximately equal semiannual principal payments following a suitable grace period on principal payments with a final maturity of five to twelve years. In certain types of projects a longer maturity may be available.

The interest rates on OPIC loans vary according to an assessment of the financial and other risks involved and the opportunity for OPIC to share in the eventual financial success of the enterprise. The interest rate on convertible notes is lower than on straight loans and thus reduces the average interest cost of total debt. Interest rates on guaranteed loans are comparable to those of other U.S. guaranteed issues of similar maturity and are subject to OPIC approval. In addition, OPIC charges the borrower a guarantee fee ranging from 1¾ to 2½ percent per annum on the outstanding principal amount.

OPIC's finance program is designed to complement and supplement the lending and investing facilities of commercial banks, local, regional, and international development banks, and such entities as the Export–Import Bank of the United States. Many of OPIC's financings involve at least one other lender, and in large projects there are typically several lending institutions involved. OPIC's willingness to commit to a substantial portion of debt requirements, to accept longer or more flexible maturities, and to finance at fixed interest rates may facilitate participation by other lenders.

Obtaining OPIC Financing. If you are interested in obtaining OPIC financing, you should provide OPIC with preliminary information in summary form. In order to establish your general eligibility and to give OPIC the basis on which it can respond, the preliminary information should include the following: the name, location, and business of the proposed project; the identity, background, and financial statements of the principal sponsors; the general marketing plan; a summary of costs and sources of procurement of capital goods and services; the proposed financing plan; and a brief statement of the contribution the business is expected to make to the foreign country's economic and social development.

If after a preliminary review OPIC is interested in financial participation, you will be asked to provide specific economic, financial, and technical information as part of the formal application for financing. The information that will be required is essentially the same as what any board of directors would need before committing its company to an investment.

The time required to review an application and to make a commitment and disburse funds is usually about four months, but can be as long as a year, depending on the complexity of the project and the degree of detail in the information submitted. One of the major factors affecting the required time is the availability of the principal documents that have been negotiated with joint venture partners, other lenders, and foreign government agencies. If necessary, bridge loans can frequently be obtained on the basis of an OPIC commitment letter.

OPIC encourages early consultation with investors so that each of a project's many elements can be coordinated with the requirements of the various investors, lenders, and host government officials, and so that as many of the requirements as possible may be met simultaneously in order to expedite ultimate implementation of the project.

International Organizations

The International Finance Corporation. The International Finance Corporation (IFC), an affiliate of the World Bank, is specifically concerned with financing private investment projects.[3] Although the IFC is usually interested only in projects over $5 million in size, it may sometimes take interest in smaller projects, especially in particularly small countries. The IFC insists upon the involvement of a foreign partner where project considerations require it and will help locate such a partner. In addition to its own equity participation, the IFC can usually arrange additional elements of a financial package through other sources. Depending on a project's need, the IFC can invest in equity, make loans, underwrite securities offerings, provide standby financing, and organize syndications of commercial bank financing.

IFC loans are usually from seven to twelve years and when held for its own account may be made at fixed or variable rates, depending on the borrower's preference. The syndicated portion of IFC financing is normally made at floating rates. Loans are usually denominated in U.S. dollars, but can be made in other currencies depending on the project's requirements.

The IFC tailors the nature and amounts of its financing to the project's needs. In keeping with its private sector orientation, the IFC neither requires nor accepts government guarantees on its investment. It does, however, assure itself that the government has no objection to the project or to the IFC's involvement in it. The IFC also seeks to ensure that foreign exchange will be available to service IFC loans and other repatriation requirements.

The IFC's staff has considerable financial, economic, legal, and technical expertise in finding solutions to problems associated with projects in developing countries. In fact, the IFC frequently provides specific technical assistance while appraising and monitoring individual projects. This help may involve advice on accounting, financial management, equipment, marketing, administration, or any other aspects of the enterprise.

Examples of small projects involving the IFC are noted in table 4–4.

The Caribbean Project Development Facility. Another institution of possible interest is the Caribbean Project Development Facility (CPDF) which was established under the auspices of the United Nations Development Program.[4] The CPDF has no funds of its own to invest, but it has access to a wide array

Table 4–4
Examples of Small Projects Involving IFC Participation

Project	Country	Project Cost (US$ millions)	IFC Investment (US$ millions)
Banana plantation	Ivory Coast	5.10	1.30
Tea corporation	Rwanda	1.30	0.30
Pulp and paper	South Korea	5.00	0.27
Equipment leasing firm	Sri Lanka	0.60	0.09
Cement and other construction materials	Jordan	4.60	0.74
Hotel	Paraguay	3.80	0.27

Source: International Finance Corporation, *Annual Report, 1984* (Washington, D.C.: International Finance Corporation, 1984), 24–35.

of potential funding sources and is thus able to create financial packages involving private and public sources, long-term and short-term money, and local and foreign currencies. It assists small and medium-sized businesses that are substantially owned by residents of Caribbean countries and territories to raise funds for new projects.

Other Regional Development Banks. There are also several regional development banks: the Inter-American Development Bank (with headquarters in Washington, D.C.), the African Development Bank (in Abidjan, Ivory Coast), and the Asian Development Bank (in Manila, Philippines). Among them, the Asian Development Bank, for instance, is involved in a variety of activities, including equity participation in projects. The bank's equity participation, which generally ranges upward from US$100,000, is especially attractive to private investors in projects in countries where there may be unusual concern about the possibility of political instability or government interference in the operations of the project.

Criteria for Selecting Source and Currency of Funds

Because of the large number of sources of funds and the possibility of obtaining funds in more than one currency, the final choice of fund sources can be complex. Exchange rates, exchange controls, and taxes (as discussed in chapter 10) need to be considered, for instance, in addition to the interest rates that determine the relative base costs of obtaining the funds.

Because the currencies of developing countries generally tend to depreciate relative to the U.S. dollar over the long term, one common financing strategy is to borrow substantial amounts in the local currency of the foreign country—from private and/or governmental sources. Such a strategy tends to offset assets exposed to exchange rate fluctuations with liabilities exposed to the same fluctuations. Outstanding unpaid balances on local loans may also serve as deterrents to some forms of government interference in the firm's operations. However, there are strong sensitivities in many developing countries about foreigners' use of their relatively scarce capital, so you may encounter some limitations on your borrowing from sources in the host country.

In any case, you may need substantial "hard currency" loans, such as in U.S. dollars or the currency of another industrial country, in order to finance shipments of equipment or initial inventory in the start-up phase of the project. The typical financing package, therefore, includes both local borrowing in the host country's currency and "hard currency" borrowing in the United States or the Euromarkets.

Export Financing

When a U.S. firm establishes production facilities in a foreign country, it typically exports substantial amounts of goods and services from the United States. Export finance opportunities are therefore also relevant to the financing of investment projects in developing countries. Again, there are numerous sources of funds in addition to your local private banker.

In particular, the U.S. goverment has several direct loan and loan guarantee programs to support exports by U.S. firms. Indeed, in recent years the U.S. Export–Import Bank has launched new programs specifically directed to the special needs of small and medium-sized firms. For instance, in cooperation with the Small Business Administration, it has established a Working Capital Guarantee Program to help exporters obtain financing for their preexport activities. It also has a Small Business Credit Program, which enables U.S. banks to offer medium-term, fixed rate loans to finance exports of small U.S. firms.

The U.S. Agriculture Department has an Export Credit Guarantee Program under the Commodity Credit Corporation that guarantees letters of credit from foreign financial institutions against default. The Agriculture Department also has an Export Credit Sales Program that enables it to buy the accounts receivable of U.S. exporters of selected commodities.

If you export from a third country—for example where you already have a foreign affiliate of your parent firm—you may be able to obtain financing for those exports from the government of that country.

Conclusion

There are numerous and diverse sources of financing for projects in developing countries, but it often takes persistence and assistance in locating them. A visit to your local banker may be an appropriate place to begin your search, but you will almost surely have to go to other potential sources as well. Your search can be greatly facilitated by specialists with experience in financing projects in developing countries and by assistance from government agencies.

Thus, on the one hand, you may find an unusually frustrating degree of skepticism on the part of your conventional and familiar financial sources. But on the other hand, you may also be surprised to discover many private and governmental organizations in the United States and in foreign countries that have funds available, that have guarantee programs, and that have the expertise to assist you with your financial problems.

Appendix 4A
Case: FEC's Funding Options

This case illustrates funding issues and alternatives that you may encounter.

The task facing decision makers at Florida Electronics Corporation (FEC) was to finance an expected $2 million plant's construction and operation in Costa Rica. Based on parent-company assets, FEC probably could borrow the entire amount from a U.S. bank. Until now, bank loans, accounts payable, and retained earnings were the main sources of credit used by the company. However, FEC's financial manager decided to investigate other financing alternatives for this project. He found the possibilities shown in table 4A–1.

By borrowing in the Eurocurrency market, FEC would be able to cut almost a percentage point off its loan cost, plus there would be no compensating balances required by the bank. Entering the Euromarket would require simply going to a local bank (in this case Southeast Bank) and requesting a Eurocurrency loan. The bank could negotiate the loan in Miami, while legally placing it on the books of the bank's affiliate in Nassau to avoid domestic U.S. restrictions. The financial manager found that he could borrow Swiss francs, deutsche marks, or other currencies in addition to the U.S. dollar. He was not sure how to evaluate that possibility. In any event, the borrowing costs are presented in the table.

By borrowing in Costa Rica with a guarantee from the parent company, FEC would pay 26 percent per year to obtain 80 million colones (worth $2 million at the current exchange rate.) The plant would have to be put up as collateral on this loan. The financial manager heard that it might be possible to negotiate a loan in colones for 18 percent per year from the Central Bank, if the project were destined to generate exports from Costa Rica, as this one was.

FEC expected that the plant would have a minimum life of ten years, so that financing for it could be done in the capital markets as well. Rates on domestic U.S. bonds and Eurobonds are shown in table 4A–1. No substantial capital market exists in Costa Rica, so local funding would be restricted to bank loans.

Note that all interest rates are quoted as annual rates. These rates would need to be renegotiated each year during the project, if one-year loans are to

Table 4A–1
Possible Sources of $2 Million, One-Year Borrowing for FEC
(in annual percentage interest rates)

| Type of Funding | Currencies | | | | | | Fees (paid up front) |
	US$	C$	FF	DM	SF	colon	
U.S. domestic bank loan (prime rate)	12.25	—	—	—	—	—	3.00
Eurocurrency loan (LIBOR quotes, not including spread)	11.69	12.30	12.25	6.00	5.13	NA	2.00
U.S. domestic bond issue (ten-year bond, issued at par)	12.97	—	—	—	—	—	2.50
Ten-year Eurobond issue	12.65	—	—	—	—	—	2.10
Costa Rican bank loan (in colones)	—	—	—	—	—	26.00	3.50
Spot exchange rate (foreign currency units per U.S. dollar)	1	1.32	9.53	3.11	2.55	45.00	—
One-year forward FX rate	1	1.33	9.57	2.95	2.39	55.00	—

be used. FEC can be expected to pay a "spread" of 1¼ percent over LIBOR quotes and 1 percent over prime, plus the fees that are one-time, up-front charges, based on the value of the loan. Assume for simplicity that all interest is paid at the end of the loan period. LIBOR is the London Interbank Offered Rate, the interest rate offered by banks in London for large deposits (Eurocurrency deposits) from other banks. The lending rate does not have a name; it is just called "LIBOR plus the spread," and it varies depending on the creditworthiness of the borrower.

Contributed by Robert E. Grosse.

Appendix 4B
Evaluating Projects Using Capital Budgeting Procedures

Y ou will need to modify only slightly your standard capital budgeting procedures in order to take into account some of the special problems associated with a project in a developing country. As in standard practice, you will need to do calculations for the initial cost of the project, the expected revenues and operating expenses, and the cost of capital for discounting the future stream of cash flows back into present value terms.

In addition, you may want to include in your calculations some figures reflecting the possibility of problems in remitting funds back to the United States, problems resulting from violence or civil disorder and problems from expropriation. As is explained in chapter 10, there are a variety of ways of dealing with these problems. One way is to obtain insurance from a private insurer or from a U.S. government agency, the Overseas Private Investment Corporation (OPIC). You can thereby protect yourself against these several kinds of risk.

An implication of this possibility of obtaining insurance is that the costs of those insurance policies can be included in your cash flow projections in the capital budgeting process. Although firms do sometimes adjust upward slightly the cost of capital rate, or adjust upward the required rate of return or hurdle rate as a way of taking into account the perception of increased risks of doing business in developing countries, such procedures can lead to unrealistically conservative capital budgeting decisions. Thus, you should instead incorporate insurance costs in your cash flow estimates. Otherwise, you might miss opportunities for profitable investments in developing countries as a result of inappropriate procedures in the capital budgeting process.

Sources of Additional Information

Business International. *Financing Foreign Operations*. New York: Business International, updated looseleaf service.

Caribbean/Central American Action, 1333 New Hampshire Ave. NW, Washington, D.C. 20036. Phone: (202) 466-7464.

Caribbean Project Development Facility, 1818 H St. NW, Washington, D.C. 20433. Phone: (202) 676-0482/3.

Delphos, William A. *Washington's Best Kept Secrets*. New York: Wiley, 1983. Chapter 7.

Diamond, Walter H., and Dorothy B. Diamond. *Capital Formation and Investment Incentives Around the World*. Albany, N.Y.: Matthew Bender, updated looseleaf service.

Dufey, Gunter. "International Financial Management." In *International Management and Business Policy*, edited by Michael Z. Brooke and H. Lee Remmers. Boston: Houghton Mifflin, 1978.

East-West Financial Services, 1667 K St. NW, Suite 380, Washington, D.C. 20006. Phone: (202) 659-5525.

Equator Advisory Services Limited, 1575 Eye Street NW, Suite 325, Washington, D.C. 20005. Phone: (202) 842-3275.

Export–Import Bank of the United States, Business Advisory Office, 811 Vermont Ave., NW, Washington, D.C. 20571. Phone: (800) 424-5201 or (202) 566-8860.

International Development Institute, 750 13th St. SE, Washington, D.C. 20003. Phone: (202) 547-8330.

International Finance Corporation, 1818 H St. NW, Washington, D.C. 20433. Phone: (202) 477-1234. Information office or appropriate regional investment department.

International Resources Group, 1015 18th St. NW, Washington, D.C. 20036. Phone: (202) 822-8817.

Marton, Andrew. "Is Smaller Better in Third World Project Finance?" *Institutional Investor* (September 1984):195–202. Names and descriptions of small merchant banks specializing in small and medium-sized projects in developing countries.

Nevitt, Peter K. *Project Financing*. 4th ed. London: Euromoney, 1982.

U.S. Agency for International Development, Bureau for Private Enterprise, Department of State, NW, Washington, D.C. 20523. Phone: (703) 235-2274.

U.S. Department of Commerce, Office of Trade Finance. *Official U.S. and International Financing Institutions: A Guide for Exporters and Investors.* Washington, D.C., 1985.

U.S. Overseas Private Investment Corporation, Finance Applications Officer, 1615 M St. NW, Washington, D.C. 20527. Phone: (202) 457-7010.

5
Managing Government Relations

I n most developing countries, governments play a prominent role in the economy. This is true even in many countries that are generally considered to have relatively open economies. You will therefore need to be familiar with government policies and procedures in the host country when you plan your project and later when your facilities are established. This chapter will provide information to improve your understanding of those economies, and it will also suggest specific guidelines and procedures for managing government relations.

Understanding the Role of Government in Developing Countries' Economies

There are several reasons for strong government participation in the economies of developing countries. An important goal in many countries is to achieve national economic independence by reducing the dependence on foreign capital, technology, enterprise, and markets, dependence characteristic of the colonial period. There is also the widespread belief that market forces alone, including world market forces, would not lead to the desired rate and pattern of national economic development. Furthermore, in the absence in most countries of an adequate local entrepreneurial class to undertake such development in the private sector, the national government may be the only agent powerful enough to undertake the task. State intervention is thus considered necessary to ensure rapid growth, industrialization, the satisfaction of basic needs, employment creation, the development of the local market

---

Linda Y.C. Lim, principal author.

and of a local entrepreneurial class, and a host of other economic, social, and political objectives.

The extent and forms of government intervention in the economy vary considerably from country to country. At one extreme are socialist or semi-socialist economies, such as that of Tanzania, where virtually all economic enterprises are state-owned and operated and where any private investment is unwelcome or even outlawed. At the other extreme are avowedly free market capitalist economies, such as that of Chile, where the government's only roles are to administer fiscal and monetary policy, to provide physical and social infrastructure, such as transport, communications, utilities, and education, and to maintain a military establishment.

Much more common than these two extremes are the mixed economies in which governments regulate internal and external trade, create various incentives and/or controls affecting private business, regulate the real estate and labor markets, and operate numerous state enterprises. In this respect, developing countries resemble the Western European industrialized nations rather than the United States.

Not only does the economic role of the government vary considerably from country to country in the developing world, it also varies from time to time within each country. While in many countries the role of government has been increasing, in others it has been declining as the private sector grows stronger and more active. Overall there is an increasing tendency in economic policy toward greater liberalization and away from controls.

In some countries the amount of government intervention may not have changed, but the type of intervention has changed as goals and policies have changed with economic development. Thus in the newly industrializing Asian countries of Taiwan, South Korea, and Singapore, for example, where the state has always been extremely active in economic affairs, the governments' focus has now shifted from enhancing the competitiveness of labor-intensive, export-oriented manufacturing to developing a new competitive advantage in capital-intensive, skill-intensive, high-tech economic activities.

Whatever the situation in a particular country at a particular time, you must expect to be greatly affected by government policies and by relations with government agencies and enterprises. You should also be prepared for frequent and unpredictable policy changes. However, for firms in certain industries at least, the amount of government intervention and the frequency of policy change may not be significantly greater than they have experienced in the United States.

Furthermore, government activities often facilitate and complement those of foreign private investors. Thus, some of the countries in which the government's economic role is greatest are also those that have been most successful and attractive locations for foreign investment.

Assessing Attitudes toward Foreign Investment in Developing Countries

Ambivalence toward Foreign Investment. Foreign investment is considered important to the economies of developing countries because it contributes scarce capital, technology, entrepreneurship, and managerial, professional, and technical expertise—all in one package. In raw material extraction and import-substituting manufacturing, the technology and skills provided by foreign investment are often crucial. In export production, foreign investment also often provides easier access to foreign markets, particularly for manufactured goods. The capital inflow from foreign investment makes a much-needed contribution to the host country's balance of payments. And foreign investment frequently provides the entrepreneurial initiative for increased economic activity that is lacking in developing countries with a weak or non-existent local entrepreneurial class.

At the same time, many developing countries and their governments have an ambivalent if not downright hostile attitude toward foreign investment. They argue that the inflow of capital generates a long-term outflow of profit remittances, interest charges, payments for licensing technology, managerial and professional fees, and occasional capital repatriation. This is a "drain" on the balance of payments, exacerbated by the tendency for foreign enterprises to be heavily dependent on imported materials and equipment. Technology is often considered to be imparted under excessively costly monopolistic terms, to be only incompletely imparted or intrinsically inappropriate (in terms of products produced or techniques used) for the developing host country. Foreigners' entrepreneurial initiative and managerial expertise, furthermore, may stifle and outcompete indigenous enterprise. Government tax holidays and other investment incentives and infrastructural provisions are sometimes considered to be unfair and extravagant subsidies that increase foreigners' profits. Foreign enterprises are believed to evade taxes by means of transfer pricing and declared book losses. Employment practices of foreign enterprises are frequently considered to be exploitative even when wages and working conditions are above (as they usually are) local standards, because they are below standards in the enterprises' home countries.

There are also popular political and ideological objections to foreign direct investment, which is seen as neocolonial domination by foreigners, the cause of continued external dependence, which is resented by nationalists desiring economic independence and self-sufficiency. Many foreign corporations are believed to use their wealth and power to intervene in the internal political affairs of host countries, as some indeed have, or at the minimum to secure extra benefits and privileges for themselves at the expense of the local population.

Opposition to foreign investment is often strongest among sections of the local business class who most directly feel and are disadvantaged by competition from foreign enterprises.

For these reasons, foreign investment, even when it is encouraged by host governments, is rarely enthusiastically welcomed by all groups in the country. Even welcoming governments frequently only tolerate foreign investment as a "necessary evil" imposed on them by external aid agencies or by the lack of domestic alternative means of economic growth.

The situation varies considerably from country to country, but overall in the developing world, attitudes seem to have shifted in recent years away from antagonism and toward tolerance and even positive feelings. This partly reflects the economic success and prosperity of several countries that have hosted a great deal of foreign investment for a long period of time, such as Brazil and the newly industrializing countries of Asia. It also reflects growing disillusionment with alternative paths of economic development, and necessity imposed by poor economic performance, causing growth to be favored over independence. Their indebtedness problems have also made governments more receptive to foreign investors. At the same time, many governments have increased their own knowledge and bargaining power vis-à-vis foreign corporations and are able to strike more favorable deals than they were in the past.

Most developing country governments are simply pragmatic in balancing the economic and political costs and benefits of foreign investment. The more fortunate or astute are able to vary their policies and marry their interests with those of foreign investors from time to time, according to national priorities and sectoral goals.

It is important to keep in mind these additional traits of host government policies: (1) Nationalist ideology and even top-level, high-profile rhetoric against foreign investment may not translate into specific policies that actively discourage or discriminate against foreign investment. In fact, foreign investment may continue to be encouraged by invitation and incentives even as political rhetoric against it increases. (2) When policies are enacted that might limit or discourage foreign investment, they are often flexibly interpreted and implemented, especially where a pragmatic need for such investment exists. (3) Even when there are controls on foreign investment and it is not strongly encouraged in certain sectors at certain periods of time, foreign companies continue to invest and reinvest, and even expand their operations, without government incentive, so long as they are prospering. Market forces and the basic strength of the host economy often have much more to do with the prospects for foreign investment than do specific government policies, which in any case may change. (See appendixes 5A and 5B.)

Incentives. Of course many countries have extensive and attractive investment incentive programs.[1] For instance, exhibit 5–1 summarizes Portugal's integrated system of investment incentives. (See also appendix 5C.)

Exhibit 5–1
Summary of Portugal's Investment Incentives

The objectives of the investment incentive program in Portugal are to stimulate industrialization in the country, reduce unemployment, develop exporting industries, give support to certain sectors assigned priority status, and to assist economic development in certain regions.

In 1980, a publication was issued on the investment incentives program, explaining the operation of the so-called Integrated System of Investment Incentives. This system incorporates six different incentive schemes:

1. A general scheme of fiscal and financial incentives
2. A special scheme of financial incentives
3. A scheme of extraordinary capital grants
4. A simplified scheme of fiscal and financial incentives for small businesses
5. A scheme of fiscal incentives for concentration of and cooperation between businesses
6. A scheme of subsidies for R&D

Alongside this system, which is managed by the central government authorities, Regional Development Companies have been set up. Legally these are near-bank institutions, aimed at promoting industrial investment by providing financial assistance for economic and social development in their respective zones of activity. . . .

Main Types of Incentives

Fiscal Incentives

1. The general regulations on incentives include the following fiscal incentives:

Tax rebate or tax exemption on transfers of real property

Exemption for three to nine years from the industrial tax and complementary tax

Accelerated writing-down allowances (rate of depreciation doubled for a period of six, eight, ten, or twelve years)

Reduction of the tax base for assessment of industrial tax (all permanent and initial formation expenses are taken into account)

Rebate or exemption from tax on profits

Rebate on or exemption from tax on interest accruing to capital invested in bonds

Rebate on or exemption from the complementary tax on such interest

Tax rebate on dividends accruing to capital invested in shares

Rebate on or exemption from duty on imports of capital goods

2.   Regulations concerning small businesses provide for exemption from duty on imported capital goods and for a reduction of the tax base for assessment to industrial tax, while under the regulations governing concentration of the cooperation between firms, tax exemptions may be allowed on transfers of real estate and on capital income. Moreover, losses incurred by a firm in the three years prior to its concentration with another firm may be allowed as a deduction where not previously deducted.

Financial Incentives

1.   Under the general scheme, the special scheme for financial incentives, and the special scheme for small and medium-sized businesses, subsidies may be given to cover interest charges.

2.   The special scheme for financial incentives distinguishes between initial investment subsidies, employment subsidies and subsequent investment subsidies where the purpose of such subsequent investment is to provide substitutes for imports of coal, iron ore, pyrites, or other mined or quarried minerals, or to export goods from certain sectors.

3.   The R&D scheme includes a subsidy to cover 50 per cent of the expenditure arising from research contracts in the three subsequent years.

4.   For certain projects of high economic importance, a capital grant may be obtained (extraordinary capital grant scheme). In this case, the firm is not entitled to benefit from the fiscal and financial incentives provided under the general and special schemes.

Nonfinancial Incentives

Assistance may be provided for the construction of infrastructures related to an investment project.

Adapted from Organization for Economic Cooperation and Development, *Investment Incentives and Disincentives and the International Investment Process* (Paris: OECD, 1983), 191–94. Used with permission of OECD.

Obtaining Information about Entry Procedures

Developing countries differ considerably in their procedures regarding the entry of foreign investment. The more sophisticated, experienced, and welcoming countries often have an established and streamlined procedure whereby government officials virtually hold the hand of the investor through all the stages of considering and setting up an investment. Other less experienced or less welcoming countries may lack established procedures, so you will have to exert more effort and take more initiatives.

The first type of host country may actively court foreign investment, bringing itself to the notice of potential investors, encouraging their interest, and smoothing their way. Officials sometimes literally knock on the doors of unsuspecting potential U.S. investors. In this case the potential host government has probably done some prior research on the desired investor and will present it with a suggested packaged of incentives to attract the investment. More commonly, host government investment officials organize or attend business seminars, send out literature and letters to publicize their offerings to potential investors, handle responses and inquiries, and then direct the potential investor to the relevant government office or agency in the host country itself. Foreign countries' investment offices are usually found in or are associated with each country's foreign embassy in Washington or are sometimes located in a separate office in New York.

In addition, you will eventually need to visit government agencies in the host country itself, since most investment promotion offices in the United States lack the authority to conduct negotiations or to offer incentives or impose controls. Their function is generally limited to information, country promotion, and referral.

You should find out what the actual practices are in a particular host country, regardless of what the rules on the books are. Common practices frequently differ from formal written policies.

In any case, you should make a visit to the host country. Before going, you should obtain as much information as possible from independent sources about the country and about the experiences of other foreign investors there, particularly in the same sector or industry. (The sources of information noted in chapters 1 and 4 may be especially helpful.) In the host country itself, attempts should be made independently to assess the accuracy of information provided by the investment promotion agency. Such factors as prevailing local wage and salary rates, the availability of different categories of skilled and unskilled labor required, employment regulations and the industrial relations environment, the availability, quality, and reliability of local suppliers, the efficiency of government agencies, and the adequacy of infrastructure should be examined. You may find it helpful to meet with fellow foreign investors who are already established, though even their opinions and information should be checked. In many countries, there are local consulting firms that specialize in foreign investment problems. In general it is good to consult with as wide a variety of local sources as possible, but you should bear in mind that many of these sources have their own interests in encouraging or discouraging a particular foreign investment project.

Negotiating Entry Conditions

Entry conditions are usually negotiated with or through a central government coordinating agency for foreign (or foreign and local) investment. However, the power of such a central agency varies from situation to situation, and sometimes it may be unable to deliver on its promises because of resistance from other government departments. Bureaucracies in developing countries are far from monolithic, being frequently divided among themselves, competitive for overlapping bureaucratic "territory," and subject to internal political manipulation and external political pressures. You should be prepared for some individual officials to demand unorthodox payments in exchange for more favorable entry conditions. All agreed-upon entry conditions should be established in writing and properly approved by the authorities.

In setting entry conditions, the outcome of negotiations depends a great deal on the relative balance of power between the individual investor and the host government. This is ultimately determined by the economics of the investment—how profitable it is likely to be for the investor under a range of different entry conditions, and how many benefits it promises to the host country that can be weighed against any possible negative social or political effects.

In a country that is reasonably familiar with foreign investment and has an established set of procedures, few negotiations may be necessary. That is to say, an investment of a certain size and type, in a certain sector, and with a certain market orientation, would automatically qualify for certain incentives or benefits. Much would depend on the government's current priorities. Thus in a country trying to create employment, a labor-intensive investment would be favored, while in a country trying to overcome a labor shortage, a capital-intensive investment would be favored.

In negotiating the length of a tax holiday, you must be prepared to vary aspects of your investment to conform with the local standard requirement—for example, a certain minimum of capital invested or a guaranteed proportion of exports. Investments that receive tax holidays or other incentives are often subject to greater government scrutiny of their activities than those that are not.

Besides tax liabilities, other subjects to be negotiated include import tariff protection for domestic market-oriented production, and import tariff exemption for materials and inputs. Here again your investment will need to meet certain specified criteria before such benefits are granted. An increasingly popular incentive that many countries now offer is the Export Processing or Free Trade Zone. The proposed investment would have to be located in the zone and be export-oriented in order to qualify for the exemption from customs duties that the zone provides.

In addition to offering certain investment incentives or benefits, host governments also impose many controls and restrictions on foreign (and local) investors that may be subject to negotiation. For example, there may be selective restrictions on foreign ownership; foreign investment may be completely excluded from some sectors, and often a minority foreign share only is permitted in resource extraction or projects supplying the local market. One hundred percent foreign ownership may be allowed for manufacturing projects that are wholly export oriented and do not use domestic raw materials. A joint venture requirement is common for many projects (see chapter 6).

Another example is restrictions on the employment of expatriate staff, including those in managerial positions; this may be the case even in 100 percent foreign-owned plants. Exceptions may be allowed for certain firms or in certain positions—for example because of the nature of the technology employed—and this is an area for negotiations. Obtaining employment passes for expatriate personnel is nonetheless often difficult; it should be negotiated in advance and not assumed.

Taking into Account Other Government Policies

In addition to policies specifically concerning foreign investment, you will of course also be affected by many other kinds of government policies. Foremost among these are foreign trade and exchange policies.

Tariffs. Customs duties are often a major source of revenue for governments in developing countries. Both imports and exports are likely to be taxed at some level. Levies on exports are usually a revenue device, since few if any countries try to discourage exports. Import tariffs, however, are often instituted to discourage specific categories of import, most notably to provide import-substituting domestic industries with protection from import competition.

In most countries import tariffs are imposed only on final products, while the import of material inputs, capital equipment, and machinery remains relatively free. This, however, has been changing as many countries increasingly insist on more domestic content in local manufactures, even those destined for export. Tariffs on raw materials, machinery, and equipment may be imposed to discourage their import and to encourage or protect nascent local production and supply operations.

Other Restrictions on Imports. In many countries imports are subject not only to tariffs, but also to various licensing and other bureaucratic procedures. You should be sure to check the local tariff classifications of products; you may find that your product is classified as a quite different type of product compared with your own definition of it. Some types of imports may be banned altogether, and often official permission is required for many other imports. In countries where foreign exchange is rationed or otherwise strictly controlled because of balance of payments problems, importers may be given limited quota allocations of foreign exchange, or they may have to "queue up" for the foreign exchange they require, which often results in costly delays. In rare extreme crisis situations—such as occurred recently in the Philippines—there may be no foreign exchange available at all, except for "vital imports." Because of the shallowness of the industrial structure in most developing countries, virtually all enterprises are likely to be import dependent to a significant degree, and the availability of foreign exchange for imports is crucial to their operations. Those who export are likely to be given priority access to foreign exchange for imports. Export-oriented multinational manufacturers are often unaffected by exchange or import problems because they import their inputs on consignment from their parent companies. (In the Philippines, for example, export-oriented U.S. electronics firms continued for the most part to operate normally despite the balance of payments crisis.)

Even where import controls are minimal, the bureaucratic procedure for clearing customs is often lengthy and inefficient. (This is further discussed in chapter 7.)

Free Trade Zones. Many if not most developing countries—certainly most of those in Asia, North Africa, Latin America, and the Caribbean—have now established Export Processing or Free Trade Zones, which are special customs areas permitting duty-free imports and exports so long as they do not pass into the principal customs territory without paying the prevailing duties. Most such zones are sited near airports or seaports. This encourages export-oriented activities—mainly manufacturing—without requiring the dismantling of trade controls elsewhere in the economy. Some countries also provide the same duty-free privileges to export-oriented bonded factories that are not located in the special zones or industrial estates. Such bonded factories are frequently sited in more interior or rural locations as part of regional industrial dispersion programs.

Exchange Rates and Controls. Foreign exchange rates and exchange controls in some countries may make it difficult to remit profits or repatriate capital. (This problem is discussed in chapter 10.)

Development Plans. Five-year development plans for the economies of developing countries are essentially plans for public investment, most of it in physical and social infrastructure and services, but also in direct production. Development plans present the government's development philosophy and priorities, and they indicate target growth rates for the economy as a whole and for individual sectors. They also indicate the resources required to achieve these targets. Besides public investment—which comes from both domestic and foreign sources—most countries also expect a large share of investment to be financed by the private sector. Plans often state the share of this private investment that is expected to come from foreign sources.

Development plans are often a good general guide to the future course of the economy and to medium-range government priorities and policies. In addition, short-run policy changes, especially tax changes, are often provided in annual government budgets.

Government Enterprises. In most developing countries, government agencies operate all infrastructural facilities: transport, communications, and utilities. Over the years the number of functions of government agencies have increased in many countries to include additional productive or commercial activities. Thus there are government and quasi-governmental banks and savings institutions, trading agencies, agricultural processing and marketing bodies, mining companies, airline and shipping companies, supermarkets and department stores, and factories manufacturing goods ranging from steel, chemicals, and automobiles to furniture, household appliances, and semiconductors. Some of these are solely government enterprises; others are publicly quoted companies in which the government has a large or majority share; still others may be joint ventures with local and/or foreign private investors. The government's share may range anywhere from 5 percent to 100 percent.

Given the number and scope of government enterprises, private firms have to deal with at least some of them on a continuing basis. The complaint is frequently made that government enterprises—or even partly government-owned enterprises—are inefficient and even corrupt, that those in commercial ventures often lack the incentive to be profitable, and that in general these bodies are more of a hindrance than a help to the private investor. On the other hand, given the inadequacy of the local private sector, government enterprises are probably necessary in many areas, and their existence can facilitate the operations of foreign investors. In recent years, some governments have sought to lessen the burden of state enterprises on the government budget by selling them off to the private sector, including some foreign investors.

Monetary Policy. Monetary policy affects the rate of inflation and the availability and cost of credit to private enterprises. In weak economies with chronic balance of payments problems and heavy dependence on foreign aid inflows, monetary austerity is often prescribed by foreign lending agencies. Interest rates are typically high in many developing countries, but not necessarily in real terms since high inflation rates also prevail. Foreign investors are often less affected by domestic credit restrictions than are local investors, since they acquire much of their capital from abroad, or from internal financing. But such restrictions on their local partners, suppliers, and customers would eventually have an impact on them as well.

Labor Policy. Labor policy will be discussed more fully in chapter 8. Here we merely note that populist and authoritarian governments usually have many labor controls, including regulations on hiring and firing, wages, union organization and bargaining, hours of work, leave provisions, working conditions, and health and safety. Although the regulations may be confusing, they are often less restrictive (from the employers' point of view) and less favorable to workers than they are in the United States and in other industrial countries.

Social Policies. The social policies of developing countries that also affect private business include policies concerning education, training, health care, medicine, housing, and recreation. They affect, for example, the skills and educational level of the work force, its physical health and productivity, social and political stability, and the extent to which private employers are expected to provide various social amenities. Thus the existence of a national health care and social insurance system may reduce the need for you to offer health and insurance fringe benefits. A good educational system reduces the need for you to engage in company-sponsored or in-plant training; subsidized public housing lowers the living wage that employers have to pay.

Getting Along with the Government

Because of the strong role of governments in developing country economies, you are likely to find yourself dealing much more with government departments and agencies after entry than you do in the United States. The government may be not only the tax collector, subsidy distributor, and regulator, but also the landlord, the provider of all utilities and services, the supplier of material inputs, the purchaser of outputs, and even the direct or indirect organizer of unions. It may also be your joint venture partner (see next chapter).

These government activities, however, are rarely coordinated, but are instead conducted by a sometimes bewildering range of government, semigovernment, and government-affiliated departments, agencies, and enterprises.

The investment promotion agency that coordinates the entry of a particular foreign investment project may be less helpful in day-to-day dealings with other government agencies, since its functions are concentrated on promoting new investments rather than on facilitating the operations of established projects. Many a foreign investor feels lost and lonely after his project has been approved and set up. This feeling will diminish over time with experience and increasing contact and familiarity with the various government agencies. However, you can anticipate several common problems.

Application of Laws. For one thing, you may find that you do not get the protection from the law that you expect from written statutes, but you may also find that you can readily obtain waivers from certain regulations. Many of the rules that govern private business are ad hoc, unclear, and flexible in their application. But there are usually conventional standards and practices that are commonly observed. You should not only follow the particular prevailing "rules of the game" for like enterprises, but you should also be prepared for the rules of their application to change, sometimes without warning. Major exceptions are usually made only for very large and important projects, and then rarely without internal political controversy in the host government and country.

Bureaucratic Delays. General bureaucratic inefficiency is another problem. Delays are common, even inevitable. Applications, requests, complaints all take time to be attended to, and several follow-up queries may be necesary. Patience, politeness, and persistence are the keys to dealing with this problem. Inefficiency is caused by many factors, including both overstaffing (and hence overlapping functions and responsibilities) and understaffing. Moreover, the pace of life and work in general may be slower than you are used to in an industrial country.

Corruption. Inefficiency may also be directly related to corruption. Indeed, in some countries special payments for the performance of certain government services are relatively common; the payments are often small to low-level officials. Some countries, however, absolutely outlaw even the most trivial gift to a public servant, like a holiday tip, and prosecution is likely to result. In all countries, large payments to higher-level officials to secure particular favors are a serious matter and should be avoided at all costs. It should be recognized, however, that beliefs about what are proper and improper payments vary considerably from culture to culture (see chapter 3).

Politics. More generally, you can best get along with the host government if you understand the government's composition and its development goals and policies. Then, if you want to influence a particular policy, you can do so by working out and presenting a reasoned case that takes into account the government's goals and that offers a compromise. More strenuous intervention, including political intervention, to force policy changes directly should not be attempted. It is best also if you distance yourself from any political groups. This will preserve the independence and neutrality of your investment as much as possible. It will protect you from being condemned for associating with an unpopular government or from being ordered out by a government in power.

Many developing countries have governments that are authoritarian and have only a limited degree of legitimacy in the eyes of the citizenry. Close cooperation with unpopular governments has had serious negative consequences for foreign investors during periods of political instability and regime change. This problem is worsened if challengers to the current government plan to implement more nationalistic policies with respect to foreign investment.

Local political leaders may have a different orientation toward public office in comparison with your previous experience. For example, if you were to seek out the mayor of a city for advice on where and how to get started, you might find yourself quickly in league with relatives and friends of the mayor who offer their services as realtors, landlords, suppliers, lawyers, and labor leaders. The services may come as a package deal. To receive the necessary municipal permits and licenses it may also be necessary to work with the mayor's designated associates. While the process may be the most expeditious, it may not always be the most beneficial in the long run.

Also, you may find that your firm can be the target of political protests. For example, if your workers feel a sense of injustice over their loss of land where your project has been located or if they feel frustrated by inadequate housing or the inequality of wage levels, then your company may be one target for those promoting greater political participation, social reforms, and national control of the economy. Among the many forms that the workers' increased political participation may take are strikes, demonstrations for political and social reform, public pressure on the government to be more nationalistic, or in some cases even armed opposition to the government.

Authoritarian governments tend to see increased political participation as subversion, not as a legitimate expression of the people's will. In cases of growing political instability, foreign companies often succumb to the temptation to appeal to the government for protection, and the government is often willing to comply. In some countries it is even against the law to strike at foreign-owned or export-oriented companies. Authoritarian governments will react to strikes and other activities that the government regards as illegal or disruptive in an authoritarian manner. In this way foreign investments can become political targets.

Finally, governments are not the people, and whatever their relations are with national governments, foreign investors should recognize that their investments have many direct and indirect effects on local communities that are sometimes not taken into account in government social benefit/cost analyses. Besides the direct benefits of local employment and of multiplier and linkage effects, investment projects may also compete with local populations for scarce land and water, and pollution may also be a problem. The balance of these factors will decide local attitudes about particular investments or about foreign investment in general.

It is not enough to accept uncritically the assumption that foreign investment is beneficial for host countries. Even if the overall effects of foreign investment are on balance positive, it is still necessary to examine the distribution of the costs and benefits within host countries. Oftentimes the adverse costs have fallen on landowners, small farmers, and workers. Your experiences in the United States may make it difficult for you to anticipate the nature and severity of the adverse impacts of your investment on particular groups in developing countries. Foreign investments can generate, in a completely unselfconscious manner, pressures that are in the long run harmful not just for parts of the host society, but also for the company itself.

Your behavior as a foreign investor may therefore affect government attitudes and policy, as it affects local perceptions of foreign investment. Firms that follow all host country regulations, do not intervene in local politics, are good employers and responsible citizens, and demonstrate a commitment to the country generally make a good impression. Beyond this, the state of the host economy and local politics largely determine policies towards foreign investment, and there is little that you can or should do about them.

Conclusion

Foreign investment produces both benefits and costs to the host country. The government will therefore usually have an ambivalent attitude toward you. The government will be at once an ally and an obstacle, both facilitator and regulator of your investment. It may also be a customer, supplier, competitor, or partner. To the government, the many benefits promised by your investment must be weighed against the perceived economic, social, and political costs. You should, therefore, be sensitive to the fact that even sympathetic host governments often have to balance economic gains from foreign direct investment against its possible domestic social or political costs.

Appendix 5A
Description of Malaysia's Changing
Policies on Foreign Investment

After attaining political independence from the British in 1957, Malaysia remained an export-oriented open economy, welcoming foreign investors and tolerating a modern sector more than 60 percent owned by foreigners. Foreign firms were welcome to invest in new tariff-protected import-substituting industries for the domestic market. Although economic growth was sustained, its uneven distribution led to popular dissatisfaction with the status quo. Large gains by opposition parties in the elections of 1969 and postelection riots in which hundreds were killed led to the institution of a New Economic Policy (NEP) in 1970.

NEP

Among other things, the NEP was aimed at restructuring ownership of the modern corporate sector to reduce the share of foreigners from 60 percent to 30 percent by 1990 and to ensure that the majority Malay ethnic group also enjoyed 30 percent ownership by that date. The remaining 40 percent would be held by other nationals, mainly of Chinese ethnic origin. This goal was to be achieved by growth rather than by redistribution.

Foreign investment in fact continued to be attracted, especially into resource-based (mainly petroleum extraction) and export-oriented (mainly electronics and textiles) industries. Complete foreign ownership was permitted in 100 percent export-oriented industries, mainly located in newly established Free Trade Zones.

But enterprises engaged in domestic resource extraction (including that for export) or production for the local market had to have majority national ownership. And most enterprises had to make sure that within five years their top management staff was of indigenous origin.

Tax holidays and other investment incentives were extended and liberally offered, and the government launched an aggressive investment promotion campaign overseas.

At home, many new state agencies (including credit agencies) and state corporations were created to own and operate productive assets and enterprises, thereby increasing not only the national but also the Malay share of modern sector ownership. In the extractive sector, production-sharing arrangements exist between the state petroleum company and private oil companies.

Market Nationalization

Towards the latter part of the 1970s, the Malaysian government also embarked on a policy of "market nationalization" of large foreign enterprises. State enterprises and state-controlled public companies bought majority shares in the stock of several foreign, mainly British, corporations, such as the resource-based conglomerates of London Tin and Sime Darby. These purchases were frequently made at a premium over market prices and were funded by external borrowing. This policy of acquiring foreign-owned stock by mergers and takeovers has continued—most recently with the Sime Darby purchase of Dunlop Malaysian Industries—but is currently being slowed by the country's adverse balance of payments position. For example, the nationalization of the two largest foreign banks in the country is being postponed for this reason.

Recent Changes

In 1982, a new Malaysian prime minister, Datuk Mahathir Mohammed, took office and initiated several changes in announced attitude and policy toward foreign investment. He first launched an "anti-British" campaign, in part a political response to British actions such as the raising of foreign student fees at British educational institutions (where Malaysians are the largest group of foreign students), in part a reaction to what he saw as continued British "neo-colonialism." Among other things, Malaysian government agencies and enterprises were to boycott British products and services. This was accompanied by a new "Look East" campaign to welcome foreign investment from Japan and South Korea and to emulate and learn from those countries' economic development experience. Japanese and Koreans became the favored foreign investors, while the British were discouraged. By late 1983, however, the attitude toward the British (more of an attitude than an explicit discriminatory policy) had softened, and by 1984 the prime minister was criticizing the Japanese for *their* "neo-colonialism" as reflected in Malaysia's large balance of payments deficit with Japan.

Yet throughout this period, and despite other government controls on private investment, such as an industrial coordination act and a foreign investment act, foreign investment in Malaysia has continued to be quite strong, attracted by the country's relatively open policies (rhetoric notwithstanding), rich resources, good infrastructure, political stability, and strong economy. In the U.S.–dominated export-oriented electronics industry, for example, multinationals have continued to expand and upgrade their operations, despite the expiry of most tax holidays, rising wages, labor shortages, and a government industrial policy that explicitly seeks to reduce "overdependence" on the electronics industry and on foreign multinationals. Some companies have chosen to establish new facilities, especially in higher technology and in R&D activities, in neighboring Singapore instead, where they receive many investment incentives not available to them in Malaysia. But even these companies continue to prosper and to reinvest in Malaysia.

Most recently, in 1984, the Malaysian government has actually relaxed one restriction on foreign investment. Enterprises employing new technological processes or producing higher-technology products using domestic resources or for the domestic market may now have a foreign share of up to 70 percent, compared with the previous 30 percent, despite the government's continued commitment to the NEP goal of reducing the share of foreign ownership. (It is likely now that for political if not economic reasons the NEP will be extended beyond the date of 1990, despite considerable if disputed success toward achieving its ownership share goals.) Foreign investment continues to be aggressively, if more selectively, courted by Malaysian government agencies abroad. It is Malaysia's nationalistic desire to achieve a "technological leap" in industrialization, on the one hand, and its balance of payments and developmental need for foreign private capital, on the other, that have motivated this pragmatic change in policy. If anything, the policy of shifting into higher-technology, capital-intensive heavy industry will increase the country's dependence on foreign investment.

Appendix 5B
Description of Singapore's Changing Policies on Foreign Investment

Though consistently open to foreign investment and welcoming 100 percent foreign ownership, the Singapore government has over time changed its priorities with respect to the type of investment that it wants. Thus, investment incentives have changed and are biased toward attracting investment in priority projects and sectors. Other government policies have also changed accordingly. For example, in the late 1960s, labor-intensive, export-oriented manufacturing was the priority. In addition to creating tax holidays and locating government industrial buildings in densely populated housing estates, the government amended labor legislation to ensure labor peace, and throughout most of the 1970s, foreign labor (both skilled and unskilled) was freely admitted, and national wage recommendations were set below market levels to guarantee an abundant and cheap supply of labor. Government social policies, particularly an extensive public housing program, also kept workers' living costs and hence their wages low.

But in 1979 a "Second Industrial Revolution" was launched, which recognized that these policies had created an excess demand for labor, resulting in labor shortages and in an ever-increasing dependence on foreign labor. The new investment policies since then have progressively favored only high-technology, capital-intensive industries, with very generous incentives especially provided to research and development. A high wage policy was instituted for three years, and annual national wage increase recommendations since then have continued to be large. Foreign labor is quickly being phased out, and labor-intensive industries are being vigorously pushed to upgrade, automate, or relocate out of the country. Labor, including unskilled labor, has become increasingly scarce and costly. Priority industries of the recent past are expected to give way to new priority industries that are now receiving the bulk of government subsidies. The government is also attempting to "privatize" social services by shifting more of the burden for providing them to private sector employers. The new industrial policies, including a national productivity movement, have meant greater state intervention in many company decisions, such as choice of technology, employee training, and industrial relations.

Foreign investors have thus had to adjust to many government policy changes, the most serious change involving the shortage and increased cost of labor. Yet it may be argued that these policy changes are necessary, and even belated, given the country's shifting comparative advantage. This in itself is the result of very rapid growth—to which foreign investment preeminently contributed. To a considerable extent, many companies responded to underlying market forces and were already restructuring their operations before the government policy changes were made. Foreign investors are also extensively consulted by the government about impending policy changes.

Appendix 5C
Points to Note in Negotiating Incentives

Probably the most important fact in negotiating incentives is that there is almost always, and almost everywhere in the developing world, a substantial gap between the letter of the law and actual practice. As one experienced corporate executive put it: "Anyone who accepts an investment law at face value is making a big mistake. The difference between how the law reads and what in fact happens can spell the difference between success and failure."

First on a checklist, therefore, must be:

• **Start with studying what the law says, but don't stop there.** Check what realistic practice is and, preferably, how other companies have fared.

• **Make sure you know how to proceed and, just as important, with whom.** In most developing countries, successful negotiating involves both what you know and whom you know.

• **Gear the tempo and sophistication of negotiation** to the caliber of the technicians who have to process your incentive applications. Working from the top is important to get approvals in principle, but there is no avoiding the paper work down the line. The degree of competence at the lower level can make a great deal of difference—and competence of lower-level officials varies widely by country.

• **Don't delude yourself that negotiating incentives is a purely economic and administrative matter;** or, for that matter, a once-and-for-all affair. Incentives have a political component and the politics change.

Incentive politics have two major aspects: first, national political, which may mean personnel changes at the top, at the ministerial as well as senior bureaucratic level; and new laws and/or regulations governing incentives. In the first instance, this will at minimum spell delay in an ongoing negotiation,

Reprinted from Business International, *101 Checklists* (New York: Business International, 1977), 61. Used with the permission of the publisher, Business International Corporation, New York.

and may mean having to start again from the beginning. If the ground rules are changed, it means a completely new situation.

The second political aspect of incentives involves competitors, particularly domestic competitors who can exert political pressures. Such pressures are difficult to deal with because they can operate both overtly and covertly. But they cannot be ignored.

• **Watch out for the fine print** in sweet-sounding incentive packages, and search carefully for the snags and loopholes that tend to bedevil incentives that look splendid on the surface. Specifically:

— Tax holidays contained in most incentive packages usually cover the early periods of an enterprise when profits are nonexistent or minimal. By the time profits become appreciable, tax holidays often run out.

— Tariff protection, usually promised for as soon as production starts up, tends not to materialize until considerably later, sometimes as much as a year or two, during which a new enterprise can take a nasty beating. And once word gets around that tariff protection has been offered to a new enterprise, customers start stockpiling, leaving the new plant with minimal sales for a number of months, sometimes years.

— Duty exemption generally is guaranteed in the incentive package, but getting duty-exempt machinery, spare parts, or raw materials out of customs is a different matter. It can take several months to pry loose duty-exempt goods from reluctant, inefficient, and/or corrupt customs.

Corporate experience with negotiating incentives in the major developing countries varies widely in different developing areas.

Sources of Additional Information

Business International. *Investment, Licensing and Trading Conditions*. New York: Business International, updated looseleaf service.

Foreign government investment promotion offices (usually in New York) and/or commercial sections of embassies in Washington.

International Center for Settlement of Investment Disputes. *Investment Laws of the World*. Washington, D.C.: ICSID, 1982.

International Negotiation Institute. *The Successful International Negotiators*. Princeton, N.J.: International Negotiation Institute, 1984.

Lambert's World of Trade, Finance, and Economic Development. New York: Lambert Publications–Business Press International, semiannual. Directory of government officials.

Price Waterhouse. *Doing Business in [name of country]*. Series on numerous countries. Updated periodically.

U.S. Department of Commerce, International Trade Administration, Country Desks for Specific Countries, Washington, D.C. 20230. Phone: (202) 377-2000.

U.S. Department of Commerce. *Investment Climate in Foreign Countries*. 4 vols. Washington, D.C.: Department of Commerce, updated periodically.

U.S. Department of State, Bureau of Economic and Business Affairs, Office of Investment Affairs, Washington, D.C. 20520. Phone: (202) 632-1128.

Wells, Louis T., Jr. "Negotiating with Third World Governments." *Harvard Business Review* 50 (January–February 1977): 72–80.

6

Selecting and Working with Local Partners

M ost investors in developing countries have local joint venture partners. In a typical joint venture partnership, you as the foreign investor would own up to 49 percent of the firm, with one or more local partners owning the balance; sometimes the local government is a joint venture partner.

This chapter will discuss government regulations concerning joint ventures, the benefits that can be derived from joint ventures, the process of finding a partner and negotiating a contract, and the kinds of problems that frequently arise during the history of joint venture arrangements.

Taking into Account Government Regulations

Most governments of developing countries require a joint venture arrangement as a condition of allowing a foreign investor into the country. They do this in order to increase local control over the investment project and also to increase the transfer of skills and technology to the local society—and for other reasons.

From the host country's point of view, the expected benefits of an element of ownership and control include: an increased national share of the income derived from foreign investment and a corresponding reduction in the balance of payments service account outflow of interest, profits, and dividends; higher local reinvestment rates, which promote growth and reduce balance of payments outflows; more linkages with other local firms, which increases the domestic value added and reduces import dependence; and greater dissemination of managerial, technical, financial, and marketing expertise and skills to locate entrepreneurs and employees. A measure of local ownership and control can also ensure that local interests and concerns are considered

Thomas L. Brewer, principal author.

in company decision making and can provide some safeguard against potential foreign abuse and exploitation.

At the same time, foreign–local joint venture enterprises have advantages over purely local firms because they give the host country more access to capital, to foreign technology, skills, and expertise, and to foreign markets. They enable a country gradually to reduce foreign ownership of the local economy, thus minimizing the political costs without giving up the economic benefits of foreign investment. In some countries joint ventures are a mechanism for developing an indigenous entrepreneurial class drawn from the majority or dominant ethnic group in collaboration with foreign investors.

Government joint venture requirements differ from industry to industry, and they change over time. Furthermore, there is normally an element of flexibility in the formal regulations so that your particular project may very well receive a waiver of one or more of the formal requirements.

In most countries your ownership share as a foreign investor may not be allowed to exceed 49 percent. A majority local share is most often required for investments producing for the domestic market—that is, in import-substituting industries that receive tariff protection—and for investments extracting domestic material resources for export, particularly in mining and lumbering. In the latter industries, host governments often retain full ownership of the assets in question, but lease their exploitation to foreign companies on a production-sharing basis. Many countries allow 100 percent foreign ownership only for wholly export-oriented ventures, such as those located in Export Processing Zones.

Where majority foreign investment (control) is permitted, however, the fine print of the law often indicates that in order for you to be able to sell your share, the favorable vote of all outstanding shares will be required. This means that it will be hard to leave a country unless you have a presigned agreement that specifically allows you to do so without a favorable vote by other shareholders. (See appendix 6A.)

Examples of Government Policies. The joint venture regulations for Thailand are summarized in exhibit 6–1. It is evident there that the extent of foreign ownership that is allowed depends on the kind of project. Although the formal requirement generally is that the foreign investor cannot own more than 49 percent of the total capital, there are exceptions. For certain industries, foreign ownership cannot exceed 40 percent. On the other hand, if the project will be doing a substantial amount of exporting, more than 50 percent of the ownership can be foreign, and in fact foreign ownership might even be as much as 100 percent. In addition, other considerations can lead to waivers of these basic requirements.

Exhibit 6–1
Summary of Thailand's Joint Venture Requirements

In considering applications from foreign investors to invest in or carry out joint ventures under promotional privileges, the Board of Investment has laid down the following general policy guidelines:

1. For investment in the field of industry where the product is intended mainly for sale on the local market, equity participation of Thai nationality must be not less than 51 percent of the total capital.

2. For investment in the fields of agriculture, animal husbandry, fishing, mineral prospecting, mining, and in service industries, equity participation of Thai nationals must be not less than 60 percent of the equity capital.

3. For investment in the field of industry producing for export to the extent of not less than 50 percent of total production, equity participation of foreign nationality may have majority control. In the case where production is intended entirely for export, the foreign participation in equity may reach 100 percent.

4. When special dispensation of any of the above conditions is requested, the Board of Investment considers the following factors:

1. the size of the capital investment necessary;

2. the level of technology;

3. the employment of local people;

4. the proposed location of the factory;

5. the economic and social importance of the project;

6. any other appropriate considerations.

In the event that an application is given special consideration in relation to any or all of the above factors, the Board of Investment may either extend the time limits for the equity proportions to be reached, or else vary the policy requirements in whatever manner is considered appropriate in the circumstances.

Reprinted from *Business Asia*, August 5, 1983, p. 245. Used with the permission of the publisher, Business International Corporation, New York.

In Oman, to give another example, foreign investment is limited to agriculture, fishing, industry, and construction, and the foreign investor's share generally may not exceed 25 percent of total capital.[1] However, if the government determines that a project is important to economic development, it may raise the foreign investment ceiling to a maximum of 49 percent. In actual practice, the exception applies to most ventures in agriculture, fishing, and industry.

In Israel, on the other hand, there is no formal restriction on foreign ownership or management. To qualify for preferred investment status, however, the enterprise must be a foreign corporation that is registered in Israel or must be a foreign limited partnership. And in any case there is a strong government preference for joint ventures.

In Pakistan, there are no legal requirements placed on the amount of equity a foreign investor may hold; the government usually expects, however, the initial expenditure in local currency for establishing the project to be met from local equity capital. In many cases, foreign investors have been allowed to hold majority equity management and control, though there have been some instances in the past when companies have been pressured to sell equity to Pakistani investors or to the Pakistani government itself.

In Indonesia the partial phasing out of foreign ownership has been formally prescribed in government regulations. Thus, at the start of a joint venture, Indonesians should own at least 20 percent of the share capital, and within ten years they should own at least 50 percent. The Indonesian partners may be private or government-owned corporations or some combination of the two. The increase in Indonesian ownership can be achieved through the capital stock market.

Obtaining Information. It is an easy matter to obtain basic information about the formal joint venture requirements for any country. The U.S. government and the governments of foreign countries have agencies that can provide you with such information.

The U.S. Commerce Department, for example, has a series of publications called "The Investment Climate in Foreign Countries," which includes a brief description of the joint venture requirements for each country. In addition, the Commerce Department's International Trade Administration has country officers with current information, including less-formalized information about the regulations of foreign countries.

Foreign governments' embassies in the United States and/or their foreign investment promotion offices can provide you with current formal information about their regulations. It is a simple matter to call or write the commercial section of the embassy of the relevant government in Washington; in some instances you may need to call or write the investment promotion office, which is often located in New York.

There are also numerous private sources of information, such as Business International's *Investment, Licensing and Trading Conditions Abroad,* or the Price Waterhouse series, *Doing Business in [country X].* In addition, major banks and consulting firms frequently have current information.

However, it is also important to obtain information from sources inside the country—from both formal governmental sources and private sources. These sources would include not only the foreign investment agency of the government, but also bankers, accountants, lawyers, trade associations, consultants, and individual firms that are doing business in the country. This kind of information can of course be obtained during your on-site visit to the country.

Obtaining Benefits from a Joint Venture

Even if a joint venture is not required by host government regulations, you may find that such an arrangement is nevertheless to your benefit. In particular, there are three main sets of benefits that you might be able to derive from a joint venture arrangement. For one thing you reduce your costs and risks. The extent to which you are able to do so of course depends quite directly on the proportions of the total investment that you and your partner(s) make. It should be noted that the value of your partner's contribution, as well as that of your own contribution, depends on more than just the amount of cash contribution in exchange for capital stock. The partner's initial contribution may also take the form of equipment, plant, or perhaps access to local capital markets.

The partner's greatest contribution, however, may lie in his or her knowledge of the local market and experience in running facilities in that country. Particularly if this is your first experience in a foreign investment project or if you have little or no previous experience as an exporter to the foreign country, the local partner's experience and knowledge can be extremely valuable to you—even essential to the success of the enterprise.

Having a local partner may also help you to have better relations with the local government, labor unions, your employees, and the local community in general. Since there is still considerable sensitivity in many developing countries about foreign control over local business, the existence of a local partner can substantially reduce the suspicion and even hostility that local people might feel toward you. So, for the sake of government relations, labor relations, and public relations, a local partner can be an important asset.

In order for your local partner to serve your interests effectively in these respects, however, he or she must be someone you can count on. You should therefore put considerable thought into the selection of your joint venture partner.

Selecting a Partner

Nongovernment Partners. In order to select a local partner wisely, you will have to assess your own needs and decide what you want from a partner. Perhaps your main interest is in obtaining local market knowledge or distribution channels relatively quickly and easily. Or perhaps your principal interest is in a partner who would help you to deal with local government regulations. Or perhaps you need experience in local production processes and labor relations.

Finding someone, even someone to begin discussions with as a prospective partner, may be a big challenge. Locating potential partners often requires persistent searching. You can obtain leads about prospective partners and information about their backgrounds, their special abilities, and their ability to meet your particular needs from local consultants, other U.S. corporations in the country, government officials, the U.S. Chamber of Commerce in the foreign country, lawyers, trade associations, and the commercial attaché in the U.S. embassy. The foreign country's investment promotion office in the United States or its embassy in the United States may also be helpful. Your own banker or accountant in the United States, if the bank or accounting firm has an office in the foreign country, is another possible source of information. There are even nonprofit organizations such as Caribbean/Central American Action in Washington that can assist you in the search for a joint venture partner.

Possible Problems. In many developing countries there is a shortage of local entrepreneurial expertise and experience, and thus a corresponding shortage of potential joint venture partners with the necessary capital and expertise. Furthermore, the ownership of wealth, the business expertise, and the local connections that make for an effective partner are often concentrated in a few individuals, families, or enterprises with intertwined interests. Some of their multiple investments may pose conflicts of interest, and they may already be invested in competing enterprises. Such potential partners may view the new investment merely as an outlet for surplus funds or as a means of diversifying their interests. Their operating interest in the actual enterprise would be marginal, and they would be only inactive or "sleeping" partners. (Such inactive or sleeping partners are not allowed in some countries.) With their multiple interests and activities, they might not have the time to provide the very forms of local assistance that make joint ventures attractive to foreign investors. If some of their other business ventures fail, the repercussions may affect the joint venture in question, which will be part of a conglomerate's holdings. When such individuals or families are involved in politics, as is often the case, further complications may arise in the event of political change.

Another problem is posed by partners who, though they may possess the necessary capital and expertise, belong to an ethnic minority or other politically weak group in the population. In Southeast Asia, the overseas Chinese frequently fall into this category, as do the overseas Indians in some African and Asian nations. The dilemma of the potential foreign partner is compounded if there are regulations requiring that the local partner be of a specific ethnic group, usually the majority. The foreign investor must trade off the economic advantages of dealing with a competent and experienced business partner against the political disadvantage of associating with a member of a group that is discriminated against.

Other Considerations. Where established individuals or enterprises that might be suitable as partners are lacking, the foreign investor may have to undertake the responsibility of "developing" a suitable partner. Eager individuals without the necessary expertise or experience may present themselves; but because of political connections or membership in the "correct" or favored ethnic group, they may have access to loan capital and/or to official influence. Assessments of character then become more important. On the other hand, competent individuals may exist who do not have the necessary capital or influence, but are likely to make good business partners—perhaps because they possess some technical knowledge or other ability.

In the selection of a local partner, much depends on the expectations of the foreign investors. Some investors prefer sleeping partners who leave them with de facto control of the enterprise while providing some risk capital and local "camouflage," if not connections. On the other hand such investors may be accused of exploiting their partners and of refusing to disseminate managerial knowledge and skills to them. Other foreign investors want an active local partner who will handle all operating aspects of the enterprises, perhaps leaving only some areas such as technology procurement, foreign marketing, and international financing to the foreign partner. Different types of local partners will be chosen in each case.

One important factor to assess is the likelihood of long-term commitment on the part of a potential partner to the enterprise.[2] Some local partners may be interested only in acquiring particular knowledge, experience, and contacts from the joint venture. Their ultimate aim is to break away and set up their own competing enterprise. Often these are the most ambitious and able partners, so a trade-off has to be made. In any case, you need to know what the prospective partner wants and how that fits your needs.

The partner's financial situation is also quite important. In addition to obtaining as much information as possible directly from the prospective partner, you will want to check with other sources. Although such information is of course often difficult to obtain in any detail, you will be able to develop some informed impressions.

Another more subtle but very important factor is your personal relationship with the prospective partner. You must be comfortable and compatible with each other, and there should be a feeling of mutual trust that will enable you to work closely together through difficult times as well as good times. You will have to trust your partner's judgment on many issues since the firm will be operating in his culture and selling in his domestic market.

You should be careful not to choose automatically a local firm with which you have already done business. For example, a local agent, distributor, or licensee may seem like the most obvious partner, and indeed it is possible that a joint venture arrangement with such a person will work out very nicely. However, the traits that make a person a good agent, distributor, or licensee do not necessarily make that same individual a good manufacturing partner—for you may need something different or something more than a familiar individual or firm has to offer. Even many years of experience with a distributor do not necessarily mean that you will know all that you should before entering into a joint venture partnership.

One kind of joint venture partner that you may want to be especially careful about is one whose experience is limited to financial affairs and who has very little or no previous experience in your particular industry. Thus, bankers and other financial people may be less desirable joint venture partners than industrialists or agribusiness firms or others who are more intimately familiar with the kind of project that you are considering.

It is also important that your partner have a good reputation in the business community and have good relations with the unions and the government.

Government Partners. There are many advantages to having a branch of the host government as a partner. Except in situations of extreme economic crisis, the government partner is creditworthy, may have access to capital at concessionary rates (from tax revenues, forced savings or bonds, government development banks, and foreign aid), can speed up bureaucratic procedures and generally facilitate relations with other government agencies, and often can offer a privileged position in a given sector or industry. The risks of the investment are reduced and political conflicts between foreign investor and host government are minimized. All this can make an enterprise run much more efficiently and profitably.

On the other hand, there are also disadvantages. Cheap capital and the security of public sector financial backing can make a state joint venture enterprise less efficient, especially if civil servants carry over inefficient and even corrupt bureaucratic practices. Government partners may also be less oriented toward earning private profit from an investment. They may be subject to political pressures that can affect management decisions.

Negotiating a Partnership Contract

You will need a local lawyer who is familiar with local government regulations and other business practices to help you draw up a joint venture contract. However, you may want to take the initiative yourself in formulating the basic terms of the contract. Your prospective local partner will not necessarily be any more familiar than you are with the particular provisions that are commonly included in a joint venture contract.

The Bargaining Process. You should be prepared for lengthy and sometimes difficult bargaining. It may take anywhere from a few months to perhaps as much as a few years to reach agreement on all relevant aspects of the contract (though repeated use of time-tested provisions can simplify the process).

One of the factors that may complicate the negotiations is that the government may take a great interest in the agreement, even if it is not a partner itself. In fact, it is not unusual for the local host government to serve as a guide, mediator, consultant, and even ultimate arbiter during negotiations. In most countries, the agreement will have to be acceptable to the government and registered with it.

Many government regulations, furthermore, will affect the operations of the joint venture even if there are not specific government regulations pertaining to the particular provisions of the joint venture agreement itself. Import restrictions, export requirements, local financing restrictions, labor practices—all of these aspects of the joint venture operations and others as well may be importantly affected by government policies. It is therefore important that the joint venture agreement be agreeable to the government and consistent with all existing and anticipated government policies.

For example, government environmental regulations prohibit new industries or expansion in some areas. If you were joining a company already in such a restricted area, you would want to make sure that you have government authorization to join the local company where it is currently operating and that additional business will be permitted.

The Content of Agreements. Although there is tremendous variation in the contents of joint venture agreements, there are several issues that commonly need to be addressed. (See also appendixes 6B and 6C.)

The Initial Contribution. One important issue, for instance, concerns each partner's initial contribution to the venture. Initial contributions commonly take the form of cash and/or machinery and equipment. Contributions of machinery can become complicated, however, by government regulations. The government may not want used machinery to be contributed, or there may be import restrictions that could limit your in-kind contribution of equipment or machinery. In such a case, one alternative would be for you to make a cash investment that would be equivalent to your evaluation of the machinery and equipment. If the joint venture is in a position to obtain an import license covering the equipment and machinery, the joint venture could purchase the machinery from you upon the legal formation of the company. Therefore, you have in effect contributed the machinery and equipment; you first contribute the cash, which is then used to purchase the machinery from you.

The Contribution of Technology. One especially difficult kind of contribution to assess is the contribution of technology, or know-how, for oftentimes there is a licensing agreement incorporated into a joint venture contract whereby the contributor of the technology receives a fee. Many governments, however, discourage licensing agreements, and in any case the government is likely to be interested in the precise terms of such an agreement. Because of the foreign exchange implications of licensing agreements, governments often restrict and monitor licensing agreements very carefully.

Control and Management. Another area that is central to a joint venture agreement is the provision for control and management. The seats on the board of directors are normally allocated according to the shares of ownership. Clearly then, in those countries in which your ownership is limited to 49 percent by law, you will not have majority voting power on the board. Furthermore, in some countries even if majority participation is allowed for a foreign investor, you would still be limited by government regulations that would prohibit you from determining the management of the corporation.

However, it is often possible to stipulate that certain kinds of decisions must be approved by you as well as by your partner(s). Thus, for example, appointments of senior managerial people, decisions concerning compensation packages, purchase orders above certain amounts, and the development of new products, or entry into new markets—all of these kinds of decisions can be made subject to your veto.

In general, though, it is good to establish clearly which partner has managerial control; this is especially true in the case of 50–50 ownership agreements. There are many ways to try to arrange a joint venture so that one partner has management control in spite of the 50–50 ownership. For example, two kinds of stock can be issued—voting and nonvoting. The bylaws can state that one partner shall have a majority of the members of the board of directors. It is also possible to state in the bylaws that in spite of the equal number of directors on the board, those directors who represent a particular partner have the authority to appoint senior managers. The bylaws may provide that in the case of a tie vote, the directors of one partner will have the authority to break the tie. In some cases it is possible to have a management contract with the partner such that the foreign investor has control. Oftentimes, however, these ways of trying to establish control will not be effective.

In many cases, such agreements are simply not even allowed by the local government or will not be enforced by it since the issue of local control of joint ventures is of paramount importance in the minds of many government officials in developing countries.

An Arbitration Clause. It is a good idea to spell out in as much detail as possible the rights and responsibilities of the partners in a joint venture arrangement. Doing so will help to minimize disagreements arising from misunderstanding. However, no agreement can anticipate every possible contingency or conflict between the partners. There should therefore be an arbitration clause for the settlement of disputes.

Termination of the Agreement. It is possible, furthermore, that at some point there will be a termination of the joint venture agreement, an eventuality that should be anticipated in the bylaws. There should be a provision for the terms under which the venture will be terminated. The provision should include completion of operations in process, the liquidation of credits and collections of payables, the sale of remaining assets, the completion of a final financial statement, and payment to the shareholders to the maximum extent possible.

Reduction of Share. Finally, the joint venture bylaws should contain a provision concerning the rights of the partners in the event of a reduction of its share by one of the partners. If you already have the maximum share legally allowable for a foreign investor, or if you do not want to increase your share of the investment even though it is legally possible for you to do so, then you still want to be able to influence the selection of the new partner. Otherwise, the old partner might sell out to a new partner with little experience or interest in the particular kind of project, or perhaps for some other reason the new partner may not be to your liking. The bylaws should therefore contain a clause indicating that the foreign investor has the right to select or veto any new partners.

No matter how carefully the joint venture contract is formulated, however, problems will arise in the operational phases of the project.

Coping with Ongoing Managerial Problems

Obviously, in order for the joint venture to succeed, it has to be to the mutual benefit of all partners on a more or less continuing basis. There may nevertheless be some circumstances in which one or both partners have to demonstrate a commitment to the long-term success of the partnership in order to weather momentary problems. Studies have shown that when partners have a strong commitment to the long-term success of the venture, they are more likely to be able to overcome short-term problems.

Some examples of common problems:

1. The reporting of profitability. A local partner may want accounting procedures adopted that will reduce his own domestic tax burden, but you do not necessarily care about the local tax burden since you can credit your foreign tax payments against your U.S. tax obligation.
2. Dividend policy. You and your partner(s) may disagree about whether to pay out large dividends or plow back profits into the company.
3. Business practices. Such issues as the choice of suppliers or even the use of questionable payments may become a source of conflict between your partner and you.[3]

One of the most important determinants of your success in coping with such problems is the ability of you and your partner to transcend cultural differences. A joint venture relationship involves personal relationships. It is therefore important that you be self-conscious about your attitudes toward the foreign culture, that you question your assumptions, that you be careful not to use stereotypes, and that you adapt to the foreign partner's culture at least as much as you expect your foreign partner to adapt to yours. You should be generally open minded and receptive to your local partner's ideas about conducting business if you expect the partnership to succeed.

It is important to establish open, honest, and direct two-way communication between partners. Sometimes this is difficult for local partners who come from a different cultural tradition—where custom and politeness, for example, may be considered more important than the truth, especially when the truth is unpleasant, or where even constructive criticism is neither offered nor tolerated. Also, negotiating styles may differ between the cultures. Both partners have to learn to communicate in or at least understand the other's cultural forms so that misunderstandings can be minimized. Mutual trust must be established. Cultural difference is a major barrier to be overcome in relations between joint venture partners in developing countries. This is true even if the local partner has been in the United States and speaks English fluently. Learning the foreign language is one way that you can try to overcome cultural barriers. As was noted in chapter 3, you cannot expect simply to impose American business practices on your partner.

With effort conflicts can usually be resolved. Resorting to arbitration, however, can be quite destructive to the relationship.

Conclusion

You may be required by the host government to enter into a joint venture agreement with a local partner. Even if you are not obligated to do so, you may find that a joint venture partner has much to contribute and can complement your own weaknesses and strengths to your mutual benefit. Great care should be exercised in selecting a partner and in drawing up a contract. You will also need patience and understanding in coping with the inevitable problems that will arise from an ongoing and evolving operation.

Appendix 6A
Checklist for Joint Venture Arrangements

A. Purpose of Joint Venture
   1. Objectives/strategy of foreign partner.
   2. Objectives/strategy of local partner.
   3. Reconciliation of objectives.

B. Contributions of Each Partner
   1. Knowledge of local environment.
   2. Personal contacts with local suppliers, customers, and so on.
   3. Influence with host government.
   4. Local prestige.
   5. Existing facilities.
   6. Capital.
   7. Management/production/marketing skills.
   8. Technical skills and industrial property.
   9. Other.

C. Role of Host Government
   1. Laws/regulations/policies.
   2. Administrative flexibility.
   3. Interest in this joint venture.
   4. Requirements for approval.

D. Ownership Shares
   1. Majority (foreign partner).

Source: Reprinted, by permission of the publisher, from *Foreign Market Entry Strategies*, by Franklin R. Root, pp. 168–169 © 1982 AMACOM, a division of American Management Association, New York. All rights reserved.

2. Minority (foreign partner).

3. 50–50.

4. Other arrangements.

E. Capital Structure

1. Legal character of venture.

2. Equity capital.

3. Loan capital (local and foreign).

4. Future increase in equity capital.

5. Limits on transfer of shares.

F. Management

1. Appointment/composition of board of directors.

2. Appointment/authority of executive officers.

3. Expatriate staff.

4. Organization.

G. Production

1. Planning/construction of facilities.

2. Supply/installation of machinery and equipment.

3. Operations.

4. Quality control.

5. R&D.

6. Training.

H. Finance

1. Accounting/control system.

2. Working capital.

3. Capital expenditures.

4. Dividends.

5. Pricing of products provided by partners.

6. Borrowing and loan guarantees by partners.

7. Taxation.

I. Marketing

1. Product lines, trademarks, and trade names.

2. Target market(s) and sales potentials.

3. Distribution channels.

4. Promotion.
5. Pricing.
6. Organization.

J. Agreement
1. Company law in host country.
2. Articles and bylaws of incorporation.
3. Contractual arrangements (licensing, technical assistance, management, and so on).
4. Settlement of disputes.

Appendix 6B
Case: An Agreement for a Joint Venture in China (PRC)

T his case concerns a large American corporation (AMC), but this discussion of the terms of its joint venture agreement with the government of China provides a good illustration of a joint venture (JV) agreement, especially one including a government.

China's domestic market potential, its attractiveness as a low-cost manufacturing site for products destined for other Asian markets, and the company's determination to have a joint venture kept American Motor Corp. (AMC) negotiating the deal for four years. The outcome is a 20-year renewable agreement . . . to set up a Beijing Jeep Corp.

AMC has 31.4 percent equity in the venture; its partner, 68.6 percent. (AMC has an option to bring its stake up to 49 percent through reinvestment of profits.) The company's PRC partner is China's top producer of four-wheel-drive vehicles, Beijing Automotive Works (BAW).

Who Contributes What

AMC is putting in US$8 million in cash and US$8 million in technology toward the joint ventures's initial investment of US$51 million. The Chinese will contribute mainly fixed assets (building, plant, machine tools) and some local currency, together valued at US$35 million.

The JV will take over part of BAW, an established operation that currently produces annually some 20,000 four-wheel-drive vehicles (built to an older, USSR–inspired design) and employs about 10,000 workers. The ultimate aim is to produce world-class vehicles (including AMC–designed Jeeps) geared to the PRC as well as to other Asian markets, and components that can be utilized in AMC's operations worldwide. To do that, the partners over the next seven years will embark on massive retraining of the workforce, introduction of modern management skills, and substantial retooling of existing production lines.

Upgrading of existing operations [was expected to] begin as the technology transfer process [got] under way. Revising the factory's painting system is likely to be one of the first tasks.

In the late 1970's, AMC was looking for a site in Asia to manufacture vehicles and components at low cost. An important spur to that search was the competition in the Asian market for four-wheel-drive-vehicles offered by Japanese firms, who had the bulk of that market. China was chosen as the site because of its tremendous untapped market potential (its poor road and highway system makes four-wheel-drive vehicles particularly attractive) and, an AMC spokesman says, the Chinese already had the aptitude, skills, and facilities to do the job.

AMC from the start wanted to establish a joint venture, convinced that other kinds of arrangements like cooperation deals, compensation trade, and subcontracting, offered neither the security of a long-term commitment nor took full advantage of AMC's strength as a manufacturer.

The JV contract does not fix the percentage of output that must be exported, but the project is definitely expected to be a net foreign exchange earner. The agreement does set out some benchmark foreign exchange targets the JV is expected to achieve on a best-efforts basis, subject to meeting rigorous quality standards, changing market conditions, and other factors.

AMC says it anticipates little difficulty meeting export commitments. Components needed by AMC affiliates are among the first items the JV will produce. As these vehicles are produced, AMC will purchase them from the JV and market and distribute them. Similarly, in the domestic market, the JV will sell finished vehicles to its PRC parent, which will handle domestic distribution.

Pricing

Pricing of products for both export and the PRC market will be handled by the JV. AMC expects that the PRC system will not put undue constraints on its setting of domestic prices that permit profitable operations. World market conditions will affect export prices.

While a new component will be introduced into the production process and the existing vehicles gradually transformed, a fully AMC designed Jeep is probably six to seven years down the road.

The JV's output will continue at about 20,000 vehicles, but it could be expanded significantly by adding a second shift or through capital expansion. Some components and intermediate products needed for the venture will be purchased from AMC in the beginning, but such imports will account for only a small portion of value added. Machinery and parts also will be imported from time to time as the upgrading process goes on.

AMC has written into the bylaws a host of provisions to protect its minority position. Since corporation policy is to operate in international ventures as a minority partner, it has developed time-tested clauses that it believes will adequately protect its interest.

Management of operations will be shared with the Chinese, but AMC designates will play a major role in the first few years of the venture's life. While certain key positions, including the presidency, will initially be filled by AMC nominees, all major executive posts will also have deputy positions. These will be filled by either a PRC or an AMC person, and the pairs will work together. The subordinate and dominant positions will be rotated between the AMC and the PRC nominees every couple of years. AMC expects to maintain a substantial foreign contingent through the life of the JV to pass on technical expertise.

The JV will have hiring and firing authority, pay higher wages than state-owned PRC enterprises, and maintain BAW's existing bonus and incentive system, with modifications.

Although the partners agreed on many basic points from the outset, negotiations still took about four years to be completed. The usual difficulties in communications, lack of language equivalents, unfamiliarity with each other's system, and the overall differences in social and economic systems contributed to drawing out the talks. Thorny issues included the problem of salary differentials between US and Chinese executives, how shares would be valued, and what proportion of technology would be deemed already utilized should the joint venture be prematurely dissolved.

Some issues that AMC negotiators had anticipated being troublesome offered no problem at all. For example, AMC's approach for valuing each side's contribution was to have an outside auditing firm (in this case, Deloitte Haskins and Sells) evaluate both Chinese assets and AMC technology contributions. The Chinese accepted the valuation with little fuss.

Reprinted from *Business Asia,* June 10, 1983, pp. 180–81. Used with the permission of the publisher, Business International Corporation, New York.

Appendix 6C
Case: Acme's Internal Proposal for a Joint Venture in Landia

T he following case is included for instructional purposes. It does not necessarily illustrate good management practices. You might want to identify the issues and alternatives needing analysis before making a decision to proceed with the project.

Establishment of Company

Financial Responsibilities

A. Acme International will provide ten pieces of reconditioned manufacturing equipment from its plant in Xenia. Acme will also be responsible for their reconditioning and shipment to Landia.
B. Mr. Saud and Mr. Shihab—the local partners in Landia—will be responsible for all other investment capital.

Certification of the Equipment

Under new law in Landia foreign invested equipment must not be older than seven to ten years, in order to receive government investment incentives. However, it is assumed that Acme will be exempt from this when it certifies that the equipment has been completely reconditioned with new moving parts.

Gaining Government Approval

An application must be filed accompanied by a feasibility report. Mr. Saud has proposed using a local accountant experienced in these matters, to prepare both the application and the report. To receive the approval would take anywhere from three weeks to nine months. When granted, the approval is valid for two years. The initial steps for establishing a company must be started within two years after the approval. The application can be submitted without any advance commitment to proceed on the project, even if the approval is granted.

Control of Company

Several alternatives concerning the control of the company have been discussed:

1. Establish the company as a joint venture between the three parties, allocating the shares as follows:
   Acme International   40%
   Mr. Saud   40%
   Mr. Shihab   20%
   Mr. Saud would actually manage the company while Acme would supply the necessary experience.

   The company would be started with the ten reconditioned pieces of equipment. Acme would explain to the government authorities in Landia that the equipment, although old, would be completely reconditioned. Acme would also cite cases indicating that using new equipment would pose an insurmountable financial burden. Acme would also mention research conducted in Pakistan and Australia that indicated that using new equipment made the payback period too long for the project to be financially feasible. To further substantiate the efficiency of this equipment, Acme would point to other manufacturers that have used such equipment.

2. Establish the company as a joint venture as in (1). However, in the event that the government does not approve the starting of the company with the old equipment, Acme could possibly bring in one new piece of equipment; the reconditioned equipment would follow shortly afterwards. Mr. Saud would assume the cost of this new equipment, without changing the proposed share structure of 40, 40, 20.

3. The next alternative would be for the company to be wholly locally owned. Acme's involvement would be as a consultant under a fee with a long-term contract. Under this arrangement Acme would also receive a percentage of the company's sales.

   In this case, it would be Mr. Saud's decision as to the type of equipment used.

4. The fourth alternative, although doubtful, in theory is possible. Again, the company would be wholly locally owned, and Acme would be retained in the same manner. However, rather than using the reconditioned equipment Mr. Saud would commission Acme to arrange to build six to ten pieces of its own new equipment.

   The above alternatives were discussed in light of Acme's wishing to have no cash investment in this project.

5. Another alternative, which has not been discussed, would be for Acme wholly to own the company, with Mr. Saud acting as manager under a fee contract, with a share of the company's sales. The plant would be started only with the reconditioned equipment, provided government approval to do so was granted.

Marketing of Company Products

Initially, the entire production output is expected to be sold to Mr. Shihab's company. Mr. Shihab has a monopoly on the utilization and distribution of containers in Landia. There will be no sales or shipping expenses in the beginning, since Mr. Shihab will consume the total output and will also take delivery at the factory. As the company expands and turns over a profit, efforts will begin to promote additional products in Landia. If this is successful, the company could also conceivably fabricate other related items.

Sources of Additional Information

Beamish, Paul. "A Strategy for Forming Joint Ventures in Developing Countries," School of Business and Economics, Wilfrid Laurier University, Waterloo, Ontario, Canada, n.d.

Caribbean/Central American Action, 1333 New Hampshire Ave. NW, Washington, D.C. 20036. Phone: (202) 466-7464.

Hall, R. Duane. *The International Joint Venture*. New York: Wiley, 1984.

Janger, Allen. *Organization of International Joint Ventures*. New York: Conference Board, 1980.

Killing, J. "How to Make a Global Joint Venture Work." *Harvard Business Review* 60 (May–June 1982): 120–27.

Reynolds, John I. *Indo-American Joint Ventures: Business Policy Relationships*. Washington, D.C.: University Press of America, 1979.

Root, Franklin. *Foreign Market Entry Strategies*. New York: AMACOM, 1982.

United Nations. *Manual on the Establishment of Industrial Joint Venture Agreements in Developing Countries*. New York: United Nations, 1971.

Walmsley, John. *Handbook of International Joint Ventures*. London: Graham & Trotman, 1984.

7

Establishing and Operating Facilities

O nce you have made the initial plans and agreements, the problems associated with actually establishing and operating the facilities become important. This chapter should help you to be prepared for the many start-up and operational problems that may arise. It considers site selection, land acquisition, infrastructure evaluation, environmental impact, supply problems, and initial employee recruitment and training.

Choosing a Plant Site

You can rent factory premises from a government agency or private landowner, or you can build your own plant. (See also appendix 7A for a checklist.)

Industrial Estates. In many countries, government agencies operate industrial estates with standard factory buildings that can be occupied right away. Such estates are usually fully equipped and well serviced, and they can be very convenient. However, they sometimes have drawbacks that you should look out for. For example, new industrial estates are costly to construct, and governments sometimes charge high rents, especially if there is a low occupancy rate and insufficient rental income. Newly established industrial estates may also be insufficiently serviced, and their administrators may be inexperienced and inefficient. Older estates, on the other hand, may be overcrowded, with insufficient space for future expansion, unreliable local utilities and transportation, and a saturated local labor market.

Government industrial estates may not be situated in the most convenient locations for your project. For example, since industrial decentralization is often a goal, many developing country governments sometimes locate new

Linda Y.C. Lim, principal author.

industrial estates in relatively remote areas where infrastructure and supporting services are not well developed. The government objectives are to avoid congestion in the major capital cities and commercial centers, to spread the benefits of industrialization more widely throughout the country, and to create regional "growth poles" in less developed areas. This has been the Malaysian government's policy on industrial location, for example, and it is now being imitated in Thailand.

There are both benefits and costs to locating in these decentralized industrial locations. Your costs, such as property rentals and labor may be lower, and additional investment incentives such as longer tax holidays may be offered. On the other hand, it may be more difficult to hire both skilled and unskilled labor because of insufficient population density in the surrounding rural area, inadequate local infrastructure such as housing and transportation, and geographical remoteness from major urban centers of education and commerce.

Frequently there is a reason for a particular region's being relatively undeveloped, such as mountainous terrain or vulnerability to bad weather. The three-month heavy monsoon rains that plague the eastern coast of peninsular Malaysia, for instance, make that area unpopular among industrial investors despite government encouragement. Transportation and communications are unreliable during the monsoon, and absenteeism rates are high among workers. Sometimes industrial estates are located in response to local political pressures. One such estate in the Philippines, for example, is located in hilly territory that is unsuitable for airport construction, has only one narrow and winding access road, and lacks a large resident labor supply.

Comparative Advantages and Disadvantages. You should be careful to note the comparative advantages and disadvantages of different locations for your particular project. For example, a labor-intensive project should be located in or near a populated area with an available labor supply, and there should be adequate transportation services for workers and goods.

Many governments plan for industry-specific siting in their zoning plans. In Singapore, for example, government agencies site light industries in multistory "flatted factories" in densely populated public housing estates, and heavy industries in a separate industrial area with deep-sea docking facilities. But the concentration of many employers in adjacent flatted factory blocks quickly absorbs the available labor supply, and some employers have resorted to "factory hopping" from one location to another in search of new sources of labor. Factories in the more remote heavy industrial area also report difficulties in hiring labor because of distance from population centers.

You may want to locate away from other firms in the same industry. Some U.S. electronics companies in Southeast Asia, for example, like to locate themselves apart from the rest, to avoid a competitive labor market.

Renting Private Factory Premises. There may be a possibility of renting private factory premises. However, you may find rentals on the private market very limited in cases where industrial development has only recently begun or where government zoning regulations or government attempts to secure for itself a monopoly of industrial real estate preclude private development. You may be able to find someone who will build a facility for you for a long-term rental contract. In any event, a rental contract should include an option to buy, especially if family inheritance of a rental property could create problems for continued renting.

Building Your Own Facilities. After several years of successful operation, you may want to build your own facilities, as part of a long-term expansion program. Buying land, though, is sometimes quite difficult. In some areas, the land area available for cultivation or industrial activity is declining. There may be other problems too.

In one instance, an agribusiness investor in Southeast Asia sought to expand its operations. Suitable areas were identified, soil samples were taken, drainage was checked, and negotiations with the host government were conducted. A joint venture partnership was entered in which the foreign investor provided the capital and management, and the host country provided the land.

The foreign investor was promised that the land was newly logged over and uninhabited. Despite what the government said, however, the land had been logged over more than fifteen years earlier. In addition, there were more than a hundred families still living inside the designated site.

The government officials responsible for the joint venture project claimed that the inhabitants were "squatters" who were occupying the land "illegally." In the strictest sense of the word, the government officials were probably correct—the settlers were squatters on government land. Yet if you asked the settlers themselves, they would claim a legal and moral right to occupy the land. They had cleared the land of stumps and brush, had built the dikes, leveled the fields, planted the fruit trees—in short, they had made the land productive.

Now they were being told to move. And more importantly from the investor's point of view, the settlers resisted pressures to move. A thorough, independent assessment in advance would have been highly desirable, since it would have made the firm aware of the need to change its plans.

Providing Housing for Employees

Some companies provide housing not just for expatriates and top management, but also for the rank and file workers, especially if the project is not in a city or within a short distance of one. This can be a costly venture, but the alternative may be less palatable. If workers are forced to fend for themselves, they may fall prey to unscrupulous landlords. The result can be a discontented work force with rapid turnover. An alternative is to provide transportation, but this can also be expensive and subject to complaints.

If workers are discontented and feel the company is in some way responsible, they can compound the problem of squatting. Workers and their families can be ingenious in their use of what looks to them to be idle company land. Makeshift homes may spring up overnight. In a situation in which wages are low and rents are high or housing is unavailable at any rent, the workers may feel morally justified in using idle land.

Using Utilities and Other Public Facilities

In urban areas and in industrial estates, utilities such as water, electricity, and phone lines, as well as transportation by roads and other means, are usually available.

In many developing countries, however, the infrastructure is not efficient or reliable, and you may have to learn to adjust to this. For example, in a city like Bangkok, where the phone lines are always jammed, many businesses resort to sending telexes or messengers on motorbikes for communication within the city itself. Bill payments are also accomplished by using messengers/collectors. In some locations, water and electricity supplies are uncertain; for example, "brownouts" or temporary reductions in electric current may be common during peak consumption periods. If your firm must have reliable supplies, you may need your own backup storage tanks or generators.

Container handling facilities or even containers may not be available in ports or airports. Where port or airport facilities are congested, extra time must be allowed for transport and delivery of goods, and routing by road or rail to more distant but more efficient ports may be desirable. It may also be necessary to keep higher inventories of parts and supplies because of the uncertain timing of deliveries.

Modification to equipment, furthermore, must often be made to suit local conditions. For instance, electric current voltages may be different from those in the United States. Also, equipment may need to be protected from tropical humidity, rust, and mildew.

Protecting the Environment and Workers

It is important to keep in mind the impact of your facilities on the workers in the plant and on the surrounding environment as well. As the tragedy in

Bhopal, India, reminds us, it is prudent to be extra cautious about protecting workers and the environment from hazards associated with any facilities.

You should be careful not to be misled in cases where government agencies and unions seem unconcerned about environmental and safety standards. Such attitudes can easily change so that you may come under pressure later to provide for greater environmental and worker protection against various hazards. In any case, it is surely more cost-effective and better business sense to make ample provisions for environmental and worker protection at the outset of the project rather than wait for accidents or outside pressure to force you to do so.

In fact, you may want to take precautions beyond those that are normal or required in U.S. facilities. You may find, for example, that you will need to do more training of workers to prevent accidents. Or you may need to exercise special care in the use of certain supplies, whose labeling may not adequately warn handlers of the dangers associated with using them. Precisely because the government and the unions may not be especially attentive to such matters, you will need to assume the extra responsibility yourself.

You will also want to have a clear understanding with any local joint venture partners about the importance of being attentive to environmental and worker safety problems, especially if the partners are not very experienced in such matters. The responsibility should be clear, and the party with legal liability should have control over the operations.

If you are a good corporate citizen with regard to environmental and health problems, you will probably find that you will enjoy better relations with the government and with local groups than will your laggard competitors.

Obtaining Supplies

Importing Supplies. Most newly established foreign firms import their materials, inputs, machinery, and equipment from the parent company in the United States or from other U.S. suppliers. Indeed, your investment entry agreement with the government may contain a schedule of items to be imported. While importing supplies may be convenient at first, there are nevertheless problems that may eventually develop:

1. In some countries, especially those with chronic balance of payments problems and tight exchange controls, foreign exchange for imports may be rationed. In extreme crisis situations, it may be practically unavailable, leading to shutdowns and layoffs, as in the Philippines in 1983 and 1984. Export-oriented firms that import their supplies on consignment for re-export after local assembly or are allowed to retain a portion of their foreign exchange

earnings for imports usually face fewer problems in this regard than do firms producing for the local market.

2. Devaluations of the local currency will raise import costs. However, devaluation will also lower prices to foreigners for your exports and make them more competitive. The accompanying internal inflation, furthermore, may enable you to increase prices for the domestic market.

3. Customs duties on imported materials may be quite high. In some cases selective duty exemption may be provided, but this could be in the form of rebates for which the application and qualification procedure is complex and time consuming. Exceptions would be free port territories, such as Hong Kong and Singapore, and Free Trade or Export Processing Zones where imported materials are admitted duty free into the zone if they are to be processed for re-export. Negotiating a single import classification agreement can also simplify the problem of processing imported items through customs procedures.

4. Even if international air and sea transportation is efficient and reliable, delays in the local delivery of imported supplies often occur. Sometimes port facilities are inadequate, so that there are delays in off-loading cargo. Off-loaded cargo may be held by customs authorities for a long time because of manpower shortages, inefficient handling systems, or other delays in processing. During this time, damage and pilferage are not uncommon. The bureaucratic procedure for obtaining goods is often extremely complex, tedious, and incomprehensible. For these reasons, foreign firms often rely on local agents to handle import supplies, but this approach is not without problems of its own. Customs procedures are usually simplified and more efficient in smaller provincial ports handling a lesser volume of cargo and in the Free Trade Zones or Export Processing Zones that many countries have set up for export-oriented manufacturers. In any case, a good agent-importer can usually reduce or eliminate the inconveniences.

5. Over time, many host governments expect or even require foreign firms to increase their local input purchases. Their aim is to stimulate local production through vertical or horizontal linkages, to save foreign exchange expended on imported supplies, to forestall tax evasion through intracorporate "transfer pricing," and to increase the domestic value-added of enterprises. However, you may be able to have a local integration program approved in advance by the government.

Using Local Suppliers. The major problem with turning to local suppliers is that there are often not enough of them, and those that do exist may be inexperienced and inadequate. The extent of the problem of course varies by country and industry; it is less where industrialization has been longer established and where there is an active local entrepreneurial class.

One solution to the local sourcing problem is for your existing suppliers to locate production facilities in the same country. Alternatively, if this is not feasible, your suppliers can set up local agent-distributors in the host country to handle imports and sales.

Over time, local suppliers, subcontractors, and supporting industries will develop, but you may have to nurture them. Many American investors have succeeded in developing and upgrading local suppliers over time. There are many long-run advantages to doing so. Freight costs are saved, delivery times are cut, inventory holdings are minimized, and the production costs of the inputs themselves are reduced because of lower labor and other costs in the developing country. Better synchronization of production between customer and supplier can also result. And it is easier for you to explain or change technical specifications and to inspect the suppliers' production process for quality, if necessary. Some companies also have a corporate philosophy to subcontract as much production as possible to external suppliers in order to reduce their own capital commitments and risks.

One firm in Singapore actively helps to set up and develop locally owned supporting industries.[1] Local firms are encouraged to become suppliers by promises of guaranteed sales and by technical training and advice by local and foreign engineers. Years of training are invested in some suppliers to help them reach the required standards. When new products and materials are introduced, the suppliers have to be retrained. Financial assistance is also sometimes given—for instance by partially deducting the cost of a machine from deliveries over five years or by buying the machines and hiring them out to the supplier. The company also recommends satisfactory local suppliers to new customers, including buyers overseas, which helps them to expand their export markets. The suppliers' success benefits the company itself because its suppliers become more viable and less dependent on it and can perhaps produce cheaper inputs because of economies of scale. The firm also encourages its suppliers to upgrade, integrate, and automate their activities, especially in Singapore's tight labor market where supply and quality problems are often caused by the high turnover of skilled workers and technicians the suppliers employ rather than by technical factors.

Before committing orders, you should check the financial viability and track record of potential suppliers and make a judgment about their business integrity and managerial ability. Credit ratings can be checked through local banks or through the U.S. Department of Commerce World Traders Data Reports; this is more important than technical capacity, which can always be augmented. At the same time, you must be prepared to gamble on some promising prospects, to be patient, and to provide developmental support where needed. There are instances where an employee of a company has quit to set up his own business making and selling supplies to the former employer, who is usually encouraging and supportive.

Because of a shortage of good local suppliers, competition among potential customers for their services may be keen. Investors must therefore be prepared for even the most carefully nurtured protégé supplier or subcontractor to use his new knowledge and experience to supply other competing firms. Some suppliers become so busy and successful that their deliveries to their original "mentors" may suffer, but this is all part of the process of market competition. Most companies in fact try to avoid having suppliers who are dependent only or mainly on them for business, and they also avoid being dependent on only one supplier for a particular item. Diversity of customers and supply sources protects both supplier and customer.

Hiring the Initial Work Force

Hiring and training workers should begin *before* your initial production date—how long before depends on the state of the local market and the level of industrial skills in a given country. Hiring and training methods must be varied from situation to situation and from time to time, depending on the local labor market and other characteristics of the local labor supply and culture.

Professional, managerial, technical, and white collar personnel can usually be hired through newspaper advertisements and interviews. You can model your job advertisement on those for similar positions in the local press. The hiring procedure for unskilled workers varies from situation to situation. Not all employers advertise positions in the newspapers as they do for skilled labor, since unskilled workers may not read them. Often, when the news of a new project gets out, many locals will take the initiative in soliciting the new employer for a job.

After your plant is established, the hiring situation may change drastically. For many developing countries with high rates of unemployment and rural-to-urban migration, the supply of labor far exceeds demand. Workers can be seen lining up at factory gates every day regardless of whether hiring is in progress. In general, word of mouth and the simple fact of the factory's physical presence is sufficient to draw workers, even long-distance migrants.

You should survey the market in advance for various types and grades of personnel to ascertain normal qualifications and remuneration, including fringe benefits. Minimum statutory standards are set by government legislation and regulation, which may be obtained from the ministry of labor or the government investment promotion body. Market offerings above the minimum will vary from firm to firm, but the general range of salaries and benefits can be obtained from a number of different sources. Besides the investment promotion body, other government agencies, such as a ministry of labor or department of statistics, conduct periodic manpower surveys. Civil service salary scales for persons of given qualifications usually set the standard that you must match or even surpass. You can consult private sector employer and industry associations, such as the local chambers of commerce or the American Business Council. And you can conduct an informal survey of employers in the same or related industries who employ similar personnel. (More information about labor relations is available in the next chapter.)

The Availability of Highly Skilled and Less Skilled Workers. The pool of adequately trained and especially of experienced personnel is still small in most developing countries, despite the existence of the "educated unemployed." As elsewhere, the employer may choose between hiring fresh graduates and training them, and hiring experienced personnel away from their existing employers. This latter practice produces awkward choices in small modern industrial or commercial sectors where "everybody knows everybody," especially in the even smaller expatriate community. "Poaching" each other's skilled staff may be frowned upon, but it is recognized as an understandable and even necessary practice in many circumstances.

The situation facing a new employer varies greatly from case to case. You may be at a competitive hiring disadvantage because you are unknown and may not be able to match the salaries of experienced managers and professionals in established firms. You may also find it hard to judge the quality and worth of these personnel as well as their current employers can. But as a new employer, you will also have some advantages. You may be sought out by experienced skilled personnel because new firms are thought to offer more opportunities for promotion, especially for employees who get in at the beginning. In developing countries even top professional and managerial personnel are often young by developed country standards (professional education and modern industrialization both being relatively recent). Their juniors thus have a long time to wait before they can achieve the same position, and horizontal mobility between firms, especially movement to new firms, is often an accepted and established means of individual upward mobility.

The hiring of less skilled production or service workers will be determined largely by local labor market conditions. Formal educational qualifications are used largely as a screening device to reduce the pool of applicants. In situations of high unemployment and/or limited employment opportunities for particular groups of workers, highly educated workers may be employed in fairly low-skill jobs. This is especially true for women. High school or junior college graduates, for example, may be employed as manual assemblers. Some employers avoid hiring the more highly educated for low-level tasks because it is felt that boredom among such workers leads to high turnover and/or labor unrest. Others welcome workers with more education than is necessary for their particular tasks because they are expected to be more productive and more easily trained. Much of course depends on the labor supply situation.

The content and quality of the formal education of low-skilled as well as highly skilled and professional workers may vary greatly from one developing country to another. The education is likely to be very different from (not necessarily worse and sometimes better than) that in the United States. Educational content and quality may even vary within a country, with urban graduates generally better educated than those from rural areas for a given educational level. Compared with schools in the United States, schools in developing countries often place greater emphasis on passive rote learning and on following rules and provide less exposure to creative thinking and individual initiative. The results may be good for ensuring a disciplined and conscientious work force at the lower skill levels, but may pose problems when independent problem solving and dynamic leadership is required at the higher professional and managerial levels.

Because of uncertainty about the educational and skill levels of the local work force, some foreign firms devise their own recruitment tests geared to the visual/manual/verbal/numerical skills required for their particular tasks. These are not always relevant or successful across cultural and linguistic boundaries, however.

Besides educational qualifications and experience, employers may have preferences for certain types of workers. Age limits, sex specifications, and citizenship requirements are usually noted in job advertisements. So are ethnic groups where relevant. For example, you may need an employee who speaks a certain language or dialect. Or the government may impose ethnic quotas; in Malaysia, *bumiputras,* who are mostly Malay indigenous peoples, must occupy a certain proportion of jobs at all levels.

Women in the Work Force. Many firms in developing countries employ women in positions where men are usually employed in the United States, and vice versa. Much depends on the relative demand, supply, wage, and skills of males and female labor; it also depends on sex roles, which are changing rapidly. In some strict Moslem countries, the practice of feminine seclusion may mean that women cannot be employed in certain jobs that involve contact with men, such as clerical work, service, and sales. Workers may thus be rigidly segregated by sex, or women may not be available for employment at all.

In many developing countries, secretaries and clerical staff are male, reflecting higher male educational attainment and the lack of alternative employment opportunities, as well as in some cases the seclusion of women.

On the other hand, in many developing countries it is common for women to be much more strongly represented in high-level professional and managerial positions and in jobs as technicians and skilled blue collar workers than they are in the United States. In Singapore, for example, women account for more than half of the journalists and statisticians, and for nearly half of the systems analysts, lawyers, accountants, and economists. Similar proportions may be encountered in the Philippines.

Even in countries where women's representation in management and the professions is not as high, there are still many highly placed women in most fields. This reflects the strong demand for skilled personnel that men alone cannot meet, as well as the access of middle- and upper-class women to higher education and to a supply of domestic help within the home from extended-family members or paid servants.

Some employers also prefer women because they may make more conscientious and stable employees than men. And sometimes women are more willing than men to work as salaried employees for foreign companies, since the men prefer to set up their own businesses. At lower skill levels, in many countries it is not uncommon for women to perform heavy manual labor as they did on the family farm.

In short, you should not be prejudiced for or against particular kinds of workers on the basis of gender or other group characteristics. The barrier to employing women is more rigid in some countries and more flexible in others as compared with the United States. Foreign investors have been credited in many cases with breaking existing sex barriers in employing women for particular high-level jobs. At the same time, certain local factors may affect your hiring choices. In some countries, especially those with plantation economies in Asia and in the Caribbean, minimum wage legislation may set a lower female than male wage for unskilled workers. In other countries, equal pay for equal work is mandated by law. Labor legislation usually requires the provision of maternity leave and benefits for female employees and, in at least two countries (South Korea and Indonesia), "menstruation leave" (one day a month), which is not always taken. There are also certain "protective" restrictions on the employment of female labor, such as the prohibition of night shift work, underground work, heavy lifting, and work with dangerous machinery.

American electronics companies in Malaysia who sought to hire young Malay women for the first time several years ago discovered that they had to devise some novel hiring procedures. The potential labor supply was rurally located, had to be drawn from a wide geographical area, had no previous experience with wage employment or knowledge of the job market, was culturally conservative, and was often not even actively searching for work.

The companies placed job advertisements in newspapers, on radio and television, on the backs and sides of buses, and on billboards and banners displayed in public places such as at football games. They also mounted an aggressive campaign of direct recruitment from the villages. Teams of recruiters would visit target villages, distributing leaflets, giving talks, and even canvassing house-to-house looking for job applicants. They promised good wages and working conditions with many fringe benefits, including safe hostels to reassure parents who were reluctant to allow their daughters to leave home and live alone near the factory. Some companies established contact with community leaders or other prominent village residents, relying on them to spread the news of the available jobs. At least one company set up a special relationship with a nearby village, to the extent that the imam, or Islamic priest, would announce job openings after Friday prayers. (In some rural villages in Indonesia, employers have even been known to retain village notables on their payroll to act as labor agents, using their local social influence and network of mutual obligations to procure labor for the factories.)

Over time, as the factories became established and well known, there was no longer any need for such direct recruitment, since informal market channels of information developed. It is more common now for workers to visit factories in search of jobs, and employers need only erect a notice of available vacancies outside the factory gates to secure themselves applicants.

Training Workers

One of the most important early tasks will be training workers. Training is a continuous process, but it is likely to be concentrated in the start-up phase of a project. Training requirements and practices vary. In-plant, on-the-job training is the most common, but when there is a large number of new employees at start-up or expansion, many firms operate separate training lines. Some firms have permanent training rooms and special trainers, while others prefer on-line training under the instruction of supervisors and experienced co-workers. Initial programs of orientation—to the company and to industrial work in general—are often the most important component of the training for unskilled workers.

Many firms bring experienced managers, supervisors, and technicians over from the United States or from a sister plant in another country for intensive training of new employees prior to the start-up of production in a new plant. Professional, technical, and skilled workers, and in some cases even unskilled operatives, may also be sent to the United States or to a sister factory in another country for training. Retraining may be necessary with expansion and technological progress. And in competitive hiring situations where trained and experienced personnel are rare, most firms will encounter some loss in training personnel who then defect to another company.

Host Government Help. In some countries government grants and other subsidies are available for training programs. Most host governments are extremely interested in the transfer of skills and technology from the foreign enterprise to the local labor force. In fact, this transfer is considered to be one of the most important benefits of foreign investment. The host government's foreign investment agency or labor ministry should have information about such programs.

U.S. Government Help. Your project may be eligible for a "Special Projects" grant or concessional loan from the U.S. government's Overseas Private Investment Corporation (OPIC) specifically to help with training costs. Again however, because of funding changes, this program is being curtailed.

Conclusion

There are distinctive problems in developing countries involving establishing facilities, obtaining supplies, and recruiting and training workers. But by adapting your operations to local conditions and cultures you should be able to find efficient and effective ways of managing the novel problems. The success of your operations in a developing country hinges on your ability to be sensitive to and aware of specific local conditions and to respond flexibly and imaginatively to those conditions. Conditions in developing countries not only differ from those in developed countries, they also differ from one developing country to the next. There are no hard-and-fast rules, no sure techniques to ensure a successful operation. Your most important assets will be an open mind, a willingness to learn, an ability to devise solutions to new and different problems, and a desire to understand and accommodate to the host country's and the local people's attitudes toward your project.

As a practical measure, you should become as informed as possible about the host country—to understand not only the economy and government policy, but also the people, lifestyle, and culture. Some facility in the local language will also aid communication with host government authorities, local partners and suppliers, workers, and the community. Local employees themselves may be of great help in interpreting local circumstances.

Above all, you must consciously adjust and adapt your firm's behavior to the local situation just as much as local people are adapting to your presence and activities.

Appendix 7A
Checklist for Physical Facilities

1. Costs of urban and suburban land (per square foot or square meter) and the availability of plant sites adjacent to urban areas with good sources of water, electric power, and transport

2. Costs for single- and multistory buildings (per square foot or square meter), and time required for normal or specific types of construction and special problems associated with construction

3. The adequacy, quality, pressure, and method of distribution of the water supply

4. Waste disposal method

5. Sources of electric power, including the availability, reliability, and costs from local public utilities; the comparative costs of local private factory power generation for the use of individual plants; and the availability and local costs of oil, coal, or other fuels

6. Availability of domestic materials in terms of quantity, quality, continuity, and price; and the names, locations, and general capacity of local suppliers

7. Availability of prices of imported materials on the local market or those obtainable by direct import

8. Availability of continuing supplies of spare parts for machinery and equipment, replacement tools, and materials for maintenance use

9. Availability of local machine shops, tool and die shops, pattern shops, plant maintenance services, forging capacity and foundry capacity

10. Subcontracting possibilities

11. Telegraph, radio, and telephone facilities

12. Sea and river, truck and road, and rail and air transport

13. Time and costs in moving goods between major cities and from raw material sources to production and consumption areas

14. Any particular packaging and handling problems

Sources of Additional Information

Chambers of commerce and other trade associations in the foreign country.

National, regional, and local government agencies in the host country, especially agencies concerned with foreign direct investment incentives and regulations, labor, power and other utilities, housing, construction, and education and training.

Pearson, Charles S. *Down to Business: Multinational Corporations, the Environment, and Development*, Study 2, World Resources Institute, January 1985. 1735 New York Ave. NW, Washington, D.C. 20006. Phone: (202) 638-6300.

8
Managing Labor Relations

I n dealing with labor relations, it is important to realize that foreign cultures are more malleable and responsive to change than many other features of a developing country. Your project may therefore profoundly change, disturb, or challenge local society; but these changes can, if properly handled, elicit constructive responses and have progressive consequences over time. In most cases, particular cultural values and practices are a rational response to specific features of society or the economy. If you understand this, then you will be able to create new incentives and patterns of behavior that can avoid, abolish, or minimize cultural conflicts.

Many conflicts between management and workers have been traced to insensitive personnel managers and/or supervisors. The role of the personnel manager is therefore crucial. Most foreign companies now prefer to hire a local person as personnel manager, since he or she will have a better understanding of local culture, and workers will be more willing to communicate their problems to such a person. The chapter considers this and other labor relations problems in detail.

Setting Terms and Conditions of Employment

Terms and conditions of employment for your workers should be set according to the norms of the host country rather than those of the United States. In developing countries, government legislation and regulations usually set minimum standards for wages, fringe benefits, working hours, leaves, and other terms of employment. Add to this a history of sometimes powerful and political labor movements, especially in Latin America, and the foreign investor often has less room to maneuver. In particular, you should be aware of local sensitivities to "imperialistic exploitation" by foreign companies, which have not always had a good record of labor relations. (See appendix 8A.)

Linda Y.C. Lim, principal author.

Wages. Government wage policies are usually oriented toward broad national goals, as well as the interests of particular groups. Minimum wage legislation, for example, is often motivated by considerations of distributional equity, or it may be a response to political pressures from the urban working class. It is most commonly found in poorer countries where market wages are very low, and thus the minimum wage is an attempt to raise wages. In Asia, such countries as Thailand, the Philippines, and Indonesia have minimum wage legislation, but more prosperous countries such as Malaysia, Singapore, and Hong Kong do not. Minimum wages are usually set above market levels and are rarely enforced because of inadequate government supervision and because mass unemployment would likely result. Often only a minority of establishments observe the minimum wage; for example, only 10 percent of urban wage workers in Bangkok and Manila receive the minimum wage or better.

However, nearly all foreign firms (and certainly those from the United States) pay at least the minimum wage to their workers, if not more. Being foreign they dare not flout local legislation, and they are expected to be able to afford to pay much higher wages than small local enterprises. And in fact, even above-market minimum wages in most developing countries are still so much lower than United States wages that most foreign firms pay them without hesitation.

Minimum wages vary by region and location within a country, being higher in large metropolitan centers and lower in small provincial towns and rural areas. In Mexico, for example, minimum wages in the industrial zones bordering the United States are the highest in the country, while in the Philippines, minimum wages in the dispersed Export Processing Zones are lower than they are in metropolitan Manila. These differences reflect both local labor market conditions and local cost-of-living variations, and are sometimes an inducement for industry to locate in less developed parts of the country where lower wages may compensate for other locational disadvantages. Some countries have lower minimum wage rates for women than for men, but in most countries the same legal minimum rate prevails for both. (The market rate usually diverges, however.)

Government-mandated cost-of-living adjustments are also part of the wage. Governments can affect wage changes by varying the minimum wage and/or the cost-of-living allowances, or they can actually recommend specific wage increases. The National Wages Council (NWC) in Singapore, for example, sets annual national wage guidelines, which the government may manipulate to influence the allocation of resources in particular ways. For many years, it kept wages below market levels in order to promote labor-intensive export manufacturing industries. Since this resulted in labor shortages, a policy of economic restructuring has sought to reduce labor intensity by recommending large wage increases to "restore wages to market levels."

The government itself employs a large proportion of the wage labor force in many countries; as a result, its wage scales frequently form the standard against which private sector wages are compared. However, foreign investors usually have no trouble matching or even surpassing government wages, especially for skilled, professional, and managerial personnel.

Social Security. Some governments require employers to make social security, pension and/or insurance payments on behalf of workers. These are usually paid into a publicly administered fund. In Singapore, mandatory employer and employee contributions to the government-sponsored compulsory savings scheme total 50 percent of the worker's wage, and therefore substantially increase total labor costs. Elsewhere many of the larger, better-established foreign and local enterprises have private company pension schemes, but in most developing countries this appears to be more the exception than the rule.

Leaves. Minimum leave provisions are legislated by governments and in most instances include weekly rest days, public holidays, annual leave, maternity leave, sick leave, and compassionate leave. The exact provisions differ from country to country, usually vary by the level of workers' seniority, and include paid and unpaid leave. Again, observation by local employers and enforcement by governments may be lax, but foreign enterprises usually do provide at least the legislated leaves.

Work Loads. Most governments also legislate daily and weekly hours of work, including maximum hours and distribution of overtime in relation to the normal working week. Shift work is also regulated: minimum rest periods are required between shift changes; the duration of rotating shifts is regulated; permanent night shift work is sometimes banned; and many countries formally prohibit night work for women. Waivers, however, can often be obtained. In general, workers in developing countries tend to work much longer hours than do workers in developed countries, except in recessions. Overtime and holiday work earn higher rates of pay, as legislated by governments.

Health and Safety Regulations. Low standards and weak enforcement of health and safety regulations are common in developing countries. But conditions in foreign enterprises are often better than the legislated norms, though still not as good as those in developed countries. Many countries restrict the types of work that women, especially pregnant women, can do.

Layoffs. Most government labor legislation also provides for proper procedure and retrenchment benefits in the case of worker layoffs. In some instances, it is extremely difficult, if not impossible, to lay off workers with seniority.

Fringe Benefits. Nonwage benefits that are commonly provided include health and medical expenses or in-factory medical care, transportation or transportation allowances, food allowances or subsidized canteens, free uniforms, and various social, cultural, and educational activities for workers. These benefits are sometimes necessary and beneficial to employers as well as to workers. For example, company transportation may have to be offered to obtain an adequate labor force, especially for more remotely sited factories, since workers may live quite far away and local public transportation systems are poor or nonexistent, making lateness and absenteeism a problem. Some company housing may have to be provided, especially to first-time female migrant workers, who might otherwise be reluctant to leave home to work. Medical care and food allowances increase workers' productivity, especially in countries where many workers may be poor and even sickly.

Profit Sharing. You may also have to provide profit sharing. For example, some countries require that the equivalent of a certain minimum number of days' wages or salary per year be paid to each employee. The minimum may be increased with each new labor contract. The stipulated amount may even have to be paid when there are no profits. Of course, each country's laws differ. But the examples in table 8-1 are illustrative of profit sharing and other aspects of labor practices in some countries.

Criticism. Local employers are likely to complain that you offer wages and benefits that are too high. This raises market wages and hence the labor costs of local employers, who can less easily afford them. Foreign employers also can outcompete local employers in hiring scarce professional and technical personnel, and this is seen as unfair.

On the other hand, even though you may offer better wages, benefits, and working conditions than local employers, you will still be subject to criticism from employees. Foreign enterprises are usually viewed as being rich and profitable, easily able to pay much more than they do. Workers also recognize that they are not getting paid the same wages and salaries as do workers in your home country plants, and they may consider this exploitation.

The workers are probably newcomers to the more regimented, more capital-intensive production processes that you may bring in; they may not be accustomed to working in factories or plantations. On top of this, workers may not be able to look forward to some day owning their own homes and

Table 8–1
Summary Profiles of Labor Practices in Two Latin American Countries

Labor Practices	Argentina	Venezuela
Workweek (hrs./wk.)	48	48 day/42 night
Overtime (premium)	50–100%	25–45 + %
Vacation time (days/hr.)	14–35	15–30
Severance pay (mos./yrs. service)	1	1 (+ 1 extra)
Social security (employer's contribution)	4.5%	7–9%
Profit sharing	None	15–60 days' pay

Source: *Business Latin America,* April 6, 1983, pp. 110–11. Used with the permission of the publisher, Business International Corporation, New York.

being able to buy lots of consumer goods. Instead, the workers may aspire to starting their own businesses in the city or returning to their native villages where they can, with luck, operate a plot of family land. They may seek the status of independence, of being the masters of their own lives. The workers may feel that if they continue as daily laborers there will be little chance for their children to attend schools of higher education and that thus there will be little chance for upward mobility for them as a family.

This condition, where workers feel little hope for advancement as long as they remain workers, is exacerbated by the obvious inequalities that foreign investment often generates. It is not uncommon for local or expatriate managers of foreign investments to live in a style that includes chauffeured luxury cars, private schools for the children, and huge homes with servants, cooks, and gardeners. When looked at through the eyes of the workers, wages that may be higher than the legally mandated minimum and higher than what locally owned competitors pay can nevertheless be viewed as unjust. Workers may conclude that a company that is profitable and that richly rewards its managers, but that pays its workers wages that do not give them social mobility or a comfortable life-style, is unjust.

Adapting to Industrial Relations Systems

Industrial relations systems and histories vary from country to country and from industry to industry. Many labor unions were politicized during the anticolonial struggle and remain actively involved in politics, providing either support for or opposition to their governments. Labor movements are generally stronger in Latin America than in Asia or Africa. (See appendix 8C, which describes labor policies in Latin America.)

Government Policies. Many governments have established industrial relations systems in which the power of labor has been substantially curtailed. Some governments have even preempted the formation of unions, taken over existing unions, or sharply reduced union powers, such as the right to strike. The export-oriented countries of East and Southeast Asia are perhaps best known for restricting labor organization. They are frequently accused of using political repression and the power of the state to ensure the passive labor movements favored by foreign investors. There are government-formed and government-backed unions and union federations in, for example, Taiwan, South Korea, Singapore, Indonesia, and the Philippines.

This does not guarantee labor peace, however. A repressive government may have the effect of politicizing and radicalizing labor movements, so that they oppose not only corporate managements, but also the government and even the existing political-economic social system—including foreign investors. Workers may be active in periodic antigovernment demonstrations.

Government policies may shift, and employers will have to adjust. One example is Singapore, where the government has been revamping a successful tripartite (government, employers, unions) industrial relations system with the goal of increasing productivity. The previously centralized system in which the state took a dominant role in establishing national-level measures that preempted or overshadowed company-level negotiations is being decentralized. Private employers will now have to take a more active role in setting wages and benefits through direct negotiations with their own workers, who are increasingly organized in house rather than in industrial unions.

Strikes. The industrial relations climate in a developing country affects foreign investors whether or not their own enterprises are unionized. Strikes in other sectors of the economy, especially in public utilities and ports, may disrupt production, imports, and exports. Strikes in the same sector or neighborhood may result in sympathy strikes that could shut down a plant that is not itself facing a labor dispute. This is particularly common in Free Trade Zones where many factories in the same industry are located side by side. Major strikes can spill over into general political unrest that adversely affects investments. Labor unrest often takes the form of spontaneous wildcat strikes and other actions taken by unorganized workers or by workers acting independently of their unresponsive "official" and officially sanctioned unions and union bosses.

Foreign Firms' Experiences. Foreign enterprises are often attractive targets for organization by both independent and government unions. U.S. investors are usually more apprehensive about unions, even government-controlled unions, than are investors of other nationalities. Despite these apprehensions, many companies in developing countries are unionized—and are not unhappy with their experience. In Singapore, for example, many U.S. companies that are not unionized in their home country have been unionized for a long time without any "trouble."

But the same firms might hesitate to accept unions in other countries. Much depends on the local situation and on the individual firm's corporate philosophy. Sometimes an employer will find that it is much better to accept a union that the workers want than continually to oppose it. This, for example, has been the experience of one U.S. electronics company in Indonesia, which has found that since accepting the union, workers are happy (and well-paid), turnover is low, and productivity has increased.

Sometimes companies devise preemptive personnel management strategies that go to great lengths to keep workers satisfied and uninterested in union organization—for example, by paying very high wages and giving generous fringe benefits.

Local Economic and Cultural Conditions. Local economic and cultural factors also influence union activity. In a tight labor market, workers may not feel the need to organize or be aggressive since they can always improve their individual situations by job hopping. But a tight labor market also increases workers' collective bargaining power. In a labor surplus situation, on the other hand, workers may avoid organizing and making demands because they fear losing their jobs. But their jobs are also all that they have so they may be inclined to make collective demands as the only means of improving their individual situations.

Conditions in Thailand. A U.S. electronics company faces dramatically different labor situations in its sister Thai and Malaysian plants even though young single women are employed in both.[1]

The workers in Bangkok, Thailand, are fully and actively unionized and lead their own union. With relatively few government restrictions, a fairly free and independent labor movement exists in the country as a whole. These women workers are mostly local urban residents, and their position as women in Thai society is strong, for they are part of a female tradition of production and family support, equality, and independent action. (Thailand has the highest rate of female labor force participation in the world.) In a surplus labor market where good jobs are scarce for both men and women, factory jobs command a high status in the urban working-class community. Most of the women are satisfied with and committed to their jobs and intend to continue work after marriage.

Conditions in Malaysia. By contrast, the workers in Penang, Malaysia, are not unionized. A long-term effort to organize them around workers' social projects for the Free Trade Zone in which the factory is located did not succeed in attracting their participation. The Malaysian government severely restricts union organization in the Free Trade Zone and in the electronics industry in particular. But the workers have also had a limited interest in union organization. They are mostly rural migrants from conservative Moslem communities, where young women are traditionally sheltered, dependent, and subordinate and where traditional patron-client relationships are strong. This is translated into a sense of obligation and obedience on the part of the worker to the employer who has provided a job.

Most of the women have a midsecondary education and aspire to white collar jobs because factory employment ranks low on the status hierarchy in a generally prosperous economy. The women are not committed either to wage labor or to their particular factory jobs, expecting to quit work upon marriage since their husands could easily find work to support a family. (See also appendix 8B.)

These cases show that industrial relations are very much dependent on local conditions. Unionization does not necessarily mean more labor unrest or labor-management conflict. The firm has found its workers in both locations to be efficient and productive.

Adjusting Labor Management Practices to Local Conditions

You should be aware that many familiar labor management practices in the United States may not translate well into countries where cultural backgrounds, incentives, and motivations are different.

Hiring on the Basis of Personal Ties. It is common for third parties to recommend workers. For example, in Sri Lanka a worker must often have an introduction from someone known to the management in order to secure a job. The police frequently fulfill this task of recommendation. In some countries, it is common for workers to recommend their own friends and relatives and even to seek employment in groups. In tight labor markets, employers often offer cash bonuses to workers who successfully persuade an acquaintance to join and stay with the firm for a minimum period of time. Where there is an excess supply of workers, personal introductions and recommendations are a means of rationing scarce jobs.

Employers are often of two minds about the merits of recruiting workers on the basis of personal ties. You may find that having a labor force that is related by ties of blood or friendship makes for a better "familylike" atmosphere in the factory and for more stable, contented, and committed workers. Or you may fear that the resulting solidarity among workers who know each other might make them more likely to organize and take labor actions against management.

In any case, the use of personal ties in hiring does impose certain tensions. For example, a recommended person may not work out and may leave or have to be fired, resulting in some "loss of face" or embarrassment for the person making the recommendation. Offering cash bonuses may cause workers to refer persons they barely know and thus cannot fully vouch for. It also puts pressure on referred persons to stay on the job even if they are unhappy lest they cause loss of income to those who referred them. Workers themselves may be pressured by relatives, friends, neighbors, and even distant acquaintances to secure them a job, sometimes in the context of traditional relations of mutual obligation within the village. And workers who join a factory because they have friends or family there may be motivated to quit along with their group when one is unhappy or decides to move.

Traditional Patron–Client Relations. In some countries, workers may transfer their tradition of patron–client relations into relations between employer and employee in the modern factory. According to this tradition, the patron (employer) and client (employee) are bound together in a bond of mutual obligation. The client is grateful to the patron for providing a job, while the patron is similarly obligated to the client for performing a service. The client is not inclined to rise up against the patron, but neither should the patron jeopardize the client's welfare, for example by firing or laying off the client.

Patron–client relations can have important consequences for labor–management relations within your company. What might appear to be nepotism—the securing of jobs, promotions, loans, and contracts for relatives, friends, village neighbors, clan members, and other acquaintances—may not represent conflict of interest, but rather the repayment and maintenance of traditional mutual obligations in a patron–client relationship.

Expectations of the patron/employer range from guaranteeing job security (not in the legal or contract sense but rather as a moral obligation) to providing personal loans to individual employees at times of need (not merely for family catastrophes, but also for weddings and festivals and more "frivolous" expenditures). Personal loans are repayable by labor (the traditional way) or by deductions from wages or salary (though this raises the awkward problem of interest charges, especially in Moslem societies, which forbid interest as usurious).

It is often best for the employer to establish at the outset the principle of no personal loans (which may be waived in extreme situations). He may wish to substitute a separate fund of company and/or employee contributions to which applications for loans may be made on a need basis (raising again the question of interest).

Punctuality and Absenteeism. Working populations that are new to industrial labor often exhibit high rates of absenteeism and a lack of punctuality. Orientation programs can be used to try to instill the habits of punctuality and good attendance into new workers—especially those with less formal schooling since schooling emphasizes these same values. (Sometimes, of course, the problem is not entirely the worker's fault, especially where public transportation systems are unreliable.) In any case, over time, workers do generally adopt new, more disciplined work habits.

Responsiveness to Monetary Incentives. Employers often pay a productivity incentive bonus over and above the minimum or basic wage. But when workers are still close to a traditional subsistence economy, they may work only until they have earned a target take-home pay and then slacken work effort thereafter. This is because in a subsistence economy workers have no motive for accumulating wealth, and so all their income is consumed. But when workers anticipate large expenses—such as for an upcoming festival or wedding or a desired durable-good purchase—they will increase productivity and income until they have earned enough to pay for it.

In some societies, the relationship between individual effort and individual return may not be fully understood or internalized. Many agricultural societies, for example, are based on collective work effort—of a nuclear or extended family, work group, community, or village—and on an egalitarian system of distribution based on individual need unrelated to individual work-effort or achievement. So it may be difficult for workers, who may be acquainted with each other, to accept unequal individual returns since to them it seems unfair.

The problem is worse where individual merit is judged at least partly on a subjective basis. In many situations supervisors are unwilling to discriminate among individual workers—because, for example, those who perform poorly would suffer a loss of "face" as well as income and in extreme cases might feel obligated to resign. Reporting average or identical performance for each worker thus defeats the purpose of an incentive system.

Individual competition is also new to many workers. Although they may respond to competitive productivity improvement schemes because they need the income, the process may generate considerable stress, tension, and discomfort for them.

Overtime Work. In many peasant societies, when subsistence needs are met, there is no great desire to work harder for more income. Workers may prefer to enjoy their leisure, or they may need the time for household and farm chores, or non–income-producing activities that are essential to the life of the community. Rather than being "lazy" in refusing to work additional hours—even at overtime pay rates—they are merely making a rational allocation of time in terms of their own preferences. Women, for example, may wish to spend more time with their children. In some countries, labor contracts limit overtime work.

There are also more practical reasons for workers' refusing to work overtime, such as fatigue (especially where workers are poor and malnourished), lack of access to public transportation after working hours, and for women, fear for personal safety when traveling home in the dark. For similar reasons, night shift work is also unpopular, though it too pays higher rates.

Sometimes workers avoid overtime because they are responsive to monetary incentives and are moonlighting at a higher-paying second job. Typically this would be a lucrative but more uncertain venture, making regular factory employment necessary for a steady and secure income, while the second job earns additional "windfall" income. Examples of second jobs include paid housework or child care, seamstressing, subcontracted piecework, petty trade and exchange (or "brokering"), helping out in small family businesses, and making and hawking food. Women are especially likely to participate in such "informal sector" activities.

Economic pressures have much to do with the willingness or unwillingness of workers to work overtime. Hong Kong and Singapore are both modern industrial city-states largely populated by ethnic South Chinese immigrants or their children and grandchildren. Yet the response to overtime work in these two cities is quite different. Hong Kong workers not only welcome overtime, they often ask for it. Their goal is to maximize income, and it reflects the Hong Kong worker's lack of security as a recent migrant in a competitive overcrowded territory with few government social subsidies and an uncertain political future. In Singapore, on the other hand, workers have become increasingly unwilling to work overtime and on night shifts. In a tight labor market and after many years of industrial experience, wages are sufficiently high that workers do not need the additional income and prefer to have their leisure instead. They also benefit from a variety of government social subsidies, such as housing, and compulsory pension fund benefits.

Avoiding Layoffs. Employers cannot afford to lose trained and experienced workers, and if they do lay off, it is not easy to rehire in the ensuing upswing. Temporary layoffs and reduced hours are therefore often used in the place of permanent layoffs, but even these milder measures may result in the permanent loss of workers who quit and find another job rather than accept the lower income. In fact, some employers have actually taken to hoarding rather than shedding workers during recessions, using the slack time to upgrade their training and skills.

Consider the following experience of a U.S. firm, which laid off some of its workers during a slump. "It was a grave mistake despite the fact that we took them back soon after," recalled the local manager. He remembered how the senior local executives sat glumly during a meeting after the workers were laid off; an American executive was puzzled to see the sullen faces. "I told him that he didn't understand the local feelings," said the local manager. Since then the company has made a promise never to lay off its workers again.[2] Layoffs, even if permitted by law, can be very costly in severance pay and in other respects. You should therefore avoid overhiring initially, but also be prepared for extra labor costs during recessions.

Turnover. You should expect high turnover rates among new employees, especially those with no previous industrial experience. The nature of the work, the discipline and pressure of the assembly line are completely different from any experience in traditional society, and many find it intolerable. Workers who stay beyond the initial period, however, are usually stable and quit only when they get a better opportunity or are unhappy about some aspect of the job (such as overtime work or an overbearing supervisor). Turnover rates are thus higher in tight labor market situations than in surplus labor markets.

When workers join an enterprise in groups, they also tend to leave in groups if one member is unhappy or has found a better job somewhere else. This is particularly common among female workers, for whom the companionship of other women is an important attraction of factory work in the first place. In some countries, women have higher turnover and absenteeism rates than men, especially where they tend to quit for marriage and child raising. In other countries—for instance, in some Caribbean and Latin American countries—married women are preferred employees because they have lower turnover and absenteeism rates and are more stable workers than men.

Labor Productivity. This result seems to depend much more on situational than cultural factors, and thus can be improved upon by the correct management policies, which will vary with individual situations. Ethnic stereotypes of productivity behavior often do not prove true where workers are subject to the same societal and company incentives and opportunities. Work habits may differ among cultural groups, but experience suggests that they can be changed with appropriate policies within the factory context.

The experience of numerous U.S. electronics companies, which have been in Southeast Asia for nearly twenty years and employ about two hundred thousand workers, may be instructive. Over time these companies have refined their labor management practices. In general they now favor the flexible, informal management style characteristic of high tech companies in the United States, emphasizing generous benefits, good personal relations, open communications from top to bottom, and a "fun" and "family" atmosphere. They also emphasize company loyalty, paternalism, and high productivity.

Many U.S. companies argue that union representation is unnecessary since they already treat their workers well, giving them better wages, leaves, and benefits than many unionized companies can manage. Staff welfare and benefits include educational training programs, sports, games and social activities, library facilities, prayer rooms for Moslems, handicraft and language classes, and community service activities.

There is great emphasis on direct communication between management and workers—for example, at weekly or monthly forums where managers inform workers about the company's progress and plans, and workers can ask any questions or make complaints and requests, which are attended to. Smaller quality control circles also have the same goal of promoting communication and increasing productivity.

While some workers do undoubtedly make use of these opportunities for communication, most do not. Some may be cynical about management's motives and sincerity, while others would still prefer a union. In most Asian contexts, young women are simply not used to speaking their minds in public (it may even be considered improper to do so). Nor are they accustomed to doing so with senior male authority figures—especially foreigners! Many, for example, balk at addressing the top manager by his first name, as that would be disrespectful in their own society.

Conclusion

Your investment project will be widely considered to be beneficial to the local society because it creates jobs, but this does not mean that there will not be labor relations problems. Nor does it mean that local people will feel any particular sense of gratitude to you. It will therefore be important for you to try to look at your project and its effects on local society through the eyes of your employees and other local inhabitants. You should be prepared to adapt labor management practices to local values and customs.

Appendix 8A
Checklist of Factors to Consider in Labor Management Practices

1. The supply of skilled, semiskilled, and unskilled labor; availability for single-, double-, and three-shift operations; availability of salespersons, clerical, and supervisory help; and the quality and supply of executive personnel

2. Labor organizations and labor–management relations, including the existence of unions and federations, leadership and membership of organizations, the ratio and importance of organized and nonorganized labor, and cultural factors affecting work habits

3. The wage structure for men and women, minimum rates and estimated average rates for skilled and unskilled workers, and fringe benefits and traditional bonus payments, if any

4. Labor laws, regulations, and policies affecting wages, hours, retirement, and termination; nationality requirements and hiring practices; health and worker's compensation insurance; sick leave; vacations and holidays (paid and unpaid); and other allowance and severance pay

5. Practices and availability of labor housing in terms of costs and other social overhead

6. The mobility of the labor force and availability of worker transportation

7. Worker efficiency and trainability. Include measurement of productivity; evaluations of working conditions and efficiency as compared with levels in other countries (skilled and unskilled) in specific fields; and determination of the existence and quality of vocational, technical, and administrative schools.

8. Special local considerations or conditions in the country, such as housing, food, health problems, and medical facilities

9. The employment of required U.S. personnel; their method of payment, allowances, taxation, and so forth; and limitations on their number

Appendix 8B
Labor Management Case: Ghosts and Beauty Queens in Electronics Factories in Malaysia—Problems and Solutions

P icture a modern electronics factory with the night shift in full swing. Hundreds of blue-uniformed young women are bent over neat rows of microscopes, assembling semiconductor chips, and piped music fills the air. Suddenly there is a loud and piercing scream, then another, and within minutes a crescendo of hundreds of voices screaming and crying can be heard. Women fall off their chairs and roll on the ground in violent convulsions, in uncontrollable fits of shaking and crying. Some display uncharacteristic aggressive behavior, while others lose consciousness. When questioned then or later, many say that they have seen a ghost or have been possessed by an unfriendly spirit.

This is an outbreak of mass hysteria, an affliction that has visited U.S. electronics factories in Malaysia with some frequency since their establishment there in the early 1970s. It occurs only on the night or "graveyard" shift and only among Malay women in the ethnically diverse labor force that also includes Chinese and Indians. Other non–U.S. factories that also employ mostly women are similarly affected. Mass hysteria outbreaks quickly became so common that they no longer make news in the local press.

Explanations

What causes this phenomenon, which, apart from being distressing to the affected workers, is extremely disruptive of work and output, the major concern of the employing firms? Researchers in industrial sociology have suggested from studies of individual outbreaks that mass hysteria is a symptom of covert conflict between labor and management at the factory. It is an unconscious form of worker rebellion against company authorities, a product of their mounting frustration, resentment, and inability to cope with the high tension of the production line. The workers feel exploited and helpless, for the absence of unions means that they have no representative organization that can voice and seek redress for their collective grievances against management.

At the same time, hysteria victims, their unaffected co-workers, their families, and their home communities attribute the outbreaks to supernatural causes—spirits inhabiting the factory grounds had been disturbed or "evil spirits possessing young women who had violated the moral code" had entered the factory. The companies are considered to contribute to the situation by not performing the right ceremonies to appease the spirits; by requiring the women to work at night, a threatening time when spirits are most active; and by encouraging or tolerating "immoral" behavior among the workers (see below). A set of traditional beliefs and behaviors comes into play here. As one researcher, an anthropologist, has stated it: "Malay girls are socialized to be submissive and loyal, in accordance with village notions of female modesty. Females are considered especially vulnerable to spirit possession and other supernatural dangers, a belief which operates as a sanction against self-assertion on the part of young unmarried women. Malay operators, in an unconscious inversion of its function, found in spirit possession (*kena hantu*) a mode of indirect retaliation on the shop floor."[3]

Mass hysteria is thus a socially accepted, if unconscious and ritualized, form of conflict expression and tension release among young Malay women. It is common not only in factories employing mainly women, but also in other female environments such as girls' schools and women's dormitories, including factory hostels. Psychiatrists tend to favor an explanation linking hysteria with sexual repression, among young unmarried women in a strongly patriarchal culture. There have been incidents of mass hysteria in factory dormitories where covert conflict existed between groups of women workers—those who adhere to the conservative traditional moral code, and a minority who openly violate this code by embracing more "modern" and "liberated," including sexually liberated, life-styles. Members of this latter group are therefore presumed by the others to be "possessed by evil spirits."

Indeed, the impact of modern factory labor on the morality of young women workers has emerged as a major issue of contention between local communities and religious authorities, on the one hand, and the employing multinationals on the other. (Some one hundred thousand women are employed in the electronics industry alone in Malaysia, the majority in U.S.–owned factories.) The migration of thousands of young unmarried Malay women from rural villages to factory employment and independent living in or near urban areas has undermined many aspects of traditional rural life and culture. This situation is aggravated by the public perception of the factory women as being prone to Western-inspired "immoral" behavior, such as the wearing of Western dress (more body revealing than traditional attire), intermingling with the opposite sex, attending discos and dance parties, and having premarital sexual relationships, unwanted pregnancies, and illegal abortions. The women are socially stigmatized and subjected to public teasing, sexual innuendo, and derisory name calling such as *Minah karan* (current) or *Minah letrik* (electric), reflecting their predominant employment in electronics factories.

Companies are frequently assigned some responsibility for this supposed immoral behavior of their workers. For example, in the early days many companies tended to clothe their workers in Western-style uniforms (short-sleeved short dresses) revealing parts of their arms and legs. Electronics companies require night shift work, when going out at night, especially alone, is considered both inappropriate and dangerous for young women. And company social activities for workers include many that are considered a bad influence on the women—such as fashion and beauty grooming classes, Western movies and women's magazines, mixed-sex social gatherings such as picnics, out-of-town trips, and disco dance parties, and worst of all, annual beauty contests sometimes involving swimsuit-clad contestants (vying, for example, for titles such as Miss National Semiconductor, Miss RCA and even Miss Electronics at the intercompany level). These activities take place in cultures in which even sports activities that involve women wearing shorts and T-shirts are frowned upon.

The truth is that these activities are not unusual in urban areas in Malaysia and are publicly available. Many Malay village women may have been introduced to them for the first time in the course of their factory employment, but research indicates that only about a third of the workers participate in company social activities, which also include "healthy" educational activities and classes on cooking, homemaking, and handicraft work. Japanese companies, in particular, encourage their female workers to be gentle, passive, and home-oriented. Extensive research also convincingly shows that the *Minah karan* stereotype is a myth, with the vast majority of factory workers continuing to lead conservative, traditional lives, and the "modern" minority influenced more by the general urban environment and by living away from home than by company social activities.

These two issues of mass hysteria and workers' morality in fact represent opposite ends of the traditional–modern cultural continuum that faces foreign investors and employers in Malaysia. In both cases, modern factory production and the spread of modern urban culture that it encourages come into conflict with traditional values and beliefs. In the case of mass hysteria, additionally, the lack of new forms of social organization (for example, unions) to deal with new problems faced by the workers causes them to resort to traditional mechanisms of conflict "resolution," which prove disruptive of modern production.

Managerial Problems

The two issues pose many problems for foreign employers, such as the U.S. electronics firms. Not only does mass hysteria severely disrupt output, sometimes repeatedly closing down an affected factory for days. It also gives the factory a bad name in the community as a place that is haunted by evil spirits or that has incurred their wrath, making it difficult to hire and retain workers. The workers' morality issue also gives all factories a "bad name," causing local friction and again making it more difficult to hire and keep workers, a major problem in a situation of periodic labor shortages. These two highly visible issues combine with local concerns over the exploitation of workers in foreign-owned factories to create a political climate potentially antagonistic to such investment and employment. It is likely that the Malaysian government's recent decision to reduce its dependence on the largely foreign-owned export-oriented electronics industry by emphasizing heavy import-substituting industry instead and its reluctance to grant new investment incentives to this industry at least partly reflect public perceptions of the industry's high social costs and low economic benefits.

Managerial Solutions

What has been the companies' response to these problems? It varies from company to company, but in the early days there was a tendency to mete out harsh treatment, including suspension or termination of employment, to victims, in the hope that this would nip the problem in the bud. Instead it generated further worker fears and dissatisfaction and community disapproval since the community attributed the outbreaks to supernatural intervention and not to the individual workers who became "possessed." Companies now are wiser, accepting that the spirit-possession behavior is unmotivated and involuntary and is considered socially acceptable. Workers are gently treated and sent home for a rest. At the same time local *bomohs,* or medicine men, are engaged to exorcise the evil spirits from the factory premises, and ritual slaughter of animals may be offered in propitiation. Sometimes this works and sometimes it does not. Local imams or Moslem priests are invited to bless new factories, which are erected only after the appropriate spirit-propitiation ceremonies have been carried out.

With the longer factory experience of both workers and managers, mass hysteria incidents have declined and have become so routine that co-workers have gained experience in dealing with the victims and limiting work disruption. In Singapore, frequent incidents in the early days of multinational electronics factories have almost disappeared, but when they do occur it is again only among Malay women and on the night shift. Short of terminating night shift work and the employment of Malay females, which is impossible in both countries, this is all that can be done, unless employers in Malaysia are willing to entertain the idea of unions—which they currently oppose and which are severely restricted by government policy—and to relax the intensity of production on the already less productive night shift.

If foreign employers in Malaysia have learned to live with ghosts, they and the community have also learned what to do about beauty queens. Following initial furors, some companies stopped holding beauty pageants or continued them without the swimsuit contest. Western-style uniforms have largely given way to workers' own customary dress or to uniforms incorporating the same features—that is, long-sleeved blouses and ankle-length skirts. Some companies have consciously cultivated closer relations with local communities, including local charity donations, holding "open house" factory visits, inviting local authorities including imams to open new buildings, installing prayer rooms for Moslems within company premises, and emphasizing more "wholesome" company activities such as education, cooking, and handicrafts. But other company social activities also continue, in part in response to the workers' own interests. Community concerns about morality have diminished somewhat as people have become better acquainted with the workers and have learned to accept their presence and behavior.

Ghosts and beauty queens continue their parades through the electronics factories of Malaysia. They tell us that factories are not only units of production; they are also social units intimately affected by the surrounding society and culture, which in turn can have an important impact on production itself.

Appendix 8C
Labor Policies in Latin America

	Wages	*Workweek*	*Overtime*	*Vacation time and bonuses*	*Severance notice and pa*
Argentina	Monthly minimum wage is P7,000,000 (P68,920:$1).	Maximum 48 hours over six days.	50% premium during the workweek. Double time on Saturdays after 1 p.m. and on Sundays and holidays.	From one to five years' service, 14 consecutive days; from five to 10 years, 21 days; from 10–20 years, 28 days; over 20 years, 35 days.	Up to five years' service one month; if over five years two months in cases of dismissal without good cause. One month's pay (not to exceed three times the minimum wage) per year of service
Brazil	Monthly minimum wage is Cr23,568 (Cr415:$1) in Rio de Janeiro, Minas Gerais and Sao Paulo.	Maximum for industry 48 hours over six-day week. In practice, office employees work 40–42-hour week over five days.	Day overtime has 20% premium, night overtime 25%. Sundays and holidays twice regular rate.	After one year, 30 calendar days. Employee may take up to 20 days in pay rather than time off. Annual bonus: 13th-month salary paid at year-end.	One month's notice if worker paid monthly, 15 days if paid hourly or weekly. Severance pay is balance of interest-bearing severance fund maintained by 8% levy on employee salaries.
Chile	Monthly minimum wage is P6,220.85 (P73.5:$1).	Maximum 48 hours over six days or nine hours and 36 minutes over five days.	50% premium for overtime. Maximum two hours overtime per day during regular workweek, unless extension authorized by government.	15 days after one year's service; after 10 years' service (not necessarily consecutive), one more day each additional three years' service, up to 35 days. Annual bonus not required but generally negotiated in collective agreements.	30 days' notice or one month's severance pay in lieu of notice. Indemnity of one month's pay for each year of service Fixed-term contracts limited to two years, but may be renewed for two additional years.

Dismissal	Social security	Pensions	Profit sharing	Other benefits
...ployers may ...miss workers ...ly and pay ...erance. Com-...nsation not ...cessary if em-...yer can prove ...ious misde-...anor in court.	Covers medical assistance, hospi-talization, etc. Employers con-tribute 4.5% of payroll; workers, 3% of pay.	Calculation based on the three high-est earning years over past five years times coeffi-cient related to age of employee. Minimum 30 years of service and paid contri-butions. Financed by employee con-tribution of 12% of pay.	None.	Collective con-tracts usually pro-vide for addi-tional benefits. Senior executives commonly receive reimbursement of club and school fees, company car and paid medical insurance.
...compensation ...or just cause—...ss negligence ...criminal activ-...—as certified ...labor court. If ...ustifiably dis-...ssed, one ...nth's pay.	Instituto Nacional de Previdencia So-cial covers medi-cal care and hos-pitalization, maternity and re-tirement. Com-pany contributes 10% of payroll, worker contribu-tions based on sliding scale.	Pensions after 30 years' service or age 65 for men, 60 for women, at 80% of benefit salary (up to 100% when meet-ing both age and length of service requirements). Costs covered by social security contributions.	None.	Employers must provide full pay for first 10 days of certified illness and 12 weeks' full pay for maternity leave (with job se-curity of two more months); family allowance equivalent to 5% of minimum wage.
...t cause in-...des immoral ...duct, unjusti-...d absences for ...re than two ...secutive days, ...) Mondays a ...nth or three ...s in one ...nth, inten-...nal damage to ...npany property ...d active partici-...ion in illegal ...kes.	New system being phased in for completion in 1986. Employer makes no social security pay-ments, but raises worker salaries. Workers may then invest up to 17% of salary in pen-sion and social se-curity funds.	Men at 65 years of age or 35 years' service, women at 60 years of age or 30 years' service. Fi-nanced through employee contri-butions to social security.	Company may distribute 30% of net profits or give workers a pay-ment equivalent to 4.75 times the monthly mini-mum wage.	Family allowance, P401.98 per de-pendent; food al-lowanc,e P438.77 per worker when food is not pro-vided by firm; prenatal care al-lowance, P401.98; trans-portation allow-ance, P358.51.

	Wages	Workweek	Overtime	Vacation time and bonuses	Severance notice and p
Colombia	Monthly minimum wage in urban areas is P9,261; in rural areas, P8,775 (P74.10:$1).	Maximum 48 hours over six days. Workers under 18 years of age not permitted to work over six hours daily.	25% over regular wages for day work, 75% for night work. Nonovertime night work carries 35% premium. Triple time for Sundays and holidays.	15 days after one year of service. Annual bonus equal to one half of monthly salary for firms with less than P200,000 capital; for those with capital above P200,000, bonus is one month's wages. 12% interest paid each January on pensions accumulated at year-end.	In cases of ju dismissal, 45 days' salary o notice. Severance pay vari with length o service in cas of unjust dismissal.
Ecuador	Minimum wage varies from S2,200 to S4,600 (S43:$1) depending on economic sector; up to S4,600, workers receive monthly COL raise of S250 plus S800 postdevaluation adjustment monthly; between S4,600 and S9,200, S800 adjustment only until monthly wage reaches S10,000 threshold.	Maximum 40 hours over five and a half days.	50% premium during daytime and before midnight. Double time on weekends, holidays and between midnight and 6 a.m.	15 days after one year; one additional day for each year over five years' service, for maximum of 15 additional days. Bonus of 13th-month salary in December, 14th-month in April (coast) or September (altiplano), 15th-month (on sliding scale) and complimentary bonus paid in 10 equal installments.	30 days' notice. Severanc pay for indefi nite term contract is 25% o one month's wages for eac year worked.

Dismissal	Social security	Pensions	Profit sharing	Other benefits
st cause for im-ediate dismissal cludes grave in-scipline, falsifi-tion of records, moral conduct d disclosure of mpany secrets. smissal requir-g 15 days' no-e includes ina-lity to perform b and chronic ness.	Covers occupa-tional and nonoc-cupational illness, maternity, disabil-ity, old age and death. Employer contributes 9.4% of salary; em-ployee, 4.7%.	75% of last year's average pay for workers with 20 years' service. Payment begins at age 55 for men, 50 for women.	None.	Family subsidy: 4% of monthly salary to workers earning less than six times the monthly mini-mum wage. Edu-cation subsidy: 2% of monthly payroll; 2% to Colombian Fam-ily Welfare Insti-tute; P810 monthly transpor-tation assistance to workers.
st cause in-des absentee-n, inability to rform work, in-bordination or lation of work es, grave per-nal injury to ployer. Worker y sue employer r failure to pay ges, for salary t or grave per-nal injury.	Covers unemploy-ment, maternity, retirement due to old age and dis-ability, death, job-related injuries and mortgages. Firms contribute 9.85% of payroll; workers, 9.35% of wages.	Pensions based on length of service, age and wage level over last five years. Amount may not exceed average wage dur-ing last year of service. Financed through social se-curity contributions.	15% of net prof-its: 10% distrib-uted among workers without regard for salary level but not to exceed 40 times the monthly mini-mum wage; 5% shared in relation to number of de-pendents each worker has.	COL adjustment of S250 monthly. Benefits subject to negotiation in-clude medical and dental service, transportation, education, and family subsidies.

	Wages	Workweek	Overtime	Vacation time and bonuses	Severance notice and p
Mexico	Minimum daily wages range from P325 (P147.90:$1) in cities such as Oaxaca, Durango and Campeche to P455 for border towns, Mexico City and petrochemical centers. Starting pay in most industries is usually above minimum.	Six days for a total of 48 hours is common. Some labor unions demanding 40-hour week, but adoption unlikely in 1983. Some individual firms already on 40-hour week.	Twice regular rate for first nine hours and triple thereafter. Sunday work has a 25% premium. Holiday pay twice regular rate.	Six days' paid vacation after one year's service, plus two days for each additional year. Many employers grant 15 days as part of fringe benefit package. Mandatory vacation bonus of 25% of one month's pay. Compulsory Christmas bonus of 15 days' salary, paid before December 20.	One month's notice after s months' service. Severan includes thre months' wag and 12 additional days f every year employed.
Peru	Minimum monthly wage is S90,000 (S1,235:$1), old rate of S60,000 retained in 1983 as a reference rate for management salaries pegged to number of minimum salaries paid by firm.	48 hours over a six-day workweek.	35% premium for late shift (6 a.m.–6 p.m.); 50% for night shift (6 p.m.–6 a.m.). Double time for Sundays and holidays.	30 calendar days after 260 full days' service. Voluntary bonus usually 15 days' pay on July 28 for national holiday. If paid for three consecutive years, bonus becomes obligatory.	Two months' notice requir after three months' employment. Se erance pay is one month's salary for eac year of servic

Dismissal	Social security	Pensions	Profit sharing	Other benefits
ʼounds for dis- ssal are incom- tence or crimi- l offense. orker may ap- al in labor urts. If unjusti- bly dismissed, orker may oose between instatement or demnification. nployers may fuse to reinstate nfidential em- oyees or work- s with less than ue yearʼs service.	Covers illness and disability, death benefits, mater- nity leave, old age, unemploy- ment and retire- ment. Costs shared by em- ployer and em- ployees. Employer contributes about 10% of payroll.	At age 65 if at least 500 weekly contributions to social security have been made. Amount varies ac- cording to num- ber of contributions.	8% of companyʼs pretax profit.	Housing fund (In- fonavit). Employ- ers contribute 5% of payroll. Train- ing programs at employerʼs ex- pense. Most firms have additional employee benefits beyond those es- tablished by law.
ʼorkers with less ian three yearsʼ rvice can be dis- issed at any me with due no- ce and severance ayment. Employ- ent over three ears requires dis- issal based on roof of serious lony, disclosure f trade secrets, c.	Covers maternity, illness, disability, old-age pensions and death. Em- ployers and em- ployees each pay 5% of monthly salaries to social security and pen- sion funds, up to a maximum monthly wage of S231,000 per employee.	Age 60 for men and 55 for women. Amount depends on total payments to fund and length of ser- vice. Maximum obtainable: S80,000 monthly. Financed through worker, employer and state contributions.	For industrial workers, 25% per year of net prof- its: 10% payable in cash, 13.5% in nonvoting stock, 1.5% to *comuni- dad*. Similar sys- tem for mining workers. Trade and banking em- ployees: 30 daysʼ pay in lieu of profit sharing.	Accident insur- ance is manda- tory; free hous- ing, school and medical services if location isolated, i.e., mining camps. Sick pay after three days covered by social security. Other benefits usually negotiated by unions.

	Wages	Workweek	Overtime	Vacation time and bonuses	Severance notice and p
Uruguay	Monthly minimum wage is P2,086.10 (P34:$1). Lower for agricultural workers.	48 hours legal maximum, but commercial and office workers in most industrial plants have 44-hour workweek, 32.5 hours for private bank employees, 40 hours for employees of state-owned banks.	Overtime rates vary by sector from 1.5 times to twice regular pay. Double the usual rate for Sundays and national holidays.	20 days' annual paid vacation and one extra day for every five years' service. Vacation bonus equal to 45% of net salary for vacation period. Annual bonus of one twelfth of yearly earnings, usually paid half in June and half in December.	Notice not required. Pay equal to one month's wag for each year of service, no to exceed six months. Extra six months' pay required dismissed worker is pregnant.
Venezuela	Legal minimum B900 (B8:$1) per month; in practice minimum is B1,500, and will remain stable as long as price controls are enforced.	Maximum 44 hours for salaried workers (40 at night); 48 hours for manual laborers (42 at night). Many labor contracts call for 40-hour, five-day workweek.	Minimum 25% premium for day overtime, 45% for night work, but labor contracts often stipulate higher rates.	15 paid vacation days annually (in practice, up to 30 days). Bonus equal to one day's pay per year of service, up to 15 days.	Two weeks' notice after s months' service, 30 days after one yea or more. Dismissal for jus cause indemn ties add up to 30 days' pay for each year of service plu one additiona month's pay. Unjustified d missal require double indemnity.

Dismissal	Social security	Pensions	Profit sharing	Other benefits
ployers may miss workers ely and pay erance. To id payment, ployers must ive serious mis- duct, criminal s or chronic senteeism.	Covers funeral expenses, 12-week maternity leave, monthly family allowance (P167 per child), unemployment, retirement and widows' pensions. Employees contribute 13% of gross salary; employers, 10% of monthly payroll.	Age 60 for men and 55 for women. Amount varies from 60% to 75% of average salary over last three years' service, depending on years of contribution to fund. Minimum 35 years' service for men and 30 years for women. Financed by social security contributions.	None.	Accident insurance costs employers 1–20% of monthly payroll, depending on risk. Health insurance covers hospital and medical care up to 70% of gross salary, not to exceed three-month minimum wage. It begins after third day of illness and costs employees 3% of monthly salary, employers 4%.
smissal justified grounds of dis- nesty and gross gligence, iong others. smissed work- can appeal to partite commis- in. If it rules smissal unjusti- d, employer has tion to rein- te worker, ap- al or pay dou- e indemnity.	Covers medical assistance and disability, death and maternity and retirement pensions. Employers contribute 7–9% of payroll (depending on industrial risk factor); employees, 4% of wages.	At age 60 for men and 55 for women, if 750 weekly social security contributions have been made. Amount varies according to number of contributions but cannot be less than 40% of reference salary.	Employers must distribute 10% of net profits to employees equal to at least 15 days' pay but no more than two months' pay (unless otherwise agreed).	Free or low-cost housing for workers required in some industries (petroleum). Other benefits, such as education, credit union programs and free lunches, offered by many firms.

urce: Reprinted from *Business Latin America*, April 6, 1983, pp. 110–11. Used with the permission of e publisher, Business International Corporation, New York.
ote: Policies may change frequently.

Sources of Additional Information

Business International. *Position Evaluation and Remuneration Service.* Information on practices in numerous countries.

Kujawa, Duane. *International Labor and the Multinational Enterprise.* New York: Praeger, 1975. Chapters 6, 8.

Labor ministries in host countries.

U.S. Department of Labor. *Labor Profiles.* Brief reports on labor conditions in various countries.

9
Marketing Products and Services

The prospect of marketing products and services in developing countries may seem daunting to marketing managers who have heard stories of international business blunders. Since this short chapter cannot teach you all the pitfalls to avoid, it would certainly be prudent for you to read two short amusing books written on this topic: *International Business Blunders* and *Big Business Blunders*.[1]

The purpose of the chapter is to give you a guide to marketing products and services in developing countries. It will teach you to learn how to learn about the opportunities and threats affecting your marketing plans. After briefly reviewing the basics of marketing as practiced in the United States, the chapter discusses social, competitive, and regulatory conditions in less developed countries that call for different priorities in marketing practices when selling goods and services in those countries.

Marketing Practices in the Context of Industrial Societies

Marketing practices in the United States and in other industrial countries are appropriate for their own cultural context. The U.S. firm usually assumes certain competitive conditions and marketing infrastructure.

Basic Assumptions. First, the United States is made up of complex social relationships, because of the diverse set of ethnic groups, religious affiliations, regional and social class differences. Social group boundaries are often ambiguous and changing. The United States also has a very complex division of

---

Kenneth David, principal author.

labor. These complexities of social life require marketers to do extensive marketing research, using sophisticated statistical techniques to segment the market and to define target markets.

Second, the United States has a highly competitive marketplace in which a large variety of products and services are available.

Third, the United States not only has well-developed facilities for transportation and communications, but also the most developed marketing technology in the world for marketing research and promotional activities.

Fourth, the U.S. government controls the process of marketing—for example, by forbidding false and misleading advertising and collusive behavior that restricts competition. On the other hand, the U.S. government does not intervene in many "normal" marketing practices such as target marketing and the creation of demand for products by intensive promotion. As we shall see, governments in developing countries do not always consider these practices legitimate.

Fifth, because of the high rate of literacy and the cultural similarity between producers and consumers, marketers count on selling to "sophisticated" buyers who can follow directions.

The Basics of Modern Marketing Practices. In modern industrial society, certain common marketing practices have evolved. The marketing goal is to satisfy customer needs and wants at a profit. Two main steps are used to achieve this objective.

The first step is to formulate a marketing plan. Marketing research is first undertaken to identify the social and economic characteristics of the population and to identify the needs and wants of the specific set of customers to whom the goods or services are being aimed. Sophisticated statistical marketing research is therefore necessary.

A marketing strategy is then developed for the target market by answering four interrelated questions: What is the package of benefits to be sold? What price is attractive? Where is the product or service to be sold? And how is the market offering to be communicated to the target market? In other words, the marketer defines "the four P's": Product, Price, Place, and Promotion. In a competitive marketplace, firms invest heavily to develop new products and new services and spend a great deal of money on promotional activities to differentiate their products or services from competitive offerings.

The second main step is to implement the marketing plan. This is accomplished by managing the process of distribution to get the goods or service to the buyer on time and in the proper amount, and by managing demand (by increasing it, evening it out over the year, or whatever), tasks that have equal priority.

Marketing in the Context of Less Developed Countries

Against this background, we can consider the social, competitive, and regulatory conditions in developing countries in order to understand the need to modify marketing practices. Several basic traits are readily identifiable, and they can be contrasted with conditions in the United States.

Societies of Less Developed Countries. First, the societies of developing countries, although unfamiliar to the U.S. marketer, are less complex and ultimately more predictable than is U.S. society. Developing countries tend to have a simpler social organization in several ways. For one thing, income is generally distributed bimodally: most people have very low incomes, while a small percentage of the population has very high incomes. Also, the division of labor is less complex.

Social relationships in these societies are less ambiguous than they are in industrial societies. A person's kinship, as well as ethnic and religious identities, define categorically and unambiguously the behavior expected of that person. Social structure is simpler because kinship and ethnic classifications correlate with social class positions and relative power in the society.

These social relationships may differ significantly from those that are familiar to an American businessperson, and they are therefore less comprehensible initially. Once known, however, social events and behavior may be significantly more predictable than they are in the United States. This is an important point to remember when marketing to developing countries. On one hand, marketing research is far more difficult and less reliable than in the United States; on the other hand, once you learn about the society, it is more predictable, and sophisticated statistical marketing research is thus less necessary than it is in the United States. Furthermore, alternative methods of effective market research exist.

For example, firms sometimes limit their productive and marketing operations to large urban areas where industrial facilities for transportation and communications are better developed. Customers, it is thought, are more easily reached in urban areas than in rural areas. If a firm studied the society's practices more carefully, however, it would discover other opportunities. For instance, in less developed countries, many large temple towns are also the sites of fairs and marketplaces. People go to these towns both to worship and to shop. By studying the connections among the natural calendar of seasons, the productive calendar, and the ritual calendar, a firm can determine when a large congregation will be at the temple/market town with money to spend. Many religions have their most elaborate festivals just after the main harvest period. In northern Sri Lanka, for example, thousands of worshipers can be counted on to attend these festivals. Local artisans can and do plan their output to meet these seasonal peaks.[2] U.S. firms can imitate their business sense. In short, rural markets are often assumed to be small, scattered, and unreachable, but only because they are unfamiliar to the foreigner.

Sellers' Markets and Competition. Second, marketing plays a necessary and essential role in countries, industries, and markets where buyers' markets and competition are present. It is of lesser importance in countries where there is (1) greater demand than supply, (2) little or no competition, (3) little diversity of products or services available, (4) a shortage of hard currency, (5) a protectionist trade policy, and (6) a system of central planning and programmed industrial production.

The topic is a complex one. For a quick review of the causes and effects of sellers' markets on marketing practices in developing countries, see exhibit 9–1.

Exhibit 9–1
The Impact of Sellers' Markets on Marketing Practices and Consumer Buying Behavior in Developing Countries

I.   Why is there a seller's market in many developing countries?

   A. Demand creating conditions:
     Government planning
     Pump priming via government projects
     Increased standard of living and more money in hands of consumers
     Greater demand for goods and services

   B. Supply restricting conditions:
     Shortage of foreign exchange
     Import restriction of consumer and capital goods
     Rigid and cumbersome control apparatus by government
     Lack of enough entries of new enterprises
     Lack of competition in the domestic market
     Short supply (and high prices) of goods and services

II. Problems of marketing in a seller's market

   A. Scarcity of goods or rationing

   B. Little or no price competition

   C. Monopoly or cartel conditions

   D. Tied distribution system

   E. Low margins for marketing in a situation of price control

   F. Limited nonprice competition

   G. Low rate of product change

H. Little opportunity to differentiate products

III. Results of seller's market in marketing behavior by firms[a]

    A. Complacency for firms: little challenge to find new products or improve current ones

    B. Real size of market is unknown

    C. Consumers face substantial risks

    D. Perishable goods are not well protected

    E. Quality control not exercised by manufacturers and middlemen

IV. Impact of seller's market and marketing behavior of firms on consumer buying behavior

    A. Businesspeople in general and merchants in particular are perceived by consumers as regularly engaged in predatory practices and chicanery

    B. Consumers shop both frequently and intensively and buy in small quantity on every shopping trip

    C. Comparative shopping is often of intraproduct and intrabrand type

    D. Bargaining is the primary method for establishing price in most markets. This is more so among lower-income people

    E. Bargaining is a social as well as economic process

    F. Consumers avoid risks in the marketplace

    G. Many consumers establish personal relationships, based on mutual trust, with selected sellers

    H. Because of the nature of their markets, consumers search intensively for information from peer and reference groups prior to making key purchases

    I. Personal sources as well as word-of-mouth advertising are the two most powerful information sources for most consumers

Adapted from Anant R. Negandhi, "Advanced Management Knowhow in Underdeveloped Countries," *California Management Review* 10, no. 3 (1968):56.

[a]Hans B. Thorelli and Gerald D. Sentell, "Consumer Ecology in the LDC: The Case of Thailand," in *Proceedings of the Academy of International Business: Asia-Pacific Dimensions of International Business* (Honolulu, Hawaii: Academy of International Business, 1979), 324–33.

Transportation and Communications Systems. The third basic trait is that the systems of transportation and communications are usually underdeveloped, especially in the rural areas of developing countries.

The marketer must, however, avoid overall stereotypes about the Third World. Differences in the availability of communications media are illustrated in table 9–1. These figures demonstrate that the U.S. firm does not necessarily face extreme problems in promoting products and services in developing

Table 9–1
Televisions, Radios, and Cinemas in Developing Countries

	Television Sets		Radio Receivers		Cinemas
	Total (thousands)	Per 1,000 Pop.	Total (thousands)	Per 1,000 Pop.	Total
Advanced developing nations averages:		199		268	
Argentina	6,300	211	6,650	222	600
Brazil	21,500	164	52,000	396	2,300
Greece	3,000	309	3,500	361	450
Philippines	2,000	41	6,000	122	787
South Korea	7,784	195	17,000	425	399
Spain	10,406	270	7,994	207	2,452
Taiwan	3,772	204	2,343	127	665
Venezuela	2,000	NA	2,305	NA	580
Less developed nations averages:		116		222	
Colombia	1,750	65	NA	NA	NA
Cyprus	110	183	125	208	65
India	2,000	3	21,000	30	10,095
Indonesia	1,500	9	20,000	124	1,193
Kenya	65	4	NA	NA	NA
Malaysia	2,000	133	2,300	164	290
Malta	110	275	200	500	26
Pakistan	1,250	14	9,000	104	625
Syria	2,400	264	5,500	604	90
Thailand	3,772	204	2,343	127	665
Turkey	5,566	119	6,291	135	450

Source: Adapted from *World Advertising Expenditures: 1985 Edition* (New York: Starch Inra Hooper and International Advertising Association, 1985), 29. Data are for 1983.

countries. It is therefore too simple to state that because of the low levels of education and poor communications, consumers are generally unaware of purchase alternatives and are unable to evaluate products when alternatives are available. As the average figures in table 9–1 show, the availability of media varies among the advanced developing nations and the less developed nations. Even in less developed nations, where there are fewer radio or television sets available, it is common for villagers to listen to the radio set belonging to a wealthy person in the village. In any case, radio transmissions get around the problem of illiteracy. (See also appendix 9D.)

Governmental Intervention. Fourth, marketers who complain about interventions by the U.S. government that restrict their business practices will probably learn something about government intervention when marketing in developing countries. In developing countries, which often have sellers' markets, foreign exchange problems, low levels of saving and investment, and other problems, regulatory agencies tend to take a dim view of marketing practices that are considered normal to U.S. firms and regulators.

In developing countries, regulatory agencies may look askance at the extensive use of middlemen in the distribution channel, for example, because local middlemen are considered parasites who raise the prices of products. Competition by extensive promotional activities rather than by price may be in conflict with the development plan of the country. This is especially true when regulators believe that lower-income consumers are spending a high percentage of their weekly income on items a foreign firm thinks of as normal shopping goods, but which regulators consider to be luxury goods. Coca-Cola was judged to be a luxury in India, for example.

The good news about governmental intervention in low-income countries, however, is that in addition to the problems there are also business opportunities from governmental intervention. As the case in appendix 9A shows, the Quaker Oats company found that government-sponsoring of products may bring about a regulated monopoly situation for the U.S. firm, even one that deals in consumer products. In deciding to go ahead with the low-cost, nutritious Incaparina product, the company weighed the inconvenience and limitations posed by the government and by possible short-term market losses in a particular country against the gains from governmental goodwill and from a longer-term market strategy aimed at addressing adjacent country markets.

Finally, government regulators can also restrict the marketing of products that wrongly assume a higher skill level on the part of the consumers than in fact exists. From the producer's point of view, the lower level of education of consumers and the cultural gap between producers and consumers make consumers appear to be "unsophisticated" and unable to follow "simple" directions.

Marketing Policy Implications for Your Firm

What are the practical policy directions that are appropriate for firms marketing in developing countries?

Marketing Feasibility Decisions: Priority to the Basic Exchange Tasks of Marketing. Marketing to less developed countries will require a reordering of priorities toward the more basic exchange tasks. Specifically, you must attend more to the basic exchange tasks of marketing (packaging, transportation, and distribution) that are appropriate to the conditions and the degree of development of transportation technology and give less attention to the promotional, demand-creation tasks of marketing.

In the course of economic development, marketing passes through four stages: (1) barter among producers, (2) direct sales from producers to consumers, (3) specialized distributing activities (grain elevators) and exchange activities (futures markets), and (4) specialized demand-regulation activities (specialized promotions). Marketing managers in the United States are brought up to operate in the fourth stage; they must adapt marketing technology for developing country conditions that are mainly in the third stage.

In defining the geographical market area served, for example, you must assess transportation available to buyers. In planning a system of goods transportation, you must manage the limitations posed by transport facilities and by lack of storage facilities, especially refrigerated storage. The case in appendix 9B illustrates an innovative way to get around problems with distribution and refrigerated storage facilities; it shows that setting up distribution facilities may indeed be a technology transfer.

Distribution decisions, however, are not just technical matters; they also include human issues that require some knowledge of the local social structure. In many developing countries, distribution tasks in the marketing channel may be organized as part of kinship or other old boy networks rather than by impersonal transactions between firms. Firms in many developing countries operate with fewer and less formal contractual business relationships than do firms in the United States. When people distrust legal contracts, they seek continuity and reliability by working largely with friends or relatives. Kin and business relationships often overlap, making it difficult for outsiders to compete even at a better price. See exhibit 9–2 for an example.

In other words, distribution channels may pose an entry barrier to competition. Where such a situation exists, it is often advisable for the investor to enter into a joint venture with a local firm.

Sequence of Decisions Regarding Product or Service Modification. Continuing with the idea that the firm must first attend to the *basics* of marketing in line with country conditions, we now take inventory of minimal product adaptation decisions. Before you consider whether the product competitively meets specific needs and wants, you need to determine whether the product meets the following threshold conditions of feasibility:

1. Does the design of the product and its packaging take into account ecological and biological limits such as humidity, temperature, altitude, and body size as well as the limits posed by the local transportation system?

Exhibit 9–2
An Example of the Importance of Social Relationships

One U.S. manufacturer of poultry feed established a facility in Spain on the basis of market studies indicating a substantial demand for feed. Only after the equipment and raw materials had been secured and the product rolled off the line did the firm discover that it was unable to sell to local poultry farmers. The problem, they learned, was that the Spanish poultry growers and feed producers had generations of personal and familial relationships and effectively barred newcomers from the market. The U.S. firm attempted to solve this problem by buying a series of chicken farms, only to discover that they had no one to buy their chickens! When last heard from, the firm was busily buying restaurants in Spain.

From "The Spanish–American Business Wars," *Worldwide P & I Planning* (May–June 1971): 30–40; subsequently retitled *Worldwide Projects.* Used with permission.

Firms have found that a variety of product and packaging modifications are necessary. Some common examples:

Modifying engines for humidity and altitude

Modifying electric cooking devices for humidity

Modifying electronic control systems for the cold of Nepal or the heat of Saudi Arabia

Modifying the sizes of machines for populations of shorter stature

Modifying packaging strength in view of locally available transport, resistance to heat and humidity

Modifying shelf life in view of locally available transport (powder instead of liquid form)[3]

2. Do the product and the instructions for using it fit with technical regulations and use patterns?

Firms must frequently modify the size, calibration, or other characteristics of their products and product directions to accord with local patterns of use. Here are some frequently occurring modifications:

Coverting to metric quantities or centigrade measurements (Conversions of dies can be expensive. One firm making measurement instruments found that a metric die cost $10,000.)

Converting to locally used electricity—50-cycle hertz instead of 60-cycle hertz, 220 volts instead of 110 volts

Replacing cylindrical bottles with other shapes such as octagonal bottles for certain drugs

In general, during the planning phase of foreign investment, you should obtain copies of all standards in English, interpret those standards and determine necessary modifications, make those modifications, and send items to testing authorities to obtain approval and certification.

3. Does the product or service and (with Union Carbide's disaster in Bhopal fresh in mind) the manufacturing process provide for: (1) environmental and human protection, and (2) advertising and directions for use that are not misleading?

You will, of course, want to reduce risk by providing products that are not dangerous to use. But in developing countries, knowing what is dangerous is often a bit trickier than it is in industrialized nations. Which standards will you use?

One way to deal with this problem is to ask yourself the following question: Does the product or service comply with *the laws and regulations of the host country?*

Technologically less developed countries often lack the facilities to set forth sufficiently accurate and precise standards for environmental and human protection. Similarly, merely being responsive to the canons of false or misleading advertising may not be adequate. If the U.S. company complies only with these regulations, the firm may be vulnerable on two counts. People or the environment may be harmed, and even if nothing harmful occurs, the firm may still be open to the accusation that it is dumping inferior goods in the Third World marketplace.

An alternative, therefore, is to use the following standard: Does the product or service comply with *U.S. standards* concerning environmental and human protection and false or misleading advertising and directions for use?

A U.S. company that follows U.S. regulations and standards may feel secure because the U.S. regulations are, in general, stricter and more accurate than are the local ones. The firm will certainly be protected against accusations that it dumps inferior goods on the Third World market. But the firm may still be vulnerable if something disastrous happens. Exporting U.S. standards is culturally shortsighted. This policy is not good enough because it assumes that the foreign consumers have a level of education similar to that of U.S. consumers and that there is cultural similarity between producer and consumer.

Yet a third alternative, then, is to follow this standard: Does the product or service comply with environmental and human protection standards and standards of freedom from false or misleading advertising or directions *when used by final purchasers?*

When marketing abroad, be sure to question your assumptions of what is a "normal" pattern of use. In order to transfer successfully the technology that is needed for your product, you must examine your assumptions about facilities and other conditions required for "normal" use. Will your product be dangerous to use if there is erratic electric current—say, 220 volt electricity with spikes up to 270 volts? Is your engine sufficiently insulated if it is to be used in a very humid area?

You must also examine your assumptions about the normal *user* of your product. Consider the literacy and cultural dissimilarity of users. (The common phrase, "lack of buyer sophistication," is a misleading way of saying "they are different and I am superior.") Consider the case of the Nestlé company, as outlined in appendix 9C. In brief, thousands of infants became seriously malnourished, ill, or even died because their mothers diluted Nestlé's milk powder to an unnourishing level or used unclean water when preparing the formula.

For a partial summary of the minimal conditions for marketing goods to developing countries, see table 9–2.

Adapting Products and Services: "Sociocultural Marketing." After meeting threshold conditions, the marketer does in developing countries what he or she does in the United States: offers a product that meets consumers' needs and wants at a profit. The question of whether and how much a firm should adapt to meet the needs and wants of consumers, buyers, or clients in another

Table 9–2
The Implications of Environmental Factors for Product Adaptation

Environmental Factor	*Product Adaptation*
Level of technical skills Level of literacy Isolation (major repairs or replacement parts difficult or expensive)	Marking and simplification of product; improvement of reliability of product
Level of maintenance	Change in tolerances
Differences in standards	Recalibration and resizing of product
Body size of users Power availability Level of labor cost	Resizing or automation or manualization of product
Level of income and interest rates	Quality and price change

Source: Adapted from Richard D. Robinson, "The Challenge of the Underdeveloped National Market," *Journal of Marketing* 25 (October 1961): 24. Used with permission.

society was introduced in chapter 3. Here, we shall give more specific suggestions for making such adaptations.

Adapt Goods and Services with a Long-Range Product Life Cycle in Mind.
A good rule of thumb is to adapt goods and services to the product characteristics used in the United States when it was at a level of economic and social development similar to that of the target market.

For example, products for washing clothes have evolved through a long-range product life cycle during this century: hand washing with scrubbing board, simple hand-operated mechanical wringer; electric clothes washer; and finally the digitalized washer. One U.S. firm found a huge target market in developing country housewives who were currently washing clothes by hand, but were ready for hand-operated washers with mechanical wringers.

Similarly, timepieces in the United States have evolved: from hand-wound watches; then to more expensive, self-winding, waterproof, shock-proof watches; and recently, to less expensive, battery-driven quartz watches. Although there are problems with supplying replacement batteries for electronic watches, there is currently a market in developing countries for hand-wound but shockproof watches.

Adapt Services to the Social and Political Context. Adapting services is partly a technical matter of adapting the range of services offered to the socioeconomic conditions in the developing country. For example, a bank offers different services in an economy with hyperinflation or in an economy with strict foreign exchange controls than it does in the United States. Similarly, winning a major engineering and construction contract in the Middle East entails entering into economic planning with government ministries and gaining the favor of highly placed personnel such as Saudi princes; it is not just a matter of offering a prospectus at an attractive price.

Adapting services is also a human matter. Since services are not tangible things, their value may not be immediately clear to the client. The perception of the quality of the service delivered is strongly influenced by the client's perception of the person or team that delivers the service. For the client to perceive the service purveyor as credible and trustworthy, good intercultural communication is essential.

Therefore, a service-providing firm does well to adapt its personnel to the foreign setting. There are three elements in particular that are needed. First, firms need a program for selecting persons who have an aptitude for intercultural communications as well as technical skills. Second, firms need a program of intensive cultural sensitivity training to ensure good communication with clients. In some industries, where the service is provided by teams, firms should be concerned with the training of teams, not just individuals, for this purpose. Some firms have strong teamwork training programs. One caution: teams can be overtrained. That is, team members can become so strongly conditioned to working well with one another that they lose their openness to the clients. Teams must be receptive to the client, especially to the client from another culture. Third, reporting and control systems must strike a balance between (1) the provision of quantitative information about the business necessary for headquarters' purposes and (2) an openness to nonquantitative trends in the foreign environment. When firms simply export their domestic reporting and control systems to a foreign enterprise, they may never hear about the changing business opportunities and threats in the foreign setting.

Pay Attention to Local Meanings. In domestic marketing, and even more so in international marketing, the marketer must speak the language of the customer. The anecdotes collected in the books on international business blunders cited earlier call attention to an essential communication task. When marketing goods and services in developing countries, the marketer must positively know whether the offering will attract or offend the customers *according to local cultural understandings.*

The marketer must be certain that customers will not be offended by the brand name, the shape, the color of the product or the package, or the wording of the directions for use. Common mistakes are to communicate sounds or colors that are objectionable intercultural puns—that is, in the local language, they may refer to something obscene, deadly, or derogatory. To give another kind of example, white is the color of mourning in much of the Far East; blue is the color of sorrow. The Greeks, however, like both colors.

You may be thinking that the foreign culture is your unseen enemy, but there are ways in which you can successfully win it to your side. For example, when planning the size of products to sell, a marketer may be confronted with a system of measures that does not resemble either the U.S. or the metric system. However, alternative cultural solutions to measurement problems are sometimes very straightforward. During field research in Sri Lanka, Kenneth David was trying to understand the quantity implied by a local word that translated as a "measure." It turned out that "measure" was the amount of uncooked rice that, when cooked, is required for a single dinner for an adult man.

In general, it is necessary to adjust both price and quantity sold to fit with local buying behavior. Referring back to section IV of exhibit 9–1, you will find some general features of buyer behavior in developing countries.

Pay Attention to Local Social Relationships. More care is required to find out whether the product or service might have unintended social consequences. A social-impact audit asks what effect the offering might have on social relationships, such as kinship, relative power, or ranking, or on political relationships.

For example, nylon fishing nets and motor launches were introduced in northern Sri Lanka in the 1960s. Because people, with hard work and some luck, were slowly able to buy the nets and launches, these items reduced the dependence of poorer fishermen on the wealthy fish merchants. Wealthy fish merchants previously owned all the equipment and treated the poorer fishermen like sharecroppers; nets and launches were introduced only over their vigorous protests. One powerful entrepreneur feuded with and reportedly murdered several of the fish merchants. A social impact audit might have anticipated that there would be serious social repercussions from the introduction of this new technology.

Not every venture requires such an audit. However, the more that the good or service is an innovation and thus represents a bundle of characteristics and features that go beyond the existing market space, the greater the potential for unintended impacts on social relationships.

You may have heard about Third World reaction to innovative goods from industrial countries as representing an imposition of alien values on Third World customers. On the one hand, it is true that new values are introduced along with the goods. The point of the social audit is to understand something of what the social reaction might be instead of leaving it to be a surprise. After all, not all impositions of different values are wrong. Three decades after the introduction of Volkswagen in the United States, the subcompact was recognized as an intelligent response to a changing energy situation.

Social consequences should also be considered with regard to pricing alternatives. In general, whether marketing abroad or at home, you take the same approach to pricing. Price is a variable, chosen with respect to other elements of the marketing mix: product or service offered, location, promotion. Pricing strategy responds to the different buying behaviors for different categories of goods: consumer nondurable or durable goods, cheap shopping goods versus luxury goods, capital goods. The U.S. firm, however, should attend to the local definitions of different goods. Buying behavior is relative. Some people may buy a Porsche as a normal shopping item, not a luxury good. Similarly, an item that may be an ordinary purchase in the United States may appear as a luxury good to a consumer in a developing country.

Responses may come from the government as well as the consumers. Firms are generally aware of two competitive price strategies for market entry: a low "penetration" price to keep out competition and build volume, and a high initial "skimming" price to catch the early buyers. The latter alternative may not be so acceptable to the foreign government, and it may step in when it perceives that a high proportion of an ordinary person's salary is being spent to acquire the item. In this sense, normal target marketing of a line of items into high-quality, high-price items versus moderate-quality, low-price items may result in what government regulators perceive as a bad allocation of its poorer citizens' incomes.

Social awareness is also necessary regarding promotion. Media use must be adapted to the particular cultural setting. For example, prime time in Islamic nations is Friday morning, the morning of their sabbath. The firm should also check on the status of mass advertising in its target country. To give another example, there are problems of mass advertising in countries like Saudi Arabia that have mainly state-controlled radio and TV stations. The firm should also bear in mind the literacy level of its target audience. A higher budget for audio-visual media (radio and TV) relative to budgets for print and billboard advertising can overcome the illiteracy problem. (See appendix 9–D for further information about advertising.)

Conclusion

To sum up, let us draw an analogy between the marketing of products and services and a speech event. In every act of communicating, there is a sender of a message, the medium chosen for communication, the message itself, and the receiver of the message. Consider your firm as a sender of its message— that is, your offering to the marketplace: your product or service, its price, and the location where it is available. The medium of communication is the promotional techniques that you use: mass advertising, promotional displays, personal selling, and so forth. In domestic marketing, the receiver of the message is your target market.

The marketing of products and services is more complicated in international marketing, particularly in developing countries, for several reasons. First, there are multiple receivers of your offering to the marketplace. You are sending your market offering to a multiple audience. In addition to consumers and competitors, the government in a developing country should be considered as part of the target market.

Second, due to language differences, the message as sent may not be the same as the message received. A perfectly innocent brand name may mean something quite different in a foreign language.

Third, your product or service was developed in the U.S. ecological, social, and technological context. To be well received, your product or service must respond to the new and different conditions in developing countries.

Appendix 9A
Case: High Nutrition Flour in Latin America

T his is a case of a responsive marketing plan that was moderately successful in the marketplace and was favorably received by host country governments.

The Quaker Oats Company is a producer and marketer of food products and animal feeds. Quaker worked with the Institute of Nutrition of Central America and Panama (INCAP) in deciding to produce and sell a food product specifically aimed at helping to solve malnutrition problems. The product, Incaparina, is a bland flour that can be used as an ingredient in drinks (as in low-calorie diet products sold in the United States), soups, sauces, pancakes, muffins, cake and bread.

The firm deviated from normal U.S. marketing practice in several respects:

1. Quaker Oats accepted a business proposition in which many business decisions were made by INCAP in return for exclusive rights to sell the product. In a sense, the firm thus became a regulated monopoly with a consumer product.

2. The firm went ahead with the project despite the fact that short-term market projections were not highly favorable. Knowing that the Incaparina project represented a small portion of its total business (5 percent), Quaker took the long-term strategic view that a favorable relationship with the governments of the region had priority over short-term return on investment.

3. In brief, the firm was marketing to the governments as well as to the consumers.

These deviations—collaboration with Third World government agencies and long-term business strategy—resulted in a strong competitive foothold for the firm in Central and South America.

Malnutrition in the Third World

Between one-half and two-thirds of the world's population is undernourished. In many Latin American countries, food intake in calories is less than two-thirds the level in the United States. More importantly, high-nutrition foods—especially foods rich in protein—are in short supply. In Latin American countries the supply of meat and milk is about one-third of the supply in the United States. Meat, eggs, fish, and dairy products as sources of protein are luxury foods for the low-income citizens of poor countries where per capita income ranges between one-fifth and one-third of the U.S. level.

Malnutrition has serious effects. Mortality rates in the Third World are twenty to forty times higher than rates in industrial countries. Preschool malnutrition retards the mental and physical development of the survivors. Thus malnutrition influences not only the individuals, but also the vigor and skill of the working population. Malnutrition is an obstacle to economic development.

INCAP's Answer

The Institute of Nutrition of Central America and Panama was established in Guatemala City by the governments of Costa Rica, El Salvador, Guatemala, Honduras, Nicaragua, and Panama. The purpose was to collaborate in finding solutions to nutritional problems.

After studying the effects and economics of protein deficiency, INCAP also noted that essential proteins are contained not only in expensive foods, but also in legumes, fish, and residues from the oilseeds of soy, cotton, and peanuts. INCAP studied ways to develop vegetable protein mixtures from local resources at low cost. After several years, INCAP's work was rewarded. Its nutritionists developed formulas containing corn flour or sorghum flour as a base, sesame, cottonseed or soy meal as a source of concentrated protein, and calcium carbonate, yeast, and vitamins. The mixtures tested well: children suffering from malnutrition recovered quickly when given the mixture.

INCAP also tested the mixture's acceptability by selling the product first in four villages, later in a small town, and finally in Guatemala City. They sold 75 grams, enough for a day's supply for a child, for the equivalent of three U.S. cents. With favorable results, INCAP selected a trade name for the product, Incaparina, and began looking for a private firm to distribute the product commercially.

INCAP prepared a resolution stating policies for licensing Incaparina. Commercial firms were required to:

Get the approval of the local government

Submit samples to INCAP for analysis and approval prior to distribution

Maintain the specified quality and submit production samples regularly

Get approval for packaging and descriptive materials

Pay for the cost of analyses and other services according to a fee schedule

Present proof of financial capacity

Describe the facilities to be used including laboratory equipment and machinery

Describe methods of distribution, storage, and transportation

Report on sources of raw material to insure uninterrupted production

Present production estimates

Obtain authorization for retail prices and discounted prices to public and private charitable institutions

Describe the arrangements for promotion, publicity, and advertising: specific promotion policies were stated for consumer protection.

In short, INCAP prescribed the entire marketing strategy for the product.

The Marketing Experience

Quaker Oats has long been interested in the development of foods to solve nutritional problems of large numbers of low-income people in developing areas of the world. The Incaparina project presented an unusual choice.

On the down side, marketing Incaparina involves considerable risk and a long payout period because margins are low and breakeven volume is high. The company had planned to market its own brand; this plan would have to be scrapped if it sold Incaparina. The company would have little strategic latitude, but would have to accept the entire business plan proposed by INCAP.

On the positive side, INCAP had gained much favorable publicity from the scientific and development community. It would have been costly and time consuming for the firm to submit its own product for extensive testing and approval by health, hospital, and medical authorities. Incaparina already enjoyed such approval. Further, in return for the obligations to INCAP, Quaker would have a major concession, for INCAP licenses were granted on an exclusive basis in each country.

Quaker obtained the INCAP license for Colombia, Venezuela, Brazil, and Nicaragua; it decided to start marketing Incaparina in Colombia for several reasons. Suitable raw materials were available at low cost. Quaker had a strong subsidiary in Colombia, Productos Quaker, S.A. This subsidiary, with more than two hundred employees, was large enough and had an organizational structure and financial resources sufficient to handle a product like Incaparina. The subsidiary used its own sales force to distribute the product through normal wholesale and retail channels: 120 wholesalers in Colombia were to sell to about 30,000 retailers. The markups were, respectively, 5 percent and 10 percent.

The project was variably successful in different countries. In Venezuela, due to lack of raw materials and higher per capita incomes than is usual in South America, the project failed immediately. In Colombia, the project hung on through five years of low sales. Ingrained eating habits were a stronger motivation than improved nutrition; consumers found Incaparina a bland and rather dull taste. However, after five years of promotions through radio and health centers, the firm turned a profit. In Brazil, after an early failure, they succeeded because consumers liked the taste and because the government gave them a very favorable competitive position. Evaluating the project on its own merits, it was a greater success with the governments than with the consumers (just the opposite of the Nestle case discussed in appendix 9C, in which the product was financially successful with consumers, but a serious mistake in the eyes of government officials).

The Quaker Oats company benefited in the long term. Such projects were part of its mission. The company felt that by acting as a good corporate citizen and accepting a project that would certainly be rejected on short-term financial criteria, it gained the goodwill of various governments. The company's overall competitive position in the region was enhanced, for it was able to introduce other, nonregulated consumer products with greater ease than were its multinational competitors. In short, the firm gained by deciding to market to the region and not just to individual countries, and it gained by deciding to market the company to the government and not just market its products to the consumers.

Adapted from Gordon E. Miracle, *Quaker Oats (A)* (Boston: Intercollegiate Case Clearing House, 1966), Case 9-511-069. Used with permission.

Appendix 9B
Case: Dairy Products in Thailand

T his is a case of a culturally responsive marketing plan that was both successful in the marketplace and favorably received by the host country government.

When Foremost Dairy Corporation and three local partners set up their first dairy products processing plant in Thailand, they were starting from scratch in a market where milk and ice cream were virtually unknown commodities. Hence, the first problem was how to make people aware of dairy products, their many uses, and the sanitary measures necessary to keep them fresh. In cooperation with the Thai government, company representatives were sent into schools to give talks on sanitation and nutrition, at the same time supplying the schools with dairy products for the students. The program was a huge success, and a demand for the products was created.

Next came the tricky question of refrigeration. How was the corner grocer to keep milk from souring and ice cream from melting? The answer was to supply every one of the tiny retail outlets—"Mom and Pop" groceries and restaurants—with a freezer, either through leasing, or more often, under terms of a conditional sales contract. If the contracts were met, the freezers were sold to the stores for one U.S. dollar. Foremost's initial capital outlay was sizeable, running into hundreds of thousands of dollars. There were many accompanying headaches, such as keeping stores from unplugging the freezers at night to save electricity and preventing their use for other products, but the effort eventually worked.

From the beginning, the firm tailored operations to the local Thai scene. Products find their way to market via crude water transportation and brightly colored company trucks. They are sold either from pushcarts, from company retail outlets, or through wholesalers.

The pushcarts, also brightly decorated in the local style with dragons and brilliant umbrellas, are supplied by the company and manned by independent retailers. These sidewalk salesmen come to a company-owned depot every morning to pick up their pushcarts and their day's supply of milk and ice cream. At the end of the day they return and pay for the amount sold, with a profit margin for themselves, of course. That margin approximates 20 percent, but the sidewalk salespeople can, and do, set their own retail price.

The company-owned retail outlets are modern soda fountains dispensing such American favorites as the chocolate sundae and the vanilla milkshake. The company builds the store, supplies the equipment, and hires and trains local people to manage the operation, to cook, and to wait on customers.

The category accounting for the biggest chunk of total sales (almost 80 percent of which are in the Bangkok area) is composed of wholesalers, small stores, restaurants, hotels, and schools. A Thai salesperson usually is assigned a territory and given responsibility for one category of outlet, such as all corner grocery stores, while another salesperson will handle all the schools.

To train its sales force, Foremost first taught trainees basic English, while expatriate instructors learned basic Thai. With such a minimal bilingual communications channel established, the salesmen-to-be were taught about dairy products. The last part of the program consisted of teaching sales techniques for which key Thai staff were sent to the United States for training, while several Americans went to Thailand to instruct the local sales force.

The patient cultural bridge building has paid off well. The firm has already replaced the original plant with a larger, more modern one. More meaningful still for the long pull, a strong brand identification was created. Today Foremost and milk are all but synonymous in Thailand.

What lessons can we learn from this case?

First, the firm engaged in social marketing in the best sense of the word. Its executives not only were successful with their venture, but they also marketed to the government and provided consumers with helpful information. They marketed to the government by seeking their approval. They provided needed public service information to school children on nutrition and sanitation, areas that were also their prime market concerns. Promotion to the government and to the consumers coincide with public service.

Second, the firm overcame inadequacies in the local infrastructure of storage and distribution by transferring appropriate refrigeration storage technology to the retail outlets and by teaching the outlet owners how to use the technology. In addition, by choosing to employ pushcart retailers, the firm made use of the local, traditional style of marketing—the bazaar.

Third, the firm used culturally responsive symbolism—dragons, umbrellas, bright colors—on vehicles for the purpose of visual promotion.

Fourth, with its two-way street of staff training—Thais trained in the United States and vice versa—the firm paved the way for continued responsiveness necessary to market products that must be directly responsive to its customers' needs and wants.

Adapted from Vern Terpstra, *International Marketing*, 2d ed. (New York: Holt, Rinehart and Winston, 1978), 117–88. Reprinted by permission of CBS College Publishing.

Appendix 9C
Case: Infant Formula in Africa

This is a case of a culturally unresponsive and ethically dubious marketing plan that was successful in the marketplace, but was considered marketing malpractice by host country governments and by international regulatory agencies. The purpose of the case is not to chastise Nestlé, but rather to illustrate a point made in the body of the chapter: Products and services must be adapted to comply with human and environmental protection standards and standards of freedom from false or misleading advertising or directions *when used by final purchasers*.

The Case and the Issue

In the early 1970s, Dr. Derrick Jelliffer, a public health specialist, declared that infant malnutrition could be linked to the use of Nestlé's baby formula. The formula is made from a milk base with vegetable fat, milk sugar, vitamins and minerals—a nutritious formula when correctly used.

The charge, however, was that the formula was incorrectly used in poor areas of the world, where parents may unknowingly mix the powdered formula with contaminated water, or to save money, dilute it too much. Moreover, breastfeeding is healthier and more economical, assuming a baby's mother is healthy and able to produce adequate nourishment for her child.

Critics have also complained that the infant formula industry compounded those hazards by marketing tactics. Although they lack medical training, employees of some formula companies have dressed as medical personnel while promoting the products from village to village. New mothers were routinely given advertising brochures and free samples while still in the hospital.

The World Health Organization called for a code of good practice in advertising baby foods in 1974. Then a new ethical code drawn up by an international baby-food makers' council appeared and was adopted by nine infant-food producers, including Nestlé. The code had been under discussion for five years. By this time, Nestlé was already engaged in a libel case. In 1974, the British aid-for-development organization War on Want published a report by Mike Muller entitled *The Baby Killer*. The picture on the first page implied that the killer was the baby's nursing bottle. Muller was indicting the industry as a whole. Later that year, another organization, the Third World Working Group (which lobbies in Switzerland in support of less-developed countries) republished Muller's pamphlet with a new title, *Nestlé Kills Babies*. The work declared that the powdered formulas should be provided in pharmacies or through doctors, but should not be advertised on the radio in languages such as Swahili, which is understood by illiterates.

The managing director of Nestlé Alimentana S.A. held a press conference to defend the company against its critics. The core of his argument was that Nestlé has two main obligations, the first of which is to make good products. He continued,

> The manufacturer's second obligation relates to the advertising he does. In my opinion, it is obvious that the advertising must not contain any false indications leading to possible error. In the developing countries there is the added fact that a fair percentage of mothers are illiterate, disregard the fundamental rules of hygiene, and do not have the means to buy our products. To begin with—let's be quite open about it—we are not responsible for this state of affairs. We can help to keep the children alive with our products, but we can't teach large sections of the population to read and write any more than we can radically change the living conditions of millions of people. The only thing the producer can do is to instruct and advise the mothers. We have been doing this for decades, and we shall improve our efforts in the light of experience as time goes on. The methods employed by our allied companies to sell milk foods for infants can be summarized as follows:
>
> Our subsidiaries take the greatest trouble to instruct expectant mothers by means of specialized brochures, tables, leaflets, and films on the care to be given to nursing infants. We have also consulted old brochures and found that for very many years we have drawn attention to the fact that breast feeding is best. We have always stressed the fact that infant milk formulas are primarily intended to supplement mother's milk, which, if the mother is feeding the baby herself, is not always sufficient to meet the infant's growing needs.
>
> These brochures have been so clearly illustrated for many years that even an illiterate can understand them.
>
> The packages contain all the relevant instructions, set out in a simple manner, for preparing the food hygienically.
>
> Mothers and expectant mothers receive advice mainly through the clinics, doctors, and consultations.
>
> To advise young mothers, we also engage the services of qualified midwives or nurses in various countries who work closely together with those responsible for consultations.
>
> Newspaper advertising seldom occurs.
>
> Slogans relating to our milk formula foods have been broadcast on the radio in various countries.
>
> The TV medium has been used only in a few countries.
>
> Inspite of everything, I am willing to admit that the War on Want report has made public opinion aware of a real problem. However, one fails to understand why the matter is blown up like this in a country such as ours where hygienic conditions are satisfactory.

A Swiss court ruled that the pamphlet's title was indeed defamatory. The judge stated that Nestlé's products were not the cause of the injuries and deaths; rather it was the unhygienic way they were prepared by the end users. The judge ordered only token fines, but he concluded that "Nestlé has to carry out a fundamental reconsideration of its promotion methods if in the future it wants to avoid charges of immoral and unethical behavior."

The matter did not rest there. In 1981, delegates from 119 countries convened a meeting of the World Health Organization. They considered an international code of conduct to restrict the advertising and marketing of baby formula. The final vote was 118 to 1. The United States was the only nation that voted against the code. Ultimately, Nestlé agreed to change its marketing practices.

Lessons

What lessons can we learn from this case?

First, firms must avoid marketing malpractice in developing countries. The practice of dressing saleswomen as nurses is misleading advertising. In the United States, actors who portray doctors in TV series are careful to announce that they are not really doctors when they appear in medically related commercials.

Second, it appears that the "Buyer, beware!" rule does not quite apply when the firm and the end users of the firm's products are from countries that differ markedly in the level of technology, education, and economic development. In such cases, acting strictly within the letter of the law is not enough. Both the statement of the managing director of Nestlé and the judgment by the Swiss judge evaluate the situation in a culturally parochial manner. They project the technological, educational, and sanitary conditions of Switzerland onto other societies. They fail to recognize that methods of communication that are perfectly suitable for their citizens are quite inadequate for many persons in poorer countries. On the other hand, in expressing the opinion that Nestlé had better reconsider its promotional methods, the judge apparently recognized that being legally innocent does not imply absence of moral responsibility.

Put another way, even if Nestlé had won its libel case, the continuing reaction of many nations, many of whose citizens were not at all adversely affected by Nestlé's actions, certainly lowered the value of that intangible but vital asset, goodwill.

Adapted from Vern Terpstra, "Nestlé Alimenta, S.A.: Can Advertising Be a Killer?" in *International Marketing*, 2d ed. (New York: Holt, Rinehart and Winston, 1978), 436–42. Reprinted by permission of CBS College Publishing.

Appendix 9D
Selection of Media for Advertising

Although selection of advertising media is a fairly straightforward activity in the United States, based on the number of potential contacts per given unit of print or broadcast media, the selection of media is not such an easy task in developing countries. The first consideration is what media are available for use.

In some countries, certain kinds of media outlets for advertising are not available. For example, in Saudi Arabia no advertising can be done on TV or radio. Furthermore, because of the high illiteracy rate, magazines and newspapers are not a good source of advertising. Billboards are not appropriate on the highways since the harsh sand and sun erode the paper on the board. Billboards placed on top of buildings in the cities, on the other hand, are the one viable source of advertising that reaches a large number of people.

In India, a country well known for tough journalism in spite of occasional government threats of press "brownouts," there are many newspapers, but only a small percentage of the populace can read. Only sixteen newspaper copies are sold per one thousand population.

Table 9D–1 indicates advertising expenditures by medium in three countries. Of course, literacy rates, social patterns, customs, and values all affect the availability and usage of various forms of media within a country. The table, for instance, indicates the relative popularity of cinema advertising in Turkey. It serves as a partial replacement for television advertising in a country that has few television sets. However, in the last few years, TV advertising has risen substantially, followed by radio ads. Fifty independent radio stations, which are not government controlled, reach local audiences, making them a good source for consumer advertising. But since national radio and TV reach 50 percent of the population, newspapers are still the number one source of advertisement. Over four hundred newspapers are in operation. The number of magazines has recently risen also. Today there are fifteen consumer and forty-two trade technical journals in Turkey. Cinema ads reach consumers in outlying areas.

Another promotional device found to be successful in many developing countries is a company-sponsored newsletter. Such newsletters can provide

Table 9D–1
Advertising by Medium in Three Countries
(percent)

Medium	U.S.	Brazil	Turkey
Newspapers	43	20	38[a]
Magazines	14	12	
TV	31	56	34
Radio	9	9	5
Cinema	2	1	8
Outdoor	1	2	9
Direct ads	NA	NA	6

Source: E. Kaynak and L. Mitchell, *Journal of Advertising Research* 7 (June 1981): 21, 29.
[a]Newspapers and magazines combined.

market contact and up-to-date information on a company's products in countries where no suitable trade journals cover the industry or where there is insufficient media coverage. They also serve as promotional and direct mailing tools to supplement local sales force calls.

For example, John Deere began its newsletter, *Furrow,* in 1895 when it found no suitable medium in which to advertise to farmers. Today the publication has a circulation of 2.5 million and is published in twenty-two different editions in ten languages. Champion Spark Plug also sought a low-pressure, low-cost way to reach its audience of auto and motorcycle dealers, service stations, and garages with predictable frequency, and in 1973, it launched *Motor Mail,* a twelve-page quarterly that today is published in eleven languages. Like Deere, Champion felt that it could provide far more effective coverage of its target market with a quarterly than it could with the same space in automotive trade publications. The cost was also significantly lower than advertising costs, averaging less than fifty cents per copy, including delivery charges. The noncommercial content of *Motor Mail* includes three technical pages about spark plugs in general—not just Champion's. Articles about developments in automobiles are also included.

Company-sponsored newsletters can be channeled to a company's own precisely identified target groups. They also provide a means of testing market reaction to new services and products and can act as a platform from which company spokespersons can speak on industry matters. Their high visibility helps the company position itself as a leader in the field.

An international newsletter's flexibility can be tailored to meet any industry's and sponsor's needs in virtually any country of the world for any product type. It may supplement an existing medium available within the country, or it may provide the only information available to target markets.

Sources of Additional Information

Cateora, Philip R., and John M. Hess. *International Marketing*. Homewood, Ill.: Dorsey Press, 1979.

Dholakia, N., and R.R. Dholakia. "Marketing in the Emerging World Order." *Journal of Macro Marketing* 2, no. 1 (Spring 1982): 47–56.

Kaynak, Erdner. *Marketing in the Third World*. New York: Praeger, 1982. (See Kaynak's bibliograpy, pp. 273–98, for a good list of specific studies about marketing in Third World countries).

Leff, N.H. "Multinational Corporate Pricing Strategy in the Developing Countries." *Journal of International Business Studies* 6 (Fall 1975): 55–64.

Leff, N.H., and J.U. Farley. "Advertising Expenditures in the Developing World." *Journal of International Business Studies* 11 (Fall 1980):64–79.

Ricks, David A. *Big Business Blunders: Mistakes in Multinational Marketing*. Homewood, Ill.: Dow Jones–Irwin, 1983.

Ricks, D., M. Fu, and J. Arpan. *International Business Blunders*. Cincinnati: Grid, 1974.

Terpstra, Vern. *International Marketing,* 2d edition. New York: Holt, Rinehart and Winston, 1978.

The Conference Board. *Adapting Products for Export*. Report No. 835. New York: The Conference Board, 1983.

Thomas, Dan R.E. "Strategy is Different in Service Industries." *Harvard Business Review* 56 (July–August 1978):158–65.

10
Protecting Assets and Returns

A ll investments involve uncertainties, and production facilities in developing countries are no exception. However, the risks of investing in developing countries are frequently different from and not as great as you might think. Furthermore, there are government programs, private insurers, and corporate strategies that can reduce the risks. As with domestic business ventures, proper analysis and thorough knowledge are essential in order to reduce the risks. In short, the risks associated with investment projects in developing countries can be managed; this chapter identifies them, puts them into perspective, and discusses ways to cope with them.

There are, to be sure, several types of problems to be considered; some of them are discussed in other chapters. (Strikes, for example, are discussed in chapter 8.) Other problems associated with your operations may develop. For instance, you might face unexpected restrictions on imports of raw materials or spare parts that you need for your production process. Or the government might impose new and higher export performance targets that require you to export a greater proportion of your output than you had originally planned. Or you may find that obtaining government permission to produce more for the local market, thus reducing your exports below the level in your original plan, may be quite difficult. Many other host government policy changes could affect your operations, much as they could even in the United States; health and safety or environmental regulations, for example, may become more restrictive.

Problems that developed in the Philippines during the mid-1980s provide a good example. One business publication noted that firms could anticipate the following difficulties in their operations in coming months: limited access to foreign exchange for financial transactions; problems in obtaining foreign exchange to pay for imports; much higher local interest rates; a substantial decline in the domestic market demand; labor unrest; higher prices for do-

Thomas L. Brewer, principal author.

mestically produced inputs; higher wages; price controls on products; and difficulties in payment collection.[1]

Many of these problems, though, will be familiar to you because they are not distinctively developing country problems; some of them occur in all countries from time to time. Much of your own experience in managing day-to-day problems in your business in the United States can therefore be transferred to a project in a developing country. The principles are similar, though the details of application may differ from country to country.

Governmental Instability

One kind of problem that investors commonly worry about is that a government regime will change, especially as a result of a coup d'état or a civil war. It is certainly true that in many developing countries governmental regimes have changed more frequently than they have in industrial countries. It is also true that the changes in governments in some developing countries have frequently occurred as a result of violence, rather than electoral procedures.

Of course, there are also many developing countries in which the government has been quite stable. This in itself, however, is not necessarily a good sign, for in many countries with stable governmental regimes a great deal of strong opposition to those regimes exists because of their repressive nature. As a result, when those governments do eventually change (as all governments do eventually), the change may be sudden, unexpected and violent; a substantially different kind of regime may come to power. So regime stability is not by itself always a good sign of a favorable investment climate.

On the other hand, you should not necessarily consider political instability a serious problem if you are planning to make an investment, because changes in governments do not necessarily lead to changes in the kinds of governmental policies that directly affect your investment. There have been many cases of changes of heads of government when government policies changed very little; the basic characteristics of the investment climate were actually quite stable in spite of conspicuous and even dramatic changes in governments.[2]

To give you an idea of how deceptive impressions can be, consider the following facts about country X.[3] Since 1960, there have been six different heads of government with tenures in office of only 2¾ years, 5¼ years, 4⅔ years, 3⅓ years, 4 years, and 6 + ? years. One head of the government was assassinated, a second was nearly killed by a would-be assassin, and a third was the target of an unsuccessful assassination attempt. Another decided not to run for reelection because of riots and other evidence of strong opposition to his candidacy, and yet another was removed from office because of allegations against him and/or his associates of involvement in burglary, tax evasion, violation of election laws, denial of fair trial to political opponents, and perjury. The partisan affiliation of the government, furthermore, changed three times in the twelve-year period 1969–81. You are probably inclined to think of country X as a politically risky one, and you would probably be reluctant to invest in it. Yet the country is—as you have perhaps already guessed—the United States.

The point, then, is that you should be careful not to allow superficial impressions about political stability to deter you from a careful evaluation of the risks involved in investing in a developing country. You should avoid the mistake made by a U.S. firm that was considering investing in a Latin American country a few years ago.[4] The company spent many months doing detailed engineering and marketing studies in preparation for establishing a plant in the country. The studies were completed and the proposal to go ahead with the project was sent to the board of directors. The day before the proposal went to the board, however, there was a coup d'état in the country. The next day the board rejected the proposal and cancelled the project permanently. Yet within a few days the political and economic life of the country was back to normal. Even though the head of the government had changed, there was actually very little change in government policies and very little if any change in the basic economic and political conditions in the country. The firm had therefore made a decision of great importance on the basis of superficial and misleading impressions about instability in the country.

Now of course you cannot simply ignore the whole issue of political instability and the risks associated with investing in developing countries. Political instability can be a problem, and there are risks involved in investing. But you need to have a clear idea of what those risks are to the extent that it is possible to do so, and you must devise ways to deal with those risks.

Expropriation

When people think about problems in developing countries, one of the first things they usually think about is expropriation (or nationalization). Although there have been instances of expropriation over the years in developing countries, you should be careful not to allow your impressions to give you exaggerated ideas about those problems.

In the first place, expropriation is probably much less common than you think. Fewer than 5 percent of the firms in developing countries have been expropriated; furthermore, expropriation has declined substantially during the past decade and will probably remain at quite low levels.[5] Also, most of the cases of expropriation were quite selective and targeted on a few industries, especially petroleum, mining, utilities, and banking. There have been a few mass expropriations in which all or nearly all of the foreign investments in a country have been taken over by a new ideologically motivated government, but those cases have been quite rare (Cuba and Iran are well-known examples). In several countries, however, even Marxist revolutionary regimes have not expropriated most foreign investments.

Even if expropriation takes place, there is usually some form of compensation paid to the investor. Although expropriation is a legally recognized right of a host country, the expropriator also has a legal obligation to pay compensation to the investor. And, in fact, compensation has usually been paid, though the extent and the time of the compensation have frequently not been to the investor's satisfaction. In addition to the possibility of compensation by the host government, opportunities for you to obtain insurance exist that will compensate you for any expropriations. (Insurance is discussed in more detail later in this chapter.)

Foreign Exchange Rates

One problem that you will encounter in connection with a project in a foreign country is that the foreign exchange rate between the foreign country's currency and other currencies, including the U.S. dollar, will change. If you have been involved in exporting, this problem will be familiar to you already, and much of your knowledge about exchange rates and their implications for your operations will be useful. However, you will need to understand some additional aspects. In particular, it is important to understand that there are several different kinds of managerial problems associated with changes in exchange rates. One is that exchange rate changes can affect individual transactions.

Short-Term Transactions. The term *transaction risk* refers to the problem of the exchange rate's possibly changing between the time that a price is set for a particular transaction and the time the transaction is actually consummated. For example, as an exporter, you may already have had the experience of agreeing to a price with a foreign customer expressed in U.S. dollars, but by the time the foreign customer has actually obtained and paid for the exported goods, the exchange rate between that currency and the U.S. dollar has changed. The foreign customer has to pay a price in his own currency different from the price that he expected at the time the initial agreement was set.

Since the price was established in terms of U.S. dollars, this change in the foreign exchange rate would not necessarily directly affect you. On the other hand, if the price had been established in terms of the foreign currency so that your foreign customer would pay a set amount in that currency, then a change in the exchange rate between the currency and the U.S. dollar would of course affect the amount that you would actually receive in U.S. dollars.

The most common way to deal with this problem is to use the forward foreign exchange markets, which enable a firm to enter into an agreement to purchase or sell foreign currencies at some time in the future at a price that is set in the present. For example, as an exporter you could set a price in a foreign currency for an export that would take place at some time in the future, and at the same time arrange with a foreign exchange trader in the United States to exchange a given amount of the foreign currency for a given amount of U.S. dollars at a price or exchange rate set in advance. You would therefore know exactly how many dollars you would be receiving from the eventual payment in foreign currency by your foreign customer.

Such a forward market hedge is widely used in U.S. export transactions. The forward markets can also be useful to you in connection with international payments associated with a foreign investment project. If your foreign project either imports or export goods or services, then the foreign project would be able to use the forward markets to reduce the transaction risks associated with individual import and export transactions.

In addition, the foreign project will presumably be remitting profits—and perhaps also fees, interest payments, and principal payments—back to the parent firm in the United States. The forward markets can also be used for such transactions as these.

Long-Term Problems. A second and in some ways more important problem associated with changes in exchange rates is a long-term foreign exchange problem. The problem here is that over the long term a change in the exchange rate of the currency of the country in which the project is located may change in such a way as to make it more difficult for the project to operate on a profitable basis. The particular ways in which exchange rates affect the long-term profitability of a particular project depend on a complex set of factors concerning the project itself and the economy of the country in which the project is located. The complexities, however, can be reduced to a few relatively simple statements.

In the first place, over the long term of several years or more, there will be a tendency for changes in the exchange rate and differences between the foreign country's inflation rate and that of the United States to offset one another.[6] As a result, the project's operations will tend to be affected in offsetting ways by exchange rate changes, on the one hand, and the inflation rate, on the other hand. For example, if the country's currency tends to depreciate against the U.S. dollar over a period of several years, then during that same period a higher inflation rate would exist in the foreign country than in the U.S. The costs that might be associated with a declining exchange rate—in a situation, for example, in which your profits in a foreign country would buy fewer U.S. dollars when you remit them back into the United States—would tend to be offset because at the same time your profits will have increased at least in nominal terms in the foreign country because of the relatively high inflation rate there.

There is no assurance that for any given country over any given period of time that the exchange rate and inflation rate effects will be approximately equal and offsetting. In general, however, the tendency for this to occur is present over the long term.

In any case, the changes in exchange rates could have offsetting effects for a given project to the extent that the project involves both imports and exports. For example, if the country's currency depreciates relative to the U.S. dollar, then the project's imports from the U.S. will become more expensive and therefore increase the operating costs of the project. On the other hand, if the project is also exporting to the United States, then the revenues of the project will increase because the exports to the United States will yield more units of the local currency per given amount of U.S. dollars spent on them.

Again, it is impossible to give assurance that such effects will exactly offset one another. The particular combination of effects on the project's costs and revenues clearly depends on the relative amounts of imports and exports associated with the project and the countries and currencies involved in those imports and exports.

Government Involvement. One of the reasons it is difficult to be more precise and reassuring about the effects of currency depreciation (or appreciation for that matter) is that there is a great deal of government involvement in foreign exchange markets in many countries. Some governments maintain overvalued exchange rates as a matter of national policy to keep imports relatively cheap because of the political popularity of such an action among consumers and import-dependent industries. Sometimes, therefore, the foreign exchange rate for a particular currency may remain at higher levels than would be expected in light of a very high inflation rate, which would otherwise tend to push the value of the currency down.

Although governments commonly try to maintain artificially high exchange rates, they eventually must change the exchange rate and/or take some other action. Sometimes, then, the exchange rate will remain at a given level, which is supported by the government, for an extended period of time, only to be drastically and precipitously devalued. Such devaluations can surely cause problems if the firm is caught unawares and has not been following widely used procedures to protect itself against such an eventuality. Appendix 10A lists measures that can be adopted in response to large, sudden devaluations.

Governments also sometimes resort to split (or multiple) exchange rates, which means that certain kinds of transactions can occur at one exchange rate while other kinds of transactions use a different exchange rate. Food imports, for example, are sometimes entitled to favored treatment whereby importers are allowed to use an exchange rate that will make it possible for them to obtain greater amounts of imported food for a given amount of local currency. In other words, the exchange rate for the favored commodities is kept at a relatively high level by the government as compared with the exchange rate prevailing for other transactions.

Another result of the exchange rate practices of many developing countries is that a parallel or black market in foreign exchange often exists. Yet another result is that these governments sometimes impose controls on exchange transactions; indeed in some cases nearly all kinds of transactions are prohibited for a period of time. The problem of such foreign exchange controls is considered in a separate section of this chapter.

Accounting Translation Problems. Yet another aspect to the problem of changing foreign exchange rates is associated with a foreign investment project. An accounting problem is created when the accounting records of the foreign firm must be converted from foreign currency terms into U.S. dollar terms for purposes of completing the accounting records of the parent firm in the United States. Because of the paper gains or losses associated with changing exchange rates, this is frequently referred to as the foreign exchange translation problem.

An accountant who is familiar with the relevant Financial Accounting Standards Board (FASB) guidelines and regulations is best qualified to handle this problem. The essence of the accounting problem is that the income, assets, and liabilities of the foreign project that are valued in the foreign country's currency will be subject to change in value over time when they are converted to U.S. dollar figures simply because of a change in the exchange rate between the foreign currency and the U.S. dollar. As a result, the consolidated reports of the U.S. parent, as expressed in U.S. dollars, may be subject to an extra element of volatility because of the changing exchange rate between the dollar and the foreign currency.

This situation can of course lead to problems to the extent that the volatility in consolidated reports creates certain impressions among potential or actual stockholders and bankers of the parent corporation. However, the problem is in essence only an accounting problem that does not reflect the true economic situation of the parent firm in the United States or of the project in the foreign country. Nor does it affect the actual dollar value of the profits that are remitted back to the United States from the foreign project.

The problem of translating the accounting records from the foreign currency into U.S. dollars is a technical one that needs the careful attention of a competent accountant. However, the translation problems need not be a central concern of the firm's executives and managers since the basic success of the project will not be affected by these technical accounting issues. The other foreign exchange rate problems, though, must receive the continuing attention of financial managers. In any case, your accountants and bankers should be able to help you to understand and deal with any such foreign exchange problems.

Foreign Exchange Controls

Many countries periodically limit in one way or another access to foreign exchange in order to make international payments. The restrictions range from preferential exchange rates for particular kinds of transactions, to the prohibition of payment of royalties, to bureaucratic delays. Investors therefore sometimes encounter exchange control problems when they want to convert local currencies into U.S. dollars and remit earnings or make other payments back to the United States. The host government may actively prevent such a transfer of funds through formalized exchange controls, or it may hinder the transfer by more passive means, such as inaction on a firm's request for permission to transfer the funds.

The most common situation prompting these host government policies is a substantial and continuing balance of payments deficit. When a country faces such a balance of payments situation, it must allow its currency to devalue, draw upon its foreign exchange reserves, or adopt internal economic policy restraints on the economy. Since these are all unpleasant measures for them to undertake, these governments sometimes restrict foreign exchange transactions as a short-term alternative.

The particular kinds of problems encountered by a firm depend on the specific nature of the foreign investment project. If the project involves production, marketing in the foreign country, exporting, and importing, then several different kinds of problems may be encountered, including controls on remittances of profits back to the parent firm in the United States, controls on payments for imports coming to the project from the parent firm, repayments of loans and interest back to the parent firm, and other types of financial transactions. Each of the several different kinds of problems that might be encountered can be considered separately.

If the parent firm in the U.S. is exporting goods or services to the foreign project, then it may be concerned about controls on the payment by the foreign project to the U.S. parent for its exports. The standard way to handle such a problem is the same as that used in common international trade practice: the exporter is the beneficiary of a confirmed letter of credit, which transfers the risk of nonpayment by the importer to a bank. It guarantees that the exporter will be paid regardless of any controls imposed on payments for imports in the foreign country. Furthermore, a guarantee of payment can be obtained in some circumstances from the U.S. Export–Import Bank. Another alternative is to sell to an intermediary, such as a U.S.–based distributor or trading company, which then sells the goods to the foreign firm.

Licensing arrangements can also be subject to exchange controls. If the U.S. parent has a licensing agreement with the foreign project, the fees that the foreign firm pays back to the United States may be subject to controls. Indeed, licensing fee remittances are sometimes subjected to very close scrutiny because the host government may suspect that such fees are being used as an alternative to the transmission of profits as a way to make payments back to the parent firm.

Exchange controls can also pertain to the repayment of principal and interest on a loan made from the parent firm or from a bank to the foreign firm. Descriptions of selected countries' controls on international payments are contained in table 10–1.

The vast majority of remittances from developing countries, however, occur quite routinely without interference by the local host government. Fur-

Table 10–1
Remittance Policies of Selected Latin American Countries

Country	Limit on Profit Remittance	Limit on Royalties and Fees	Limit on Capital Repatriation	Limit on Leads and Lags
Argentina	Tax on dividends greater than 12% of capital	18% tax	Not allowed for three years	5% lead payment maximum
Brazil	Same as above	Maximum of 5% of sales	NA	NA
Chile	None	Maximum of 5% of sales	Not allowed for three years	90–120 day lead or lag allowed
Colombia	Maximum dividend 20% of capital	Prohibited	None	Not permitted beyond 180 days
Ecuador	Same as above	Prohibited	Not allowed for three years	NA
Mexico	Tax on dividends	Up to 5–6% of sales	None	None
Peru	Maximum dividend 20% of capital	Prohibited to parent firm	None	NA
Venezuela	Same as above	Same as above	None	None

Source: Adapted from Business International, *Financing Foreign Operations, Part III*, May 1984, vol. 2, *passim*. Used with the permission of the publisher, Business International Corporation, New York.

thermore, guarantees of freedom from such problems can often be obtained from the host government during entry negotiations, and insurance against currency inconvertibility can often be obtained from a U.S. government agency or from a private insurer. There are several measures a firm can take in advance to minimize the effects of exchange controls if they are imposed, the same kinds of measures that are appropriate in anticipating a devaluation. In any case, controls are frequently only temporary, short-term measures sometimes lasting for only a few days, and bankers can usually provide assistance in coping with payment problems.

Taxes on Remittances

Once you have taken foreign exchange controls into account, you should consider the costs of various forms of funds transfer. Taxes are usually an important cost factor. The tax cost tends to be the highest on dividends that are taxed by both home and host countries. Royalty fees and interest payments generally are tax deductible in the paying country and are taxed in the receiving country, leaving a net lower transfer cost than dividends. Except for a few tax havens, most countries impose a corporate income tax of 40–50 percent, though some countries impose a lower rate and some a higher one.

An additional complication is that the tax laws of the foreign country and the United States are both pertinent. The United States has tax treaties with many foreign countries that are designed to reduce the total tax burden and to simplify the tax effects on firms with foreign investments. In addition, the United States gives a credit for corporate income tax payments made to foreign governments against the parent firm's tax liability in the United States. Furthermore, only that portion of the firm's profits that are actually remitted back to the United States are subject to U.S. taxation. (See chapter 5 for further information about taxes in host countries.)

Insurance and Guarantees

Treaties and Other Agreements. The United States government has treaties and other agreements with many developing countries in order to diminish some of the problems U.S. firms face in those countries. The exact provisions of those treaties and agreements differ somewhat from country to country. However, in recent years new bilateral investment treaties have been negotiated to strengthen the protection afforded to U.S. investors.

The treaty with Egypt, for example, contains four key provisions that are designed to strengthen the position of U.S. investors there.[7] One area covered is the treatment of investments. The agreement says that the Egyptian government agrees to permit U.S. investments to be established on terms that are no less favorable than the terms that the government gives to its own nationals or to investors of any other country. Although some sectors such as airlines, shipping, banking, and insurance can be excluded, the intent of the agreement is to cover most types of investments. The agreement also provides that the country will not impose performance requirements that would include, for example, quotas for exporting goods or for obtaining goods and services locally.

A second provision is that no foreign investment will be expropriated except under due process of local laws. It must be nondiscriminatory and accompanied by prompt, adequate, and effective compensation. (The compensation would be equivalent to the fair market value of the investment involved, and it would not be reduced because of the events that led to the expropriation or because of unproven claims.) Another provision states that there will be compensation in cases of war or other armed conflict between the country and a third country, or damages because of revolution, a state of national emergency, insurrection, riot, or terrorism.

A third area that the treaty covers is rights of investors to transfer funds related to the investment freely and without delay into and out of the host country. These transfers would include, for example, compensation deriving from an investment dispute, payments made under a contract, including the payment of principal and interest on a loan, expenses related to the management of an investment, royalties and other payments derived from licenses, proceeds from the sale of an investment or liquidation of the company, and additional contributions to capital.

Finally, the treaty provides that in the case of a dispute between the investor and the host government initial attempts would be made to resolve the dispute through consultation and negotiation, including the use of nonbinding third-party procedures. If this does not result in a settlement, then the dispute would be settled through the terms of any investment entry agreement that has been reached between the investor and the government. Or failing this, the dispute could be submitted to the International Center for the Settlement of Investment Disputes, an affiliate of the World Bank.

Of course such a government-to-government agreement does not provide you with an ironclad guarantee that a host government will not discriminate against you in some way, establish controls on foreign exchange transactions, or even expropriate your facilities. However, government-to-government agreements do make it possible for the U.S. government itself to issue insurance and guarantees directly to you as an investor to protect you against certain kinds of problems.

OPIC Insurance. In particular, the U.S. Overseas Private Investment Corporation (OPIC) issues insurance against three kinds of problems: (1) the inability to convert local currency into dollars for remitting profits or for returning the original investment back to the United States; (2) the loss of an investment as a result of expropriation, nationalization, or confiscation by the foreign government; and (3) losses due to war, revolution, insurrection, or civil strife.[8] OPIC programs are available to cover U.S. private investments in more than ninety developing countries. The list of eligible countries is available from OPIC on request.

Coverage is available for new investments only. But this requirement includes the capital needed for enlargement or modernization of existing plant and equipment or the additional working capital for an expanded business. In some circumstances an investment involving acquisition of an existing enterprise is eligible for coverage if further capital contributions for expansion of the firm are to be made.

Coverage is limited to 90 percent of a proposed investment so that the investor has to face a possible loss of 10 percent of the total investment of the insured project. However, insurance is available for retained earnings and interest that acrue on the insured investment. OPIC typically issues insurance commitments equal to 270 percent of the initial investment, of which 90 percent is for the investment itself and 180 percent for standby commitments to cover earnings or interest as accrued. The insurance coverage may be issued for up to twenty years, depending on the nature of the investment.

The inconvertibility coverage is designed to ensure that earnings, capital, principal, interest, and other eligible remittances, such as payments under service agreements, can continue to be converted into U.S. dollars—at least to the extent that they are transferable under policies in effect at the time the insurance was issued. The coverage pertains to both "active" restrictions—such as exchange control authorities' denying access to foreign exchange on the basis of new, more restrictive regulations—and "passive" restrictions—such as the failure of authorities to act within a specified period (often sixty days) of an investor's application for foreign exchange. The inconvertibility coverage also protects the investor against adverse discriminatory devaluation of the local currency.

The OPIC coverage against expropriation includes not only the traditional form of expropriation, but also what are sometimes described as creeping expropriations.

The coverage against war, revolution, insurrection, and civil strife covers loss due to actions occurring within the country in which the project is located. A formal declaration of war is not needed in order for a loss to be covered.

OPIC insurance contracts require a premium to be paid annually. Premiums are computed for each type of coverage separately; the premiums vary somewhat according to the nature of the project. Typical projects pay about 0.3 percent on the amount of coverage per year for inconvertibility coverage, about 0.6 percent on expropriation coverage, and about 0.7 percent on war, revolution, insurrection, and civil strife coverage.

OPIC shows preference to smaller-sized investors and therefore sometimes provides special assistance and/or exempts them from certain OPIC regulations. In general, however, investors are asked to provide information on the project's developmental effect on the host country, including information relating to job creation, the development of skills, the balance of payments effects, the taxes to be paid to the host government, and the contribution to basic human needs. Furthermore, the project is expected to contribute to competition in the private sector and not involve monopolistic elements. A proposed investment will also be assessed by OPIC for its effect on employment in the United States and on the U.S. balance of payments.

Private Insurers. There are private insurance companies that will provide you with coverage against expropriation, currency inconvertibility and other types of loss that you may face (see appendix 10B for details).

Although the period of coverage tends to be shorter than the twenty years provided by OPIC, the coverage provided by private insurers is otherwise quite flexible. Insurance policies can be tailor-made to the needs of specific firms and projects. Since it is not tied to U.S. government foreign policy goals, the coverage provided by private insurers may be available in cases where OPIC coverage is not. Fees are also less standardized; premiums can range from a small fraction of 1 percent per year of the amount of coverage to over 1 percent per year. The precise premium depends on the country involved, the nature of the investment project, and other factors.

It is advisable to discuss the possibility of obtaining insurance in the planning stage—before your project is established. Your local insurance broker may not be familiar with the various policies and coverages available, but there are several major brokers with specialized knowledge and experience—some with regional offices around the country. You may want to consider the possibilities for obtaining insurance coverage for additional risks beyond the three standard "political risks" of war, expropriation, and exchange controls.

Advisory and Consulting Services. There are also several private organizations that circulate updated forecasts of political and economic developments in various countries and also provide consulting services to help firms clarify the nature and extent of prospective changes in government policies. (See Sources of Additional Information at the end of the chapter.)

New International Agency. As this book was going to press in 1986, a new organization was in the process of being created in Washington. Called the Multilateral Investment Guarantee Agency (MIGA for short), it is intended to complement the programs of the U.S. Overseas Private Investment Corporation, similar programs of other national governments, and private insurers. Its activities would include issuing guarantees against currency inconvertibility, expropriation, and other types of non-commercial risks. Although the initiative for its creation has come from the World Bank, MIGA would be an independent, autonomous agency. As of this writing, its future remains uncertain, but it could evolve into a major facilitator of investment in developing countries through its guarantees and other programs.

Deciding Whether to Stay or Leave

Political and/or economic conditions in the host country may become so problematic that you will have to consider the possibility of abandoning your project. However, you should be careful not to give up too easily. Reading the account in exhibit 10–1 of developments in Turkey and the responses by various firms suggests that patience and skillful management may enable you to weather difficult circumstances and eventually even increase your investment—and your return.

Exhibit 10–1
Foreign Investment in Turkey

Turkey's foreign investment environment grew increasingly problematic during the late 1970s, and there was an uneasy adversarial relationship between foreign investors and the Turkish government. Foreign investors generally considered the Turkish government to be hostile, obstructionist, and discriminatory toward them. They even believed that the government was often violating its own laws in dealing with them. The government, on the other hand, accused the investors of bad faith, paranoia, deception, and even criminal behavior. The government tried to keep foreign investors in line by using increasingly rigid controls. Neither side trusted the other. Each side traced its problems to the other side's attempts to obtain unfair or illegal gains at its expense. Each side believed the other side to be breaking the rules of the game and cheating.

Several foreign firms pulled out of Turkey during 1978-79 because of this situation—and also because of the country's serious international debt problems. Most of the foreign firms, however, stuck it out despite the increasing difficulties of doing business in Turkey, and their perseverance eventually paid off.

Because of the country's traditional inward-looking industrialization, foreign investors had originally been attracted to Turkey to meet primarily domestic demand. They were guaranteed protected seller's markets by the Turkish government. However, they were pressured to increase local content, and they were also told to become significant exporters. They were criticized for not building large enough capacities to benefit from scale economies, but they were also seriously restricted in their expansion by bureaucratic and political obstacles. In fact, isolated from all foreign competition and enabled to sell profitably all they could produce in domestic markets, foreign investors were not motivated to reduce unit costs. One U.S. businessperson reflected the typical foreign investor's good fortunes in saying: "I could throw anything I make out of my office's sixth-story window, and it would be sold before hitting the ground."

But as Turkey's international payments position deteriorated in the late 1970s, conditions worsened. The government put heavy pressure on foreign investors to decrease the imports and increase the exports of their operations. This government pressure was coupled with a strong political, even ideological opposition (from the extreme right as well as the extreme left) to the foreign business presence in the country. Soon after coming to power in January 1978, a new government began to impose increasingly rigid and unrealistic performance requirements on firms with foreign equity. But it also created numerous legal and administrative obstacles that made it very hard for foreign investors to meet the performance requirements.

Foreign investors were also blamed for relying too heavily on domestic credits instead of borrowing overseas and thus relieving Turkey's foreign exchange and domestic savings bottlenecks. They were criticized for under valuing their imported inputs and for resorting to many illegal business practices. But the government restrictions on their profits and their profit transfers, as well as other legitimate business objectives, left them with little choice if they were to continue operating in Turkey. In light of these developments, Turkey acquired a reputation as one of the riskiest countries in the world for foreign investors.

Yet foreign investors were on the whole actually quite successful in adapting to the unfavorable investment environment in Turkey. Their adaptation was based on many creative ways to neutralize the government's discriminatory, obstructionist, and often contradictory policies. That adaptation was undoubtedly made easier by the fact that their most serious complaint against the Turkish government was the same one that most Turkish private businesspeople had against the government: short-sighted, incoherent, unpredictable, and excessive government intervention.

They benefited from the experiences of their Turkish counterparts or partners. Moreover, the ambitious government intervention, aimed at directing economic activity at all levels, was not very effective. The government whose authority was split and diffused among different government agencies, was simply incapable of realizing most of its interventionist aims, since it lacked the resources and coordination required to enforce its directives. Furthermore, most foreign investors were able to cope with both their adversarial relationship with the Turkish government and the country's international financial problems by a variety of strategies and tactics.

As the country's economic crisis dragged on, though, some foreign investors began to lose hope and leave the country. But most foreign investors viewed their difficulties as being temporary and hoped to ride them out in the near future. They were pessimistic about the short-run but optimistic about the long-run.

Those who stayed all survived. They were able to cope with both their adversarial relationship with the Turkish government and Turkey's two-year long international insolvency. They proved correct in their assessment of Turkey's significant long-term potential as a host country.

That potential began to be realized after January 1980 when Turkey made a fundamental change in managing its economy. A new government regime assigned great importance to foreign trade and investment, which has proved to be a boon to foreign investors who survived the crisis of the late 1970s. Foreign investment in Turkey today is highly attractive. Those investors who were already in the country in early 1980 have benefited handsomely from their perseverance and farsightedness. They have been well compensated by Turkey's fundamental transition from one of the least to one of the most hospitable countries in the world for foreign investors. Their increasingly risky adventures in Turkey during the late 1970s helped them to begin building increasingly profitable ventures in the early 1980s.

This discussion of the Turkish case is adapted from Asim Erdilek, "The Dynamics of the Foreign Direct Investment Environment in Turkey: Political Risks in the Past and the Present," in *Political Risks in International Business: New Directions for Research, Management and Public Policy,* ed. Thomas L. Brewer (New York: Praeger, 1985), and from Erdilek, *Direct Foreign Investment in Turkish Manufacturing—An Analysis of the Conflicting Objectives and Frustrated Expectations of a Host Country* (Tübingen, West Germany: J.C.B. Mohr, 1982).

Conclusion

The problems associated with investment projects in developing countries are generally manageable. Some of them will be familiar to you from your experience as a businessperson in the United States. Others will be novel and perhaps unsettling. There are government and private organizations, however, that can help you to manage many of those problems. These programs, plus your own commitment and skills, should enable you to pursue your business interests with success and satisfaction.

Appendix 10A
Coping with Devaluation: The Case of Uruguay

Managers of Uruguayan subsidiaries are still struggling to adjust to the November 1982 peso devaluation, but after revaluing stocks and tightening collection practices they are only getting by. The brighter side is that imports are no longer competitive; when demand picks up, managers expect a stronger market for their local production.

Throughout the Uruguayan economy's boom years, companies took on heavy dollar liabilities. Executives were, however, aware of the risks involved in accepting dollar-denominated debt against an overvalued local currency. Managers sheltered their firms against devaluation by taking out insurance, albeit at considerable peso expense. The Central Bank guaranteed coverage and made it available for suppliers' credits as well as for financial operations.

Moreover, after the devaluation, companies learned to appreciate the value of financial managers with experience in the region. According to one executive, nationals in Uruguay and other countries in the Southern Cone of South America are particularly skilled at dealing with high inflation and interest rates, and they know how to work with overvalued currencies.

Multinational corporations tackled the cash management problems created by the devaluation in a variety of ways. A petrochemicals company, for example, immediately revalued its imported stock at their anticipated replacement cost. It also changed its collection practices, pressing clients for payment of outstanding bills before selling them new merchandise. Shortening payment terms helped to compensate for exchange rate volatility.

Another firm skirted the problem of time lags in the import–collection–replacement cycle by calculating replacement costs at a rate that covered stocks against loss.

Sharply increased liability has, however, forced some companies to shelve investment plans. The severity of Uruguay's recession has compelled firms to cut operations to the bone. But all is not gloom and despair. An executive in the fertilizer industry captured the mood when he said, "We have not abandoned our investment plans; we have adjusted them."

According to one executive, "The effects of the boom–recession–devaluation cycle will be felt for another four or five years. And the agricultural and industrial sectors will have to be restructured ." In general, the automotive, service, and construction sectors were hardest hit.

Nevertheless, the devaluation has had positive effects. Imported stocks appreciated, leaving companies with peso profits (when those profits are translated into dollars, however, the gains disappear). Dollar debts have diminished, and exports are competitive once again. Nonessential imports have been cleared from the local market. Companies should be therefore in a good position to profit from the economic recovery.

Adapted from *Business Latin America*, February 22, 1984, p. 59. Used with the permission of the publisher, Business International Corporation, New York.

Appendix 10B
Some Private Sector Underwriters of Political Risk Insurance

American International Group, Inc.
Political Risk Division
99 John Street
New York, NY 10038
(212) 700-8185

Chubb Group of Insurance Companies
Political Risk Department
15 Mountain View Road
Warren, NJ 07060
(201) 580-2000

INAMIC, Ltd.
60 Broad Street
28th Floor
New York, NY 10004
(212) 422-4377

U.I.C. Ltd.
One World Trade Center, Suite 2049
New York, NY 10048
(212) 466-9222

Sources of Additional Information

Association of Political Risk Analysts, 1133 Fifteenth St. NW, Suite 620, Washington, D.C. 20005. Phone: (202) 293-5913.

Barovick, R.L. "Bilateral Investment Treaties: Ensuring Fair Treatment for U.S. Investors in the Third World." *Business America* 5 (August 23, 1982):3–5.

Brewer, T.L. "Political Risk Assessment for Foreign Direct Investment Decisions: Better Methods for Better Results." *Columbia Journal of World Business* 16, no. 1 (Spring 1981):5–12.

Stern, R. "Insurance for Third World Currency Inconvertibility Protection." *Harvard Business Review* 60(May–June 1982):62–64.

U.S. Overseas Private Investment Corporation (OPIC), Insurance Application Officer, 1615 M St. NW, Washington, D.C. 20527. Phone: (202) 457-7059.

Notes

Chapter 1. An Introduction to the Opportunities

1. The statistical data and forecasts for individual countries and country groups are from the World Bank's *World Development Report, 1983* (New York: Oxford University Press, 1983).

2. Coopers & Lybrand, *1985 Annual Report on the Worldwide Economic and Business Climate* (Washington, D.C.: Coopers & Lybrand, 1985), 9.

3. William A. Delphos, ed., *Washington's Best Kept Secrets: A U.S. Government Guide to International Business* (New York: Wiley, 1983).

4. The comparative rates of return are reported in Brent D. Wilson and Indra Guertler, "A Comparison of Returns on Foreign vs. Domestic Investments for U.S. Companies," unpublished paper, Brigham Young University and Babson College.

5. The returns for joint ventures in India are summarized in "Doing Business Collaborations in India," *OPIC Topics* (Fall 1984):2.

Chapter 2. Planning the Project

1. Rosalie Tung, "Selection and Training of Personnel for Overseas Assignments," *Columbia Journal of World Business* 16 (Spring 1981):68–78.

2. Kenichi Ohmae, *The Mind of the Strategist* (New York: McGraw-Hill, 1982).

3. Vern Terpstra and Kenneth David, *The Cultural Environment of International Business*, 2d ed. (Cincinnati: South-Western Publishing Company, 1985).

Chapter 3. Managing Cultural Problems

1. David A. Ricks, *Big Business Blunders: Mistakes in Multinational Marketing* (Homewood, Ill.: Dow Jones–Irwin, 1983).

2. Jagdish N. Sheth, "Cross-cultural Influences on Buyer–Seller Interaction/Negotiation Process," *Asian Pacific Journal of Management* 1 (1983):46–55.

3. Kenneth David, field research in India.

4. Thomas Peters and Robert H. Waterman, Jr., *In Search of Excellence* (New York: Harper & Row, 1982); Andrew M. Pettigrew, "Strategic Aspects of Management of Specialist Activity," *Personnel Review* 5 (1975):5–13; Louis Pondy, "Leadership is a Language Game," in *Leadership: Where Else Can We Go?* ed. M. McCall and M. Lombardo (Durham, N.C.: Duke University Press, 1978).

5. Alan Wilkins and Joanne Martin, "Organizational Legends" (Research Paper No. 521, Graduate School of Business, Stanford University, 1979); Joanne Martin, "Stories and Scripts in Organizational Settings," in *Cognitive Social Psychology,* ed. A. Hasdorf and A. Isen (New York: Elsevier, 1982).

6. Joanne Martin and Caren Siehl, "Organizational Culture and Counter-Culture: General Motors and Delorean" (Research Paper No. 633, Graduate School of Business, Stanford University, 1981).

7. Terrence E. Deal and Allan A. Kennedy, *Corporate Cultures* (Reading, Mass.: Addison-Wesley, 1982); Peters and Waterman, *In Search of Excellence.*

8. See chapter 1 of Vern Terpstra and Kenneth David, *The Cultural Environment of International Business,* 2d ed. (Cincinnati: South-Western, 1985).

9. Deal and Kennedy, *Corporate Cultures.*

10. Yves Doz and C.K. Prahalad, "How MNCs Cope with Host Government Intervention," *Harvard Business Review* 58 (March–April 1980):149–57.

Chapter 4. Obtaining Financing

1. Andrew Marton, "Is Smaller Better in Third World Project Finance?" *Institutional Investor* 18 (September 1984):195–202.

2. Overseas Private Investment Corporation, *Finance Handbook,* pamphlet.

3. International Finance Corporation, *IFC,* pamphlet.

4. Caribbean Project Development Facility, "Report to the CGCED Steering Committee on CPDF Operations," March 29, 1985.

Chapter 5. Managing Government Relations

1. See especially the analysis by Stephen Guisinger, "Investment Incentives and Performance Requirements: A Comparative Analysis of Country Foreign Investment Strategies," study prepared for the International Finance Corporation, July 1983.

Chapter 6. Selecting and Working with Local Partners

1. The descriptions of the foreign investment regulations of Oman, Israel, Pakistan, and Indonesia are from U.S. Department of Commerce, International Trade Administration, *Asia,* vol. 3 of *Investment Climate in Foreign Countries* (Washington, D.C.: 1983).

2. The importance of commitment is emphasized in Paul Beamish and Henry W. Lane, "Need, Commitment, and the Performance of Joint Ventures in the Developing World" (Working Paper Series No. 6483, School of Business and Economics, Wilfrid Laurier University, Waterloo, Ontario, Canada, 1984).

3. Business International, Checklist No. 47, "Solving Joint-Venture Partner Problems," in *201 Checklists* (New York: Business International, 1979).

Chapter 7. Establishing and Operating Facilities

1. Linda Y.C. Lim and Pang Eng Fong, "Vertical Linkages and Multinational Enterprises in Developing Countries," *World Development* 10, no. 7, (1982): 585–95.

Chapter 8. Managing Labor Relations

1. Myrna Blake, "Constraints on the Organization of Women Industrial Workers," in *Women in the Urban and Industrial Workforce, Southeast and East Asia*, ed. Gavin Jones (Development Studies Centre Monograph No. 33, Australian National University, Canberra, Australia, 1984), 149–62.

2. *Malaysian Business*, August 1, 1984, p. 17.

3. Aihwa Ong, "Global Industries and Malay Peasants in Peninsular Malaysia," in *Women, Men and the International Division of Labor*, ed. June Nash and Maria Patricia Fernandez-Kelly (Albany: State University of New York Press, 1983), 439–62.

Chapter 9. Marketing Products and Services

1. David A. Ricks, M. Fu, and Jeffrey Arpan, *International Business Blunders* (Cincinnati: Grid, 1974); and David A. Ricks, *Big Business Blunders* (Homewood, Ill.: Dow Jones–Irwin, 1983).

2. Kenneth David, field research in Sri Lanka.

3. Virginia M. Yorio, *Adapting Products for Export*, Research Report No. 835 (New York: The Conference Board), 11.

Chapter 10. Protecting Assets and Returns

1. Business International, *Business Asia*, October 12, 1984, p. 3.

2. Thomas L. Brewer, "The Instability of Governments and the Instability of Controls on Funds Transfers by Multinational Enterprises," *Journal of International Business Studies* 14, no. 3 (Winter 1983):147–57.

3. Thomas L. Brewer, "Conclusion," in *Political Risks in International Business*, ed. Thomas L. Brewer (New York: Praeger, 1985), 338–39.

4. Interview with Ralph Diaz of Business International.

5. Stephen J. Kobrin, "Expropriation as an Attempt to Control Foreign Firms in LDCs: Trends from 1960–1979," *International Studies Quarterly* 28, no. 3 (September 1984); reprinted in Brewer, ed., *Political Risks in International Business*, 71–94.

6. This is referred to as Purchasing Power Parity.

7. R.L. Barovik, "Bilateral Investment Treaties," *Business America* 5 (August 23, 1982): 3–5.

8. Overseas Private Investment Corporation, *Investment Insurance Handbook* (Washington, D.C, n.d.).

Index

About the Authors

Thomas L. Brewer is on the faculty of Georgetown University's School of Business Administration in Washington, D.C. He specializes in strategic planning, international finance, and government–business relations, including U.S. government programs concerning investment projects in developing countries. He has published numerous articles and books on international business and international relations, and consulted on such international business issues as strategic planning for agribusiness projects and foreign government procurement practices.

Kenneth David is a professor of anthropology and international business at Michigan State University. Trained in sociocultural anthropology at the University of Chicago, he later took an M.B.A. and doctoral training in international business and business policy at Michigan State University and the University of Michigan. He co-authored the widely used *Cultural Environment of International Business* (1985). He now researches and consults on business problems requiring social and business analysis.

Linda Y.C. Lim is an international and development economist from Singapore, with degrees in economics from Cambridge University, Yale University, and the University of Michigan. She is an assistant professor in the Graduate School of Business Administration at the University of Michigan. Since 1984 she has been research director of the University of Michigan's Southeast Asia Business Education and Resources Program. She has published widely and consulted on business practices in Southeast Asia and other developing areas.